Mediating Vulnerability

COMPARATIVE LITERATURE AND CULTURE

Series Editors
TIMOTHY MATHEWS AND FLORIAN MUSSGNUG

Comparative Literature and Culture explores new creative and critical perspectives on literature, art and culture. Contributions offer a comparative, cross-cultural and interdisciplinary focus, showcasing exploratory research in literary and cultural theory and history, material and visual cultures, and reception studies. The series is also interested in language-based research, particularly the changing role of national and minority languages and cultures, and includes within its publications the annual proceedings of the 'Hermes Consortium for Literary and Cultural Studies'.

Timothy Mathews is Emeritus Professor of French and Comparative Criticism, UCL.

Florian Mussgnug is Reader in Italian and Comparative Literature, UCL.

Mediating Vulnerability

Comparative approaches and questions of genre

Edited by
Anneleen Masschelein, Florian Mussgnug and
Jennifer Rushworth

First published in 2021 by
UCL Press
University College London
Gower Street
London WC1E 6BT

Available to download free: www.uclpress.co.uk

Collection © Editors, 2021
Text © Contributors, 2021

Cover image: Bronzino Underbelly (Galleria Borghese), Liz Rideal, 2018. Digital print on silk georgette.1/3, 178x134 cm.

The authors have asserted their rights under the Copyright, Designs and Patents Act 1988 to be identified as the authors of this work.

A CIP catalogue record for this book is available from The British Library.

Any third-party material in this book is not covered by the book's Creative Commons licence. Details of the copyright ownership and permitted use of third-party material is given in the image (or extract) credit lines. If you would like to reuse any third-party material not covered by the book's Creative Commons licence, you will need to obtain permission directly from the copyright owner.

This book is published under a Creative Commons Attribution-Non-Commercial 4.0 International licence (CC BY-NC 4.0), https://creativecommons.org/licenses/by-nc/4.0/. This licence allows you to share and adapt the work for non-commercial use providing attribution is made to the author and publisher (but not in any way that suggests that they endorse you or your use of the work) and any changes are indicated. Attribution should include the following information:

Masschelein, A., Mussgnug, F. and Rushworth, J. (eds). 2021. *Mediating Vulnerabilty: Comparative approaches and questions of genre*. London: UCL Press. https://doi.org/10.14324/111.9781800081130

Further details about Creative Commons licences are available at http://creativecommons.org/licenses/

ISBN: 978-1-80008-115-4 (Hbk.)
ISBN: 978-1-80008-114-7 (Pbk.)
ISBN: 978-1-80008-113-0 (PDF)
ISBN: 978-1-80008-116-1 (epub)
ISBN: 978-1-80008-117-8 (mobi)
DOI: https://doi.org/10.14324/111.9781800081130

Contents

List of contributors   vii

Introduction: on/off limits   1
Anneleen Masschelein, Florian Mussgnug and Jennifer Rushworth

Part 1: Human/Animal   17

1. What if they could speak? Humanized animals in science fiction   19
   Simona Micali

2. Rewriting the myth: consideration of the Minotaur in Georgi Gospodinov's *The Physics of Sorrow*   38
   Nicole Siri

3. A vulnerable predator: the wolf as a symbol of the natural environment in the works of Ernest Thompson Seton, Jack London and Cormac McCarthy   52
   Kateřina Kovářová

Part 2: Violence/Resistance   69

4. Retelling the Parsley Massacre: vulnerability and resistance in Danticat's *The Farming of Bones*   71
   Eleonora Rapisardi

5. Toni Cade Bambara's vulnerable men   82
   Tuula Kolehmainen

6. *The Secret Agent* – fictionalizing history: Joseph Conrad and Stan Douglas 99
   Sandra Camacho

7. New worlds: violent intersections in graphic novels 116
   Jessica Gross

Part 3: Image/Narrative 133

8. Ludic space in horror fiction 135
   Onni Mustonen

9. Graphic stories of resistance: a comic memoir of becoming 149
   Pinelopi Tzouva

10. The cryptographic narrative in video games: the player as detective 168
    Ana Paklons and An-Sofie Tratsaert

11. Narrating pornographic images: photographic description and ekphrasis in *De fotograaf* by Jef Geeraerts 185
    Karen Van Hove

Part 4: Medium/Genre 201

12. Through the doors of time: media interactions and cultural memory in *El Ministerio del Tiempo* 203
    Katie Ginsbach

13. Vulnerability as duality in speculative fiction 223
    Eva Dinis

14. No, poetry is not out of date: notes on poetic writing and digital culture 238
    Jan Baetens
    Translated by Marie-Claire Merrigan

    Afterword: Covid-19 or the vulnerability of the future 252
    Florian Mussgnug

Index 258

List of contributors

Anneleen Masschelein is Associate Professor in Literary and Cultural Studies at KU Leuven. She has published extensively on contemporary cultural theory and intellectual history. Her book *The Unconcept: The Freudian uncanny in contemporary theory* (2011) is a systematic genealogy of the uncanny. More recently, she has published a volume on the *Interview as Creative Practice* with Rebecca Roach (Special issue of *Biography*) and she edited *Writing Manuals for the Masses* (2020) with Dirk de Geest.

Florian Mussgnug is Professor of Italian and Comparative Literature at University College London. He has published widely on twentieth- and twenty-first-century literature, with a particular focus on literary theory, experimental literature and narrative prose fiction. His book *The Eloquence of Ghosts: Giorgio Manganelli and the Afterlife of the Avant-Garde* (2010) was awarded the Edinburgh Gadda Prize in 2012. He is co-investigator for the five-year AHRC-funded research project 'Interdisciplinary Italy 1900–2020: Interart/Intermedia'.

Jennifer Rushworth is Associate Professor in French and Comparative Literature at University College London. She is the author of two books, *Discourses of Mourning in Dante, Petrarch, and Proust* (2016) and *Petrarch and the Literary Culture of Nineteenth-Century France* (2017). She was also the recipient of the Malcolm Bowie Prize 2015 and the *Paragraph* Essay Prize 2016. Her principal research interests are mourning, medievalism and music.

Jan Baetens is Professor of Cultural and Literary Studies at KU Leuven. His recent publications include *Novelization. From Film to Novel* (2018) and *The Film Photonovel. A Cultural History of Forgotten Adaptations* (2019). He co-edited the *Cambridge History of the American Graphic Novel* (2018) with Hugo Frey and Steve Tabachnick. A published poet in French, he has novelized Jean-Luc Godard's *Vivre sa vie* (English translation in PLACE: https://www.place-plateforme.com/hors-serie-2.html).

Sandra Camacho has a PhD in comparative studies from the School of Arts and Humanities, the University of Lisbon, where she developed the thesis 'From Analogue to Image Retrieval: Concepts of archival art in Daniel Blaufuks'.

She holds a master's in art and multimedia from the Faculty of Fine Arts, the University of Lisbon and an MA in contemporary art from Sotheby's Institute of Art, the University of Manchester. Her research interests are archival art, the digital archive, media archaeology, intermedia and interarts studies.

Eva Dinis is a PhD student at the School of Arts and Humanities, the University of Lisbon. She is currently developing her research on 'The Speculative Fiction of Maria Judite de Carvalho and Margaret Atwood – Interrogative Genre'. She is a member in training of the Centre for Comparative Studies (CEC) and is part of the City and (In)security in Literature and the Media (CILM) project.

Katie Ginsbach was awarded her PhD from the University of Wisconsin-Madison and is an assistant professor of Spanish at St. Norbert College in De Pere, Wisconsin. She specializes in contemporary peninsular literature, with a focus on representations of history in modern-day Spain. Her most recent scholarship analyses the popular Spanish television show *El Ministerio del Tiempo* and examines how cultural codes and transmedial extensions allow individuals to collectively reshape their relationship to the past. She is currently working on a book chapter that focuses on the historical novel *Hombres buenos* by Arturo Pérez-Reverte.

Jessica Gross is Associate Professor of English at the University of Health Sciences and Pharmacy in St. Louis, Missouri, where she teaches her courses Comics and Mental Illness, Global Comics and Comics and Conflict. Her research interests include comics, graphic medicine, mental illness, war, violence and conflict in literature, and Filipino, Singaporean and Francophone literatures. Her previous publications on comics include a chapter in *Literatures of Madness: Disability studies and mental health* and her edited collection, *Invisible Made Visible: Comics and mental illness*, co-edited with Leah Misemer, is forthcoming.

Tuula Kolehmainen is a doctoral candidate at the University of Helsinki. The title of her thesis is 'Like Men They Stood: Male vulnerability as resistance to stereotypes in fiction by African American women'. She has published an essay on Jhumpa Lahiri's short fiction in the *Keltaiset esseet* collection (2016) and an article on Toni Morrison's *Tar Baby* in the journal *American Studies in Scandinavia* (2018). As a stand-up comedian herself, she is passionate about humour in all its forms.

Kateřina Kovářová is a PhD candidate at Charles University, Prague and a lecturer at the University of South Bohemia in České Budějovice. Her PhD research focuses on the interdependence of American nature and culture in Cormac McCarthy's fiction. She has published essays in the collections *Speculative Ecologies: Plotting through the mesh* (2019) and *Transnational Interconnections of Nature Studies and the Environmental Humanities* (2020).

Simona Micali is Associate Professor of Comparative Literature at the University of Siena. She has published four books and several essays on modern and contemporary fiction, science fiction, and the fantastic. Her latest book is *Towards a Posthuman Imagination in Literature and Media: Monsters, mutants, aliens, artificial beings* (2019). She also edited a special issue of *Contemporanea* on 'Raccontare il postumano'.

Onni Mustonen is a Helsinki-born cultural journalist and critic specializing in popular culture, horror fiction and comics. He has written several articles in Finnish publications, as well as international journals such as *Thinking Horror*. In addition, he is the copyeditor of *Sarjainfo*, a magazine published by the Finnish Comics Society. He has authored a number of comics and is published in the esteemed Finnish comics anthology *Kuti*.

Ana Paklons is a research assistant at KU Leuven Science & Technology and a member of the Institute of Cultural Studies and CS Digital, coordinating multiple projects concerning digital education, and undertaking research on the intersection between affect theory and video game studies. She holds a bachelor's degree in history and art history and a master's in ancient history and cultural studies from KU Leuven. Her MA dissertation analysed the use of video games in museums as an educational and marketing tool.

Eleonora Rapisardi is a PhD student in the Graduate Center for the Study of Culture in Gießen, Germany. She is also affiliated to the Catholic University, Lisbon. Her doctoral dissertation concerns diasporic literature in the United States from Cuba, Haiti and the Dominican Republic, with specific regard to polyphony and decolonial epistemology.

Nicole Siri holds a joint PhD in comparative and French literature from the University of Siena and Université Paris 3 - Sorbonne Nouvelle. Her doctoral thesis focused on the representation of labour in the novel from a theoretical perspective. Her main research interests include cultural history, cultural theory, material culture studies, psychoanalysis, Marxist criticism and the nineteenth- and early twentieth-century novel, with expertise in the French novel.

An-Sofie Tratsaert is a junior rigger at Larian Studios and graduated from Howest University. She previously obtained a bachelor's degree in Japanology at KU Leuven and is in the process of finishing a master's degree in cultural studies at KU Leuven. Her MA dissertation analyses a new narrative in indie horror games.

Pinelopi Tzouva has a background in psychology, social and cultural anthropology and cultural studies. She is currently working on her PhD dissertation at the University of Tartu, Estonia, which combines perspectives from literature and anthropology to address breast cancer narratives in the context of actor–network theory and new materialism.

Karen Van Hove is a PhD fellow funded by the FWO (Research Foundation, Flanders) and works in the Dutch literature department of KU Leuven. She obtained a master's degree in Western literature and a degree in literary theory from KU Leuven. She specializes in modern and contemporary Dutch literature and has a special interest in narrative theory. Her doctoral research focuses on interactions between literature and pornography in the 1960s and 1970s, especially in the work of C.C. Krijgelmans, Jef Geeraerts, Louis Ferron and Heere Heeresma.

Introduction:
on/off limits

Anneleen Masschelein, Florian Mussgnug
and Jennifer Rushworth

Vulnerability signifies a susceptibility to being wounded (from the Latin *vulnus*, wound). It suggests both fragility and openness, and it is this ambivalence which this volume explores. Thinking about vulnerability raises questions about representation: who or what is represented as vulnerable? How is vulnerability represented? How do the vulnerable make representation in different forms? This connection between vulnerability and representation lies at the heart of our chosen focus on *Mediating Vulnerability*, that is, on the intersection between vulnerability studies and media studies, within the broader field of comparative literature. On the one hand, we explore how representations of vulnerability change across different media. On the other hand, in a meta-literary twist, we are interested in media as themselves vulnerable, particularly as a result of changing generic expectations over time and place. In other words, we argue that the works analysed in this volume are not only vehicles for representing different forms of vulnerability but are themselves potentially vulnerable given the intrinsic porosity and contingency of media and genre.

Vulnerability theory has developed since the final decades of the twentieth century as a distinctive, multidisciplinary cluster of philosophical, ethical and legal enquiry. In the works of pioneering thinkers such as Martha Nussbaum and Judith Butler, vulnerability was addressed as a concept that cannot and ought not to be defined in any one way: firstly, because it requires a broad theoretical and political attention that cannot be held exclusively by any single academic discipline; and secondly, because it is a relational term and therefore one which needs to be understood through other terms and paradigms, such as power, violence, agency and passivity.[1] Thinking about vulnerability, according to this approach, brings to the fore subjectivities and narratives that are always already shaped by an intimate awareness of relations of power and dependency. Building on this position, recent scholars of vulnerability have insisted that political advocacy by and on behalf of vulnerable individuals and communities can only be imagined as an open, continuous practice: a mobilizing critique of power, in Julietta Singh's words, which displaces binaries and 'resists foreclosures by remaining unremittingly susceptible to new emergent figurations'.[2] As political philosopher Estelle Ferrarese writes at the outset of her book *Vulnerability and Critical Theory*, '[a] vulnerability only ever arises as the hollow side of a power to act'.[3] Similarly, philosopher Lucia Corso theorizes the study of vulnerability as a critique of the imagined wholeness of the law, in the political discourse of modernity. Shifting the focus from legal definitions of vulnerable groups to what she calls 'ontological vulnerability', Corso urges her readers to ponder the fragility of the human, not as a conceptual boundary that defines the abstract, interchangeable, autonomous individual of liberal moral-political theory, but as a shared vital dependency on human and more-than-human systems. In this way, she suggests, experiences and encounters with vulnerability can stretch the limits of our imagination towards responsible and responsive sensitivity.[4]

In the chapters that follow, our contributors respond to the demands that have been formulated by philosophers and political theorists, from the perspective of literary and cultural studies. We address specific and diverse contexts that create and shape vulnerability as an experience and as a concept. Much of our discussion is focused on the late twentieth and twenty-first centuries. In this respect, the book reflects an increasing academic attention to vulnerability, in recent years and across disciplines, and a heightened sense of our own vulnerability as a result of multiple factors, whether specific events (such as 9/11, often invoked as a critical turning point in the field of vulnerability studies) or ongoing crises (the Covid-19 pandemic, at the time of writing; the ever worsening climate emergency).[5] We contend that literary and cultural studies can make a unique contribution to these discussions, since they necessarily embrace a plurality of approaches to vulnerability, from the literal to the metaphorical, from the historical to the theoretical and from the reflective to the self-reflexive. Comparative literature in particular is ideally placed to draw attention to the ways in which vulnerability is mediated by form and language – by narration, style, genre and medium. At the same time, it is also highly aware of the vulnerability of specific categories, particularly those of media and genre but also of its own status as a discipline.

Discussions of vulnerability, in literary and cultural studies, have long been attentive to other disciplinary fields, and especially to philosophy, political theory, law, bioethics and the environmental humanities. In recent years, this nexus of different perspectives has been explored, with exemplary acumen, by the contributors to the 2016 volume *Vulnerability in Resistance*, edited by Judith Butler, Zeynep Gambetti and Leticia Sabsay. In their introduction, the editors challenge:

> two assumptions pervasive in several popular and theoretical discourses. The first holds that vulnerability is the opposite of resistance and cannot be conceived as part of that practice; the second supposes that vulnerability requires and implies the need for protection and the strengthening of paternalistic forms of power at the expense of collective forms of resistance and social transformation.[6]

Butler, Gambetti and Sabsay unequivocally reject the equation of vulnerability with 'victimization and passivity' and instead propose vulnerability as 'one of the conditions of the very possibility of resistance'. Similarly, the chapters in the present volume are devoted to considering vulnerability and resistance as interrelated rather than opposed concepts. Resistance emerges as a keyword chiefly, though not only, in the chapters collected in part 2, 'Violence/Resistance'. In this way, vulnerability becomes a site of possibility rather than of impossibility and of agency and activity rather than of passivity – even a site of empowerment and not only disempowerment.[7]

A further aspect of the approach of Butler, Gambetti and Sabsay to vulnerability is to define it as 'relational and social'. They write:

> if we argue . . . that vulnerability emerges as part of social relations, even as a feature of social relations, then we make (a) a general claim according to which vulnerability ought to be understood as relational and social, and (b) a very specific claim according to which it always appears in the context of specific social and historical relations that call to be analyzed concretely.[8]

In defining vulnerability in this way, these authors highlight that vulnerability is caused and may be exacerbated by specific socio-political situations. Their second point above underpins the emphasis in this volume on specific, concrete case studies in each chapter, with attention to different socio-historical contexts.

If vulnerability is relational, this volume adds to this that it is also mediated. Vulnerability is expressed in various forms and modes, beginning with the nature photos that we see daily when we open our computers, to narratives in all possible forms, modes and genres. Many terms that emerged in the debate on vulnerability have also been used in contemporary discussions of genres and genre ecology. Jay Bolter and Richard Grusin's influential work on remediation, for example, has shown that 'old media' and their genres do not just disappear but are remediated and transformed by new media.[9]

The concept of vulnerability has prompted unprecedented attention to the fundamental and precarious interrelatedness not just of human beings, but also of species, objects and cultural forms. This turn to vulnerability is exemplified by the growing interest, in literary and cultural studies, in what Steven Vertovec describes as the 'fluidity of constructed styles and practices: syncretism, creolization, bricolage, cultural translation and hybridity'.[10] Moving away from static taxonomies of genre and form, researchers have come to view aesthetic form as a process of constant unfolding, revision and adjustment to different mediatic, cultural and spatiotemporal contexts. Artists have explored ephemeral forms of cultural practice that are transformed and redefined by every new articulation (performances, interactive hypertexts and so forth). Simultaneously, scholars have championed new and diverse forms of knowledge dissemination, such as open-access platforms, websites, co-authored writing and catalogue essays. Engagement with these media is seen as an effective way to break new ground, set the terms of a debate and create new disciplinary orientations. From the perspective of the environmental humanities, these new relations between practice and inquiry are best described as an ecology: a dynamic nexus of heterogeneous forces and practices.

A sense of vulnerability is also triggered by new political and societal pressures, in research and higher education and in the mutual interaction between disciplines and media. Disciplinary demarcations and expertise are perceived as immanent, ever-modulating force relations. For comparative critics, this rapid transformation of research environments impacts on our experience as cultural mediators of disciplines, regions and languages. Comparative literature has always championed linguistic and cultural diversity and the importance of locally embedded traditions. This characteristic attentiveness to space and to cultural difference emerges from many of the contributions to this volume. The contributors argue that artistic practice has the power to shed new light on the way in which situated images and practices can function both as sites of emerging knowledge production and as vaults of experiences on the verge of disappearing. Attention to the vulnerability of this interaction allows us to explore diverse texts and cultural contexts not only in terms of their history, geographic specificity or contemporary relevance, but also as figurative openings and re-imaginings of the future.

Across these different contexts, our volume is organized according to related pairs of concepts, which are brought together by the ambiguous punctuation mark '/'. With this mark, we intend to suggest not binary opposition, but patterns of entanglement that are shaped by emergent fault lines: moments where related concepts rub against one another, creating instances of creative friction. The first of these fault lines is our introductory title 'On/off limits', which raises a variety of questions: what are the limits of vulnerability? Is vulnerability necessarily limiting? How does vulnerability entail a questioning of boundaries and norms? The 14 chapters themselves are then organized in four parts: 'Human/Animal', 'Violence/Resistance', 'Image/Narrative' and 'Medium/Genre'. In each case, the fault lines emerge from diverse objects, media and genres in contemporary narratives and cultures. The volume begins with a literary (that is, a textual) focus, before expanding out to other media, with particular attention to graphic novels and comic books (chapters 7 and 9), video games (chapters 8 and 10) and film and television (chapters 6 and 12). All contributions are united in starting from a comparative analysis of specific objects, leading to more general questions about the relevance of cultural forms in understanding the manifold elements of the vulnerability currently facing the world. Chapters address an appropriately wide as well as focused range of topics, including animal studies; child abuse and trauma more generally; victimhood and nationhood; race, terrorism and genocide; breast cancer and care; cultural memory; and digital culture and the future of poetry.

Within literary studies, vulnerability has been particularly considered in relation to modern and contemporary fiction.[11] Here, the work of Jean-Michel Ganteau is especially important.[12] Our volume also turns, at the outset, to twentieth- and twenty-first-century fiction, including writers such as Cormac McCarthy and Margaret Atwood. As is argued in particular by Eva Dinis in her chapter on Atwood (see chapter 13), contemporary fiction is made vulnerable by its being caught up in questions of genre; in the case she addresses, this refers to the relationship between science fiction and speculative fiction and the power structures of generic names.

The exploration of vulnerability in literary studies is also engaged in other theoretical turns, in particular the 'animal turn'. Exemplarily,

Anat Pick's 2011 book *Creaturely Poetics* addresses, in the words of its subtitle, *Animality and vulnerability in literature and film*.[13] Pick's book points to a key question, that of potential connections between vulnerability and particular species. Vulnerability has, in turn, been presented as a defining characteristic of both human and animal life. The American philosopher Daniel Callahan writes that 'we are as human beings intrinsically vulnerable. We are vulnerable to time and nature . . . and we are vulnerable to each other.'[14] Yet these vulnerabilities are shared not only by humans but also by non-human animals. Indeed, Catriona Mackenzie, Wendy Rogers and Susan Dodds write in the introduction to their edited volume on *Vulnerability* (2013) that 'our bodies are animal bodies, which are liable to affliction and injury'.[15] Conversely, the recognition that animals, too, are vulnerable is a key argument in animal rights. To recall a much-quoted phrase from Jeremy Bentham, 'the question is not, Can they reason? nor, Can they *talk*? but, Can they *suffer*?'[16] The result of the 'animal turn', alongside interest in the post-human and the Anthropocene, is to understand that humans and animals are not distinguished but rather connected by their vulnerability. Part 1 of this volume is devoted to forms of vulnerability that involve the 'Human/Animal', again understood not as opposites but rather as permeable states that are explored, here, particularly in science fiction and nature writing.

In the first chapter, 'What if they could speak? Humanized animals in science fiction', Simona Micali explores the figure of the 'humanized animal', defined as 'animals which think, speak and behave as humans', in a selection of modern literature from H. G. Wells's *The Island of Doctor Moreau* (1896) and Mikhail Bulgakov's *The Heart of a Dog* (1925) to Philip K. Dick's *Dr Bloodmoney* (1965) and *Deus Irae* (1976), Pierre Boulle's *La Planète des Singes* (1963; *Planet of the Apes*) and, most recently, Margaret Atwood's *MaddAddam* trilogy (2003–13). Micali draws attention to the way in which the animals in these texts are uncanny not only in their humanness – often manifested in their use of language – but also in the way their humanization is always somehow incomplete or lacking. In this way, Micali demonstrates how, in depicting these vulnerable and threatening subjects, science fiction interrogates anthropocentrism and human exceptionalism.

In the second chapter, 'Rewriting the myth: consideration of the Minotaur in Georgi Gospodinov's *The Physics of Sorrow*', Nicole Siri considers a modern, Bulgarian rewriting of a famous Classical myth, that of the Minotaur. In Gospodinov's rewriting (first published in Bulgarian in 2011 and in English in 2015), the mythological Minotaur enclosed in a labyrinth and to whom virgins are sacrificed is replaced with an herbivore

Minotaur whose life story is defined, instead, by the neglect he experienced on being disowned by his parents and abandoned as an infant. As Siri shows, Gospodinov presents the Minotaur as a victim and as a child, thereby highlighting his human traits. When put on trial by Minos (the husband of Pasiphaë, whose alliance with a bull produced the Minotaur), this Minotaur attempts to defend his legitimacy and to expose the injustice of the way he has been treated. Both human and animal, the Minotaur is doubly vulnerable through his childhood and through his powerlessness in the face of the law (represented by Minos). In *The Physics of Sorrow*, in Siri's reading, the story of the Minotaur ultimately has two purposes: firstly, it serves as a way to speak about child abuse; and secondly, it is a challenge to any presumed or attempted human–animal divide.

The third chapter, Kateřina Kovářová's 'A vulnerable predator: the wolf as a symbol of the natural environment in the works of Ernest Thompson Seton, Jack London and Cormac McCarthy', continues the theme of anthropomorphized animals by focusing on the wolf in short stories by Seton ('Lobo the King of Currumpaw' from *Wild Animals I Have Known* (1898); 'Badlands Billy, the Wolf That Won' and 'The Winnipeg Wolf' from *Animal Heroes* (1905)), in London's novels *Call of the Wild* (1903) and *White Fang* (1906) and in McCarthy's novel *The Crossing* (1994). Focusing on texts that are temporally distant from one another, Kovářová argues for a changed relationship between humans and the environment that is discernible in the changing literary representation of wolves. Kovářová makes a powerful argument that literary representation affects real-life attitudes and encounters, suggesting that the demonized wolf figure of earlier, particularly North American representations is consonant with practices such as wolf-trapping that were, in the time of Seton and London especially, not only legal but even encouraged and lucrative, since wolves were seen as a threat to livestock. In contrast, more recent times have seen wolf reintroduction and preservation programmes, which Kovářová sees as reflected and supported in the more ethical position espoused in McCarthy's *The Crossing*. For Kovářová, recognizing the wolf as vulnerable goes hand in hand not only with recognizing the vulnerability of the natural environment (to which the wolf may point metonymically), but also with understanding our own human vulnerability and responsibilities, as a result of the interconnectedness of human and animal worlds. While Butler, Gambetti and Sabsay have argued that vulnerability is relational and social, Kovářová's analysis of the mutual vulnerability of environment and inhabitants is also indebted to the moral, feminist philosophy of Catriona Mackenzie, Wendy Rogers and Susan Dodds.[17]

The second part of the volume, 'Violence/Resistance', contains four chapters which consider the relationship between vulnerability, violence and resistance. Following Butler, Gambetti and Sabsay, as noted above, resistance and vulnerability are not considered as antithetical in these cases, but as interrelated concepts. In the fourth chapter, 'Retelling the Parsley Massacre: vulnerability and resistance in Danticat's *The Farming of Bones*', Eleonora Rapisardi focuses on Edwidge Danticat's novelistic treatment of the Parsley Massacre, in which between 15,000 and 20,000 Haitians were killed on behalf of the regime of the Dominican dictator Rafael Leonidas Trujillo. Focusing on Danticat's novel of 1998, Rapisardi argues in a compelling fashion that it is in fictional narratives, rather than in official historical accounts, that the voices of the most vulnerable subjects can be heard. Rapisardi follows Susana Onega and Jean-Michel Ganteau in focusing on 'the way in which victimhood and vulnerability are constructed by reference to the perception and literary representation of such notions as race or nationhood'.[18] In dialogue with the work of Guillermina De Ferrari,[19] Rapisardi also contends that, far from being disempowering, vulnerability is – in her words – 'a powerful paradigm by means of which vulnerable groups can reclaim their own existence and rewrite their own epistemology', in fiction as well as in history.

The fifth chapter, Tuula Kolehmainen's analysis of 'Toni Cade Bambara's vulnerable men', continues the focus on the relationship between race and vulnerability begun in the previous chapter, albeit in a different context. Kolehmainen turns her attention to two short stories in Bambara's *Gorilla, My Love* (1972), namely 'The Hammer Man' and 'Raymond's Run'. Kolehmainen shows how Bambara challenges gendered stereotypes by contrasting the feisty female narrators with vulnerable male characters who have unspecified but apparently non-physical disabilities. In showing the male characters as dependent in various ways upon women, Bambara projects ideas of strong femininity but – as Kolehmainen suggests, inspired by the analysis of David T. Mitchell – falls into the trap of presenting disabled characters as props or 'crutches'.[20] Nonetheless, Bambara does portray the intersectional vulnerability of these disabled characters who – by being Black and male – are particularly vulnerable to police intervention and other forms of discrimination.[21]

The sixth chapter, Sandra Camacho's '*The Secret Agent* – fictionalizing history: Joseph Conrad and Stan Douglas', focuses on violence and resistance through considering acts of terrorism, firstly the bombing of the Greenwich Observatory in 1894 as narrated in Joseph Conrad's *The Secret Agent* (1907) and secondly Stan Douglas's six-screen film installation which adapts the plot to Lisbon *circa* 1975, with the new target of the

Marconi installation in Sesimbra. Like Rapisardi in chapter 4, Camacho is interested in the relationship between fiction and history, although in her case this interest also embraces transmedial adaptations. Camacho demonstrates in particular the vulnerability of the spectator through the use of the multiscreen, as well as the vulnerable boundaries between the personal, the political and the public in Conrad's novel and Douglas's adaptation.

The seventh chapter, Jessica Gross's 'New worlds: violent intersections in graphic novels', takes as its focus 'The Rabbits' by Shaun Tan and John Marsden (1998) and J. P. Stassen's *Déogratias* (first published in French in 2000). 'The Rabbits' narrates the conflict between British imperialists (figured here as colonizing rabbits) and indigenous Australian peoples (figured as an unnamed, indigenous species of small, brown, tree-dwelling animals). *Déogratias* is an account of the Rwandan genocide, with a focus on a young Hutu man (the eponymous protagonist) who takes part in the killing of Tutsis. As Gross demonstrates, both graphic novels share an awareness of violence as an irreversible, transformative force in the world. In this respect, Gross's case studies hark back to Kovářová's discussion of wolves (chapter 3), since the major challenge is how different groups (in 'The Rabbits', different species) can learn to live together in the same environment that has been irreparably damaged by different forms of violence. While the animals of 'The Rabbits' are strongly anthropomorphized, the protagonist of *Déogratias* suffers from psychotic episodes in which he identifies as a dog, in a return to the theme of 'humanized animals' expounded by Micali in the opening chapter of this volume. Once more, vulnerability emerges in Gross's chapter as blurring the boundary between human and animal, as relational and social and as bound up with the possibility of resistance.

The third part of the volume is devoted to 'Image/Narrative', although violence and resistance continue to be present as themes in this section, and image analysis already evidently underpins chapters 6 and 7. Chapter 8, Onni Mustonen's 'Ludic space in horror fiction', offers a comparison of H. P. Lovecraft's horror novella 'The Shadow over Innsmouth' (1936) and the Japanese video game *Silent Hill 2* (2001), published by Konami. Mustonen's interest is in the construction of space in these two distinct media, with an understanding of the vulnerability of both reader and player as created and enhanced by the experience of imagined spaces.

Pinelopi Tzouva's 'Graphic stories of resistance: a comic memoir of becoming' (chapter 9) picks up on the focus on graphic novels from Gross's chapter, in this case examining Miriam Engelberg's autobiographical

Cancer Made Me a Shallower Person: A memoir in comics (2006). Tzouva shows how Engelberg's memoir stands apart from other accounts of cancer (breast cancer, in particular) that are typically characterized by an overly glamorized, positive-thinking emphasis on survival. In contrast, Tzouva reads *Cancer Made Me a Shallower Person* as a micro-political utterance and as a work of minor literature (in the terminology of Gilles Deleuze and Félix Guattari).[22] Tzouva's analysis of this comic as a story of resistance is also in dialogue with Jack Halberstam's revalorization of failure.[23] Ultimately, Tzouva argues that cancer is a particular experience of bodily vulnerability that Engelberg captures in a work where text and image are not only in dialogue but mutually transformative, where language is deterritorialized and where text can itself function as image.

Chapter 10, Ana Paklons and An-Sofie Tratsaert's 'The cryptographic narrative in video games: the player as detective', continues the focus on video games, the horror genre and the player's involvement of Mustonen's contribution (chapter 8). The two authors take as their primary material the popular indie horror video game series by Scott Cawthon, *Five Nights at Freddy's* (2013–). In relation to this game, Paklons and Tratsaert highlight a secondary narrative that exists alongside the main narrative, which players call 'the hidden lore' and which they term 'the cryptographic narrative'. This second narrative does not contribute to plot or to the completion of the game. Nonetheless, these authors argue that the cryptographic narrative has a specific function and structure and, moreover, that the player has greater agency but also greater vulnerability through participation in this second narrative.

Karen Van Hove's 'Narrating pornographic images: photographic description and ekphrasis in *De fotograaf* by Jef Geeraerts' (chapter 11) is focused upon a 1972 novel published by Geeraerts under the penname Claus Trum, with the publisher Walter Soethoudt. Challenging the typical association of pornography with visual media (VHS, DVD, online), Van Hove points to a flourishing industry of pornographic books in the 1960s and 1970s, in Europe and in America. The specific example Van Hove chooses relates to a photographer and often describes photographs, the setting up of scenes to be photographed and relationships between the photographer and his subjects. Thus, Van Hove understands this particular novel as characterized both by photographic description and by ekphrasis, as well as by what she proposes as a hybrid form between the two, with implications also for non-pornographic texts. Van Hove shows how images can be constructed in narrative and suggests that such descriptions are designed to arouse the reader. Here, the reader's vulnerability is argued to be pleasurable, although Van Hove also considers the issue of the 'male gaze' that connects ekphrasis and pornography, presenting the female body as particularly vulnerable in this regard.

The fourth and final part of the volume is devoted to 'Medium/Genre'. To open this section, Katie Ginsbach considers a popular Spanish television series in 'Through the doors of time: media interactions and cultural memory in *El Ministerio del Tiempo*' (chapter 12). Like the chapters by Rapisardi and Camacho, Ginsbach is interested in the relationship between fiction and history. More particularly, Ginsbach analyses the way in which different media, present in the TV series, emblematize different historical moments, convey a sense of time and act as containers of cultural memory. Moreover, Ginsbach also shows how fans interact with the series through different media, considering the involvement of the viewer in a way that is reminiscent of the role of the player investigated in previous chapters, in particular that of Paklons and Tratsaert. The past is thus brought to life in the present, though not in a traumatic way (as in Rapisardi's consideration of the Parsley Massacre) but rather in a playfully anachronistic but educational spirit. Where the vulnerability of the present to a return of the past had been traumatic in other chapters, here this vulnerability is a form of ludic openness that allows for a reassessment and reshaping of temporal relationships.

Chapter 13 sees a return to Atwood's *MaddAddam* trilogy in Eva Dinis's 'Vulnerability as duality in speculative fiction'. As anticipated above, Dinis's contribution concerns the relationship between Atwood and science fiction, a genre from which Atwood has tended to distance herself. Dinis considers the relationship between science fiction and the subgenre of speculative fiction (Atwood's preferred term), as well as the way in which certain genres not only reflect on vulnerability (as is typically the case with science fiction, concerned with the vulnerability of possible worlds and their various inhabitants) but are themselves in a different sense vulnerable in terms of their status and categorization. Like other chapters in this volume, Dinis argues for the ambivalence of vulnerability, that is, the inherent dichotomy between potentially undesirable fragility and potentially desirable openness. In support of her analysis, Dinis draws on vulnerability studies, genre theory and Atwood's own theoretical writings in *In Other Worlds* (2011).

The final chapter, Jan Baetens's 'No, poetry is not out of date: notes on poetic writing and digital culture' (chapter 14), considers current trends in contemporary French-language poetry, with particular attention to the writings of Olivier Cadiot and Pierre Alferi. Jacques Derrida claims in an interview on 'Che cos'è la poesia?' ('What is poetry?') that poetry is an inherently vulnerable genre: 'no poem that does not open itself like a wound, but no poem that is not also just as wounding'.[24] Baetens explores what happens when poetry meets digital culture, not only in the sense of the possibilities of digital poetry but also, as Baetens argues, in the sense that digital culture changes our relationship to all media, whether they are themselves digital or not. Thus, rather than considering exclusively screen-based poetry, Baetens is more interested in what he calls demediatization and transmedialization as products of digitization, the former defined by Baetens as 'a creative procedure that favours components that can move as freely as possible from one medium to the next' and the latter, instead, as a phenomenon of fragmentation and serialization across media, as previous chapters (in particular that of Ginsbach) have also examined.

The volume ends with an afterword on 'Covid-19 or the vulnerability of the future' by Florian Mussgnug, which reflects on the challenge of the coronavirus pandemic. Mussgnug considers in particular how vulnerability affects our imagining of possible futures, while calling the very possibility of a future into question.

***

This volume is the result of long-standing discussions that started during two international doctoral summer schools convened by the Hermes Consortium for Literary and Cultural Studies, a network of 11 doctoral schools in Belgium, the Czech Republic, Denmark, Finland, Germany, Great Britain, the Netherlands, Portugal, Spain, France and the United States. The earlier of these two summer schools, 'Contemporary Genre and Media Interactions', took place in Leuven in June 2016, with generous support from Belspo (Belgian Science Agency) and KU Leuven. The more recent summer school, 'Vulnerability', was jointly hosted by the Italian Institute of Germanic Studies (Istituto Italiano di Studi Germanici) and by University College London. It took place at Villa Sciarra-Wurts in Rome in June 2018. On this second occasion, our sponsors included the Faculty of Arts and Humanities at University College London (Dean's Strategic Fund) and the UCL Global Engagement Office. We further benefited from close partnership with the Italian National Research Council (CNR) through the CNR-funded large collaborative research project Progetto di Ricerca di Rilevante Interesse Nazionale (PRIN 2015–17): 'Soggetto di diritto e vulnerabilità: modelli istituzionali e concetti giuridici in trasformazione', convened by Baldassare Pastore. This led to the organization of a further conference, which took place in parallel with the 2018 Hermes summer school, and which was organized by Lucia Corso and Giuseppina Talamo, with generous funding from the University of Enna

'Kore'.²⁵ We are grateful to all institutions and colleagues who through their active support provided important opportunities for encounter and dialogue for senior researchers and doctoral students from many parts of the world.

We are grateful to all the contributors, who have responded enthusiastically to our invitation to rethink the relation between vulnerability and media. Our thanks also go to our colleagues who took part in both conferences as keynote speakers and panel chairs: Brigitte Adriaensen, Susana Araujo, Stephan Besser, Klaus Brax, Fernando Cabo Aseguinolaza, Jim Collins, Lucia Corso, Antonio Gil, Giandomenico Iannetti, Katherine Ibbett, Jens Kugele, Elizabeth Kovach, Peter Leary, Luca Marcozzi, Timothy Mathews, Jean-Christophe Mayer, Simona Micali, Baldassare Pastore, Aarathi Prasad, Martin Procházka, Heta Pyrhönen, Ellen Sapega, Karen-Margrethe Simonsen and Jakob Stougaard-Nielsen. We thank KU Leuven and the Italian Institute of Germanic Studies for logistical and technical assistance.

The following colleagues in particular deserve our gratitude. Gert-Jan Meyntjens, Heidi Peeters and Arne Vanraes assisted with the practical organization of the Leuven summer school and provided feedback on earlier drafts of the chapters. We are grateful to Roberta Ascarelli, academic director of the Italian Institute of Germanic Studies from 2015 until 2019, for welcoming Hermes to the picturesque setting of Villa Sciarra-Wurts. We thank Tamar Garb for suggesting the theme for the 2018 summer school and Alastair James Shibby Bromwich for his patient and precious help with bookings and financial conundrums, as well as Melissa Oliver-Powell for her help at the summer school in person. Liz Rideal's artwork has inspired much of our thinking about vulnerability and mediation, and we are proud and grateful that her 'Bronzino Underbelly (Galleria Borghese)' can feature on the cover of this book. Timothy Mathews, the co-editor of the Comparative Literature and Culture Series, was a cherished source of advice throughout the editorial process, providing inspiring and illuminating comments at every stage. Finally, we wish to thank our anonymous readers and the effortlessly energetic Chris Penfold, our commissioning editor at UCL Press, who made this project less vulnerable than it would have been without them.

Notes

1. Nussbaum, *Fragility*, 343–72; Butler, *Precarious Life*.
2. Singh, *Unthinking Mastery*, 22.
3. Ferrarese, *Vulnerability and Critical Theory*, 1.
4. Corso, 'Vulnerabilità e concetto di diritto'.

5. On the relationship between 9/11 and vulnerability, see especially Butler, *Precarious Life*. For a useful literature review on climate crisis and vulnerability, see Ford, Pearce and McDowell, 'Vulnerability and its discontents'. For a similar undertaking in the social sciences, see Virokannas, Liuski and Kuronen, 'The contested concept of vulnerability'.
6. Butler, Gambetti and Sabsay, 'Introduction', 1.
7. See, accordingly, Koivunen, Kyrölä and Ryberg, *The Power of Vulnerability*.
8. Butler, Gambetti and Sabsay, 'Introduction', 4.
9. Bolter and Grusin, *Remediation*.
10. Vertovec, *Transnationalism*, 3.
11. Inevitably, all edited volumes have their own limits. This is another form of the limits alluded to in the title of this introduction. In our project, one limit has been the focus on modern and contemporary artistic forms, at the expense of attention to earlier periods. Exceptions in secondary criticism to this trend include Greene, *The Vulnerable Text*; Tylus, *Writing and Vulnerability in the Late Renaissance*; McCoy, *Wounded Heroes*; Leonard, *Tragic Modernities*; Bulotta, *Vulnerability*; Gragnolati, Lombardi and Southerden, 'Introduction'.
12. Ganteau, *The Ethics and Aesthetics of Vulnerability in Contemporary British Fiction*.
13. Pick, *Creaturely Poetics*; see also Pick, 'Vulnerability'.
14. Callahan, 'The vulnerability of the human condition', 115.
15. Mackenzie, Rogers and Dodds, 'Introduction', 4.
16. Bentham, *An Introduction to the Principles of Morals and Legislation*, 283.
17. See Mackenzie, Rogers and Dodds, 'Introduction'.
18. Onega and Ganteau, 'Introduction', 10.
19. De Ferrari, *Vulnerable States*.
20. See Mitchell, 'Narrative prosthesis and the materiality of metaphor'.
21. On the vulnerability of Black men, Kolehmainen is particularly in dialogue with Curry, *The Man-Not*.
22. Deleuze and Guattari, *Kafka*.
23. Halberstam, *The Queer Art of Failure*.
24. Derrida, 'Che cos'è la poesia?', 233.
25. The proceedings of this conference have since been published. See Corso and Talamo, *Vulnerabilità di fronte alle istituzioni*.

Bibliography

Bentham, Jeremy. *An Introduction to the Principles of Morals and Legislation*, edited by J. H. Burns and H. L. A. Hart. London: The Athlone Press, 1970.

Bolter, Jay David, and Richard Grusin. *Remediation: Understanding new media*. Cambridge, MA: MIT Press, 1999.

Bulotta, Donata, ed. *Vulnerability: Memories, bodies, sites / Vulnerabilità: Memorie, corpi, spazi*. Perugia: Morlacchi, 2016.

Butler, Judith. *Precarious Life: The powers of mourning and violence*. London: Verso, 2006.

Butler, Judith, Zeynep Gambetti and Leticia Sabsay. 'Introduction'. In *Vulnerability in Resistance*, edited by Judith Butler, Zeynep Gambetti and Leticia Sabsay, 1–11. Durham, NC: Duke University Press, 2016.

Callahan, Daniel. 'The vulnerability of the human condition'. In *Bioethics and Biolaw*, edited by Peter Kemp, Jacob Dahl Rendtorff and Niels Mattsson Johansen, 2 vols, II, 115–22. Copenhagen: Rhodos International Science and Art Publishers, 2000.

Corso, Lucia. 'Vulnerabilità e concetto di diritto'. In *Vulnerabilità di fronte alle istituzioni e vulnerabilità delle istituzioni*, edited by Lucia Corso and Giuseppina Talamo, 3–13. Turin: Giappichelli Editore, 2019.

Corso, Lucia, and Giuseppina Talamo, eds. *Vulnerabilità di fronte alle istituzioni e vulnerabilità delle istitutzioni*. Turin: Giappichelli Editore, 2019.

Curry, Tommy J. *The Man-Not: Race, class, genre, and the dilemmas of Black manhood*. Philadelphia: Temple University Press, 2017.

Deleuze, Gilles, and Félix Guattari. *Kafka: Toward a minor literature*, translated by Dana Polan. Minneapolis: University of Minnesota Press, 1986.

Derrida, Jacques. 'Che cos'è la poesia?' In *A Derrida Reader: Between the blinds*, edited by Peggy Kamuf, 221–37. New York: Columbia University Press, 1991.

Ferrarese, Estelle. *Vulnerability and Critical Theory*, translated by Steven Corcoran. Leiden: Brill, 2018.

Ferrari, Guillermina De. *Vulnerable States: Bodies of memory in contemporary Caribbean fiction*. Charlottesville: University of Virginia Press, 2012.

Ford, James D., Tristan Pearce, Graham McDowell and others. 'Vulnerability and its discontents: The past, present, and future of climate change vulnerability research'. *Climatic Change* 151 (2018): 189–203.

Ganteau, Jean-Michel. *The Ethics and Aesthetics of Vulnerability in Contemporary British Fiction*. London: Routledge, 2015.

Gragnolati, Manuele, Elena Lombardi and Francesca Southerden. 'Introduction: Dante unbound: A vulnerable life and the openness of interpretation'. In *The Oxford Handbook of Dante*, edited by Manuele Gragnolati, Elena Lombardi and Francesca Southerden, xxiii–xxxv. Oxford: Oxford University Press, 2021.

Greene, Thomas M. *The Vulnerable Text: Essays on Renaissance literature*. New York: Columbia University Press, 1986.

Halberstam, Jack. *The Queer Art of Failure*. Durham, NC: Duke University Press, 2011.

Koivunen, Anu, Katariina Kyrölä and Ingrid Ryberg, eds. *The Power of Vulnerability: Mobilising affect in feminist, queer and anti-racist media cultures*. Manchester: Manchester University Press, 2018.

Leonard, Miriam. *Tragic Modernities*. Cambridge, MA: Harvard University Press, 2015.

Mackenzie, Catriona, Wendy Rogers and Susan Dodds. 'Introduction: What is vulnerability, and why does it matter for moral theory?' In *Vulnerability: New essays in ethics and feminist philosophy*, edited by Catriona Mackenzie, Wendy Rogers and Susan Dodds, 1–26. New York: Oxford University Press, 2014.

McCoy, Marina Berzins. *Wounded Heroes: Vulnerability as a virtue in ancient Greek literature*. Oxford: Oxford University Press, 2013.

Mitchell, David T. 'Narrative prosthesis and the materiality of metaphor'. In *Disability Studies: Enabling the humanities*, edited by Sharon L. Snyder, Brenda Jo Brueggemann and Rosemarie Garland-Thomson, 15–29. New York: The Modern Language Association of America, 2002.

Nussbaum, Martha. *The Fragility of Goodness: Luck and ethics in Greek tragedy and philosophy*. Cambridge: Cambridge University Press, 1986.

Onega, Susana, and Jean-Michel Ganteau. 'Introduction'. In *Victimhood and Vulnerability in 21st Century Fiction*, edited by Jean-Michel Ganteau and Susana Onega, 1–18. New York: Routledge, 2017.

Pick, Anat. *Creaturely Poetics: Animality and vulnerability in literature and film*. New York: Columbia University Press, 2011.

Pick, Anat. 'Vulnerability'. In *Critical Terms for Animal Studies*, edited by Lori Gruen, 410–23. Chicago: University of Chicago Press, 2018.

Singh, Julietta. *Unthinking Mastery: Dehumanism and decolonial entanglements*. Durham, NC: Duke University Press, 2018.

Tylus, Jane. *Writing and Vulnerability in the Late Renaissance*. Stanford, CA: Stanford University Press, 1993.

Vertovec, Steven. *Transnationalism*. London: Routledge, 2009.

Virokannas, Elina, Suvi Liuski and Marjo Kuronen. 'The contested concept of vulnerability: A literature review'. *European Journal of Social Work* 23 (2018): 1–13.

Part 1:
Human/Animal

1
What if they could speak? Humanized animals in science fiction

Simona Micali

From *Aesop's Fables* to Disney's *Zootopia* (2016; also known as *Zootropolis*), the fictional imagination has offered countless stories of 'humanized animals' – animals that think, speak and behave as humans. Their characterizations and narrative roles cover a vast range, from fantastic beings who may act as helpers or antagonists in fantasy tales to generic animals, which are clear allegories of human types or qualities. In all these cases, the figures are the product of the universal practice of anthropomorphization, a cognitive and imaginative mechanism that functions as a filter both in our perception of and in our speculation about non-human beings and entities.[1] Recent studies in cognitive psychology, anthropology and ethics have shown that anthropomorphism may have an important role in shaping our attitudes and behaviour towards other species, thus gradually dismantling the centuries-long scientific arguments against it. Yet it is quite evident that anthropomorphizing animals does not automatically affect our consideration of animals per se. This is clearly demonstrated by the fact that the continuous practice of seeing and imagining animals with human features has not hindered in the least the equally continuous exploitation, maltreatment and slaughter of animals for our own purposes.

In this chapter I will leave aside anthropomorphized animals and focus instead on works of fiction in which the humanization of animals is meant in a literal sense, namely, science fiction (SF) stories involving figures of animals that have undergone a process or a procedure through which they have acquired some human features. These figures are not a particular case of the more general category of anthropomorphic animals. Indeed, the assumed plausibility of their origin radically changes their ontological and fictional status. Mickey Mouse and Philip K. Dick's post-atomic mice are not variations of a single figure, but completely different creatures. The former is the inhabitant of a fantasy world in which animals are assumed to be analogous to humans, and the rules of 'make-believe' require us to accept this purely imaginary premise for the whole time of our experience. On the contrary, Dick's mice are the inhabitants of a fictional world which is a credible and very realistic transformation of the one we live in, due to some exceptional (yet epistemologically possible) condition or event. The narrative pact requires us to accept this new world as possible not only temporarily, within the limits of the work we are reading, but also in the general sphere of our real world. If we assume that a humanized mouse is actually *possible*, it stops being a nice, cute creature and becomes instead a more disturbing, problematic being. More importantly, its characterization and fictional behaviour necessarily affect the way in which we regard actual mice, as they draw our attention to some features or potentialities in mice which we may previously have disregarded or underestimated. In short, it produces what Darko Suvin has defined as 'cognitive estrangement', that peculiar mechanism produced to a greater or lesser extent by any SF work.[2] By inviting us to see possible developments in or alternatives to the world we live in, SF enhances our critical understanding of what is real by highlighting or interpreting, or else by criticizing, particular aspects which we do not usually perceive clearly or thoroughly understand, or which we take for granted. In the case of humanized animals, I will argue that their SF occurrences always tend to be problematic, even when they are not openly threatening or *unheimlich* (uncanny), to evoke the Freudian term. They usually share some common features, including a peculiar and estranging use of language, a strongly pathetic profile and a controversial legal status. All these features, which are clearly connected to our notion of the 'vulnerable subject', refer to the same general category of the 'subhuman', that is, creatures outlined and perceived according to the human standard and yet regarded as insufficient or underdeveloped versions of it – as *not fully, not yet human*.[3] In other words, humanization is never complete. It is even suggested that humanization may never be able to be fully accomplished, thus leaving the test subject stuck in an ambivalent, intermediate condition between humanness and animality, which disturbs us since it obviously questions the very boundary between human and animal, thus hampering the functioning of what Giorgio Agamben has defined as 'the Anthropological Machine'.[4]

   Mutant animals are fascinating, fantastic creatures and therefore very popular in the SF imagination across multiple media. From

Godzilla to Jurassic Park's dinosaurs, from the evolved monkeys of the *Planet of the Apes* film saga to the cyber-animal Rocket Raccoon in the Marvel comic *Guardians of the Galaxy*, we could illustrate a rich typology of characterization, modes of representation and narrative roles. Yet in this chapter I will direct my attention almost exclusively towards literary representations. My impression is that in all media involving visual representation the humanizing effect relies primarily on the physical aspects of the creatures: human features, clothes, an upright position, voice and so on. When represented visually, the animal's humanness is somehow normalized and becomes almost a foregone fact, no longer disturbing, in a manner similar to what happens in anthropomorphic representations. Instead, in literary representations the visual aspects are clearly secondary, mediated elements and humanization concerns primarily language and agency, in the sense that the humanized animal manifests itself mostly and above all by the way it speaks and acts, and by the motives and emotions which produce its speech and actions. Therefore, literary speculation mainly involves not so much the way in which the creature is characterized by the narrative but the way in which it positions itself in relation to the other characters, the plot and the narrative itself. In short, my interest is directed towards the humanized animal not as an *object* of fictional representation, but rather as a possible *subject* within fiction.

In the following pages, I will discuss the features of some of these very peculiar creatures, which I believe may both usefully highlight some implications of the theme of vulnerability in literature and connect it to the emerging discussion of non-human animals as 'vulnerable subjects' in Human–Animal Studies.[5]

Victor Frankenstein meets Charles Darwin

The theme of humanized animals clearly finds its origin and epistemological ground in Darwin's theory of evolution, of which it emphasizes the implicit questioning of anthropocentrism and speciesism. In fact, both H. G. Wells's *The Island of Doctor Moreau* (1896) and Mikhail Bulgakov's *The Heart of a Dog* (1925) can be easily read as rewritings of Mary Shelley's *Frankenstein* – probably the most influential archetype of modern SF – in light of the popularization of the theory of evolution. While Shelley's arrogant scientist defied God's authority to instil human life in inanimate matter, the post-Darwinian scientists compete with Him in trying to reproduce instantaneously the ages-long work of evolution which has transformed the beast into an intelligent, ethical creature. Yet, just like Frankenstein, they will be severely punished for their hubris, as the creatures will reject their mastery and revolt – although the consequences will be tragic in the moralistic Wells, but much milder in the disenchanted and ironic Bulgakov.

H. G. Wells wrote *The Island of Doctor Moreau* in the wake of the dispute raised by the first protests against the practice of vivisection in Victorian Britain.[6] Despite his being a man of science and a student of Thomas Henry Huxley, Wells seems to take a firm stand against experimentation on animals in his portrait of the fanatic Moreau – who, as the protagonist Prendick suddenly recalls, had been 'howled out of the country' by the scandal raised regarding his experiments on living animals and had chosen to exile himself on a deserted Pacific island.[7] Here he is totally alone with his assistant Montgomery and a large number of wild animals upon whom he is totally free to carry out his research work, which is aimed at transforming them into human beings, by manipulating their bodies through surgery and their minds through hypnosis and terror. Nevertheless, it is not vivisection in itself which arouses Prendick's (and the reader's) moral judgement (as he remarks, 'there was nothing so horrible in vivisection'), but the fact that Moreau's experiments are 'wantonly cruel'.[8] The scientist will in fact explain that he regards the infliction of physical pain on his subject as totally irrelevant in view of his noble scientific goals:

> 'You see, I went on with this research just the way it led me. That is the only way I ever heard of research going . . . You cannot imagine the strange colourless delight of these intellectual desires. The thing before you is no longer an animal, a fellow-creature, but a problem. Sympathetic pain – all I know of it I remember as a thing I used to suffer from years ago. I wanted – it was the only thing I wanted – to find out the extreme limit of plasticity in a living shape.'
>
> 'But,' said I, 'the thing is an abomination –'
>
> 'To this day I have never troubled about the ethics of the matter. The study of Nature makes a man at last as remorseless as Nature.'[9]

If experimenting on animals does not raise ethical issues, inflicting unnecessary pain on a 'fellow creature' does. The ambivalence is therefore connected to the question of how much pain is inflicted and how 'necessary' we consider it to be. Wells's narrative strategies actually illustrate this ambivalence. The narrator, Edward Prendick, is a gentleman and himself an amateur natural scientist, therefore he is in the best position to appreciate Moreau's intellectual passion. From this narrative perspective, in our first encounter with the large number of brutes who inhabit the island we regard them as weird, underdeveloped or degenerated human beings, whose beastly countenances and behaviour trigger horror and disgust. Here is the description of the first of Moreau's creatures Prendick encounters:

> He was, I could see, a misshapen man, short, broad, and clumsy, with a crooked back, a hairy neck, and a head sunk between his shoulders . . . The facial part projected, forming something dimly suggestive of a muzzle, and the huge half-open mouth showed as big white teeth as I had ever seen in a human mouth. His eyes were bloodshot at the edges, with scarcely a rim of white round the hazel pupils . . . I had paused halfway through the hatchway, looking back, still astonished beyond measure at the grotesque ugliness of this black-faced creature. I had never beheld such a repulsive and extraordinary face before.[10]

At first Prendick supposes they are men on whom Moreau has run some devilish experiment. When he finds out the truth, he undoubtedly disapproves of Moreau's experiments, which he regards as an unacceptable manipulation of the laws of Nature; yet he still feels aversion for the test subjects, which he considers as 'bestial monsters, mere grotesque travesties of men', to be distrusted and feared.[11] The animal in them is still too clearly visible; 'the unmistakable mark of the beast' excludes them from the range of our sympathy. Moreover, the humanness of these 'Beast Folk' – as he calls them – is precarious, since the animal component remains latent and is ready to take over at any time.[12] Their violent drives, their dullness and their inability to manage complex concepts and speech are markers of their persistently animal nature. In fact, once Moreau's control over them finally comes to an end, each species rapidly regresses from its acquired subhuman condition to its original animal one. On an allegorical level, the story may thus be read as a fantastic transposition of the theory of atavism, in which Wells was particularly interested. According to this theory, the evolution leading from animal to man is not a one-way path; rather, the animal's genetic traits remain dormant within the human gene pool and may re-emerge at any time, thus pushing us back towards our animal ancestors. The underlying vision which Wells's fantasy evokes is that of progressionary evolutionism, the popular version of the Darwinian theory, which presumes humans to be at the top of the 'evolutionary ladder', the culmination and *telos* of the million-years-long evolution of living species. The resurgence of animal traits is therefore seen as a throwback of evolution, a regression from what is more perfect and valuable to what is incomplete and less worthy.

What challenges Prendick's self-confident speciesism, that is to say his trust in the natural superiority of man and his right to dispose of other species at will, is being confronted with the expression of their pain. When Moreau starts to perform his surgery on a puma, the continuous cries of the beast are 'such an exquisite expression of suffering' that he finds himself unable to bear them.[13] Later on, he will be touched by the manifest suffering of the Beast Folk in repressing their natural animal drives. The animal is revealed to be a vulnerable, pathetic creature, and the acknowledgement of its pain triggers our empathy and brings about the sense of an interspecies community which stops us from considering it as ontologically different from ourselves. But this can happen only if we are allowed to *hear* the animal. As Prendick remarks, '[i]t is when suffering finds a voice and sets our nerves quivering that this pity comes troubling us'.[14] Empathy may be triggered exclusively if the animal is granted the right to a voice. Eventually Prendick will definitively reject Moreau and will passively assist when the Beast Folk take their bloody revenge on their God-torturer. Notwithstanding his instinctive aversion to them, Prendick chooses to betray his fellows and stand with the subhuman creatures, thus becoming in practice a defendant of animal rights.

Listening to a dog's voice

Significantly, the moving cry of an animal in pain opens one of the most bizarre works of early twentieth-century SF, Mikhail Bulgakov's *The Heart of a Dog* (*Sobachye syerdtsye*): 'Ooow-ow-ooow-owow! Oh, look at me, I'm dying.'[15] The voice of the animal this time is not filtered through the perception of a first-person narrator but addresses us directly, requiring us to unexpectedly empathize with the animal Other and to share the vision, opinions and emotions of the stray dog Sharik, the owner of the title's heart.[16] Sharik has a rich emotional and intellectual life; he understands perfectly what humans say – although he does not grasp their thoughts and motives completely – and can even read. However, he has no means of expressing himself to other species; we readers are the only beneficiaries of his perspective. Most importantly, Sharik is not just the primary focalizing character of the novel, he is the only one. His perspective is the only one we are allowed to share. When he ceases to be himself – that is, when he starts his humanizing process – we are not allowed access to any other point of view. The story is then recounted through the technique defined as 'external focalization' and we see and hear what happens from a totally external, impassive perspective.

This narrative strategy is the most original element of the novel and grants it its bizarre quality. The story in itself can be read as a satirical rewriting of *The Island of Doctor Moreau* – and, further back, of Shelley's *Frankenstein* as well. The renowned surgeon Filipp Filippovich Preobrazhensky is in fact dragged into his foolish experiment neither by Frankenstein's Promethean arrogance nor by Moreau's fanatical scientific passion. He and his protégé, Dr Bormenthal, are simply experimenting with new ways of achieving bodily rejuvenation, for which their rich patients are willing to pay whatever honorarium they request.[17] The great scientist has put his genius to the service of the vanity of the upper class and sacrifices poor Sharik to it with a light heart. He had picked up the dog in the street and misled him into thinking he had finally become a bourgeois pet. In this case, humanization is produced as an unexpected side effect of the experiment. By substituting the dog's pituitary gland and testicles with that of a young thief who had recently died, the result is not a renovation of the canine body, but its total transformation into a complete human being. The transformation of the body is paralleled by a surprisingly rapid acquisition of the ability to speak, but the utterances of the creature are not what we would expect. The first word he utters is 'Nesseta-ciled', which is easily deciphered as the reversal of 'delicatessen'; then he calls his creator a 'bloody bastard', causing him to faint; the third utterance anticipates his main passion in life, 'liquor'; finally, all possible swear words follow in an endless litany.[18] Dr Bormenthal, who is keeping the clinic log, entirely mistakes what is happening and thinks that what they are watching is the actual humanization of the dog Sharik himself:

> As I see it, the situation is as follows: the implanted pituitary has activated the speech-centre in the canine brain and words have poured out in a stream. I do not think that we have before us a newly-created brain but a brain which has been stimulated to develop. Oh, what a glorious confirmation of the theory of evolution! Oh, the sublime chain leading from a dog to Mendeleyev the great chemist! A further hypothesis of mine is that during its canine stage Sharik's brain had accumulated a massive quantity of sense-data. All the words which he used initially were the language of the streets which he had picked up and stored in his brain.[19]

This new being maintains very few traits of his former animal self, namely terrorizing cats, his voracious appetite and the tendency to catch lice. Surprisingly, however, he develops the psychological and moral traits of the man from whom the organs were taken, who unfortunately had been a scoundrel, ignorant and shameless. In short, the two scientists will have to acknowledge that what they are dealing with is not a humanized Sharik, but the revived dead thief in the body of Sharik. While the dog Sharik had been 'naughty' but funny and loyal to his master, the citizen Poligraf Poligrafovich Sharikov – as he chooses to call himself – is rude and stubborn, harasses the housemaid, steals money and drinks alcohol.[20] What is worse, he gangs up with the proletarians who have occupied part of the elegant building in which Preobrazhensky lives and have been trying to expropriate part of his luxurious apartment. He himself thus becomes the nemesis for the reckless scientist. The monster which this new Frankenstein has brought to life is an impudent proletarian who calls him 'Dad' and 'comrade' and threatens to destroy the wealth and very bourgeois life of his master.[21] Nor can he be banished, as Frankenstein's Creature was, because he cleverly defends his right to being taken care of by the man who brought him to life. But this time, the creator will be wiser than his predecessors and will find a way to reverse his unfortunate creation. When the criminal police, 10 days after the sudden disappearance of Sharikov and with news of a violent fight heard from Preobrazhensky's flat, go to arrest the doctor for murdering the man, they find the creature almost entirely returned to a canine state:

> from the door into the study appeared a dog of the most extraordinary appearance. In patches he was bald, while in other patches his coat had grown. He entered like a trained circus dog walking on his hind legs, then dropped on to all fours and looked round. The waiting-room froze into a sepulchral silence as tangible as jelly. The nightmarish-looking dog with the crimson scar on the forehead stood up again on his hind legs, grinned and sat down in an armchair.[22]

The regression of the subhuman creature back to the animal condition solves all legal and practical issues. As a humanized being, Sharikov shared all human rights and any abuse of him would have had to be legally prosecuted. As an animal, he is instead the property of Preobrazhensky, who is entitled to dispose of him as he wishes.[23] Thus, the novel implicitly exposes the animal condition of what has been defined as 'situational vulnerability'.[24] Moreover, the creature has by now conveniently lost any ability to communicate with humans. As Preobrazhensky explains to the astonished policemen, '"[s]cience has not yet found the means of turning animals into people. I tried, but unsuccessfully, as you can see. He talked and then he began to revert back to his primitive state. Atavism."'[25] It is hard to believe that here Bulgakov is not parodying the tragic story of Moreau's abominable experiments. If in Wells the process from Beast to Man had been indisputably assumed as an enhancement of the intellectual and moral status of the creatures, in Bulgakov such an anthropocentric vision appears at best questionable, if not openly invalidated. All the human characters, Sharikov included, are portrayed as arrogant, selfish and devoid of any compassion; our sympathy and compassion go exclusively to the dog Sharik.[26] We cherish and take pity on his reappearance on the last page of the book, reinstated as the house pet, yet definitely damaged in mind and body from the experiment.

The freak children of the bomb

Language, and especially the possibility of interspecies communication, holds a crucial role in fantasies exploring the possibility of a different relationship between human and non-human animals. As Gary Steiner has remarked, the anthropocentric vision can be summarized in the assumption that 'all and only human beings are worthy of moral consideration, because all and only human beings are rational and endowed with language'.[27] From this perspective, the stories we are dealing with, and more generally the works of SF involving communication with animals, explore the possibility of bridging the species gap by enabling animals to express themselves through human language, thus removing one of the main anthropocentric biases which have oriented our vision of (and relationship with) non-human animals.[28]

In the two novels mentioned above, speaking animals were exceptional cases, creatures produced in single specimens by a post-Darwinian Frankenstein trained in surgery and natural biology. In the wake of the bombing of Hiroshima and Nagasaki, both scientists and SF writers learned not only that genetic mutations could be produced either by the million-year-long work of evolution or by lab experiments, but that they might also be an appalling side effect of nuclear fallout. Post-atomic scenarios of the 1960s and 1970s offer us worlds richly populated by mutated or evolved animals, and conversely by regressed or degenerated humans. In this sense, the nuclear holocaust works like a sort of genetic spell which upsets and mixes up the genetic make-up of the living world, causing sudden deviations, contaminations and devolutions, as well as evolutionary leaps.

In the novels of the most visionary SF writer of these decades, Philip K. Dick, the post-apocalyptic narrative is intertwined with, and counterbalanced by, what we could define as a 'regressive utopia', resuming the model of the small pre-industrial community. In fact, the catastrophe works as a sort of blank slate on which we can start over again, retrieving the naturalness and humane solidarity of 'the good old times' which preceded the degeneration of modern and technological capitalism. A strong emphasis is thus given to the opposition between images of decay and images of healing; it is suggested that a decaying humanity and the wounded Earth may be healed only by means of this re-founded communal solidarity, within humanity itself but also within the larger family of all living beings, all the old, new and mutated or damaged species. In *Dr Bloodmoney* (1965), many animals have evolved to be sentient and some have even gained the ability to use human language. Some of them seem like pathetic imitations of humans, such as Terry, the good-natured talking dog, of whom the whole community of Marin County is fond. When the new schoolteacher, Barnes, meets him, he cannot make out the words Terry struggles to utter:

> It was a hideous sound, and Barnes shivered; it sounded like [...], a damaged person trying to work a vocal apparatus which had failed. Out of the groaning he detected – or thought he detected – a word or so, but he could not be sure. Bonny, however, seemed to understand.[29]

Other animals have developed more dangerous abilities and appear to be a threat to humans. Cats, who have developed their own language and at night are heard 'mewing to one another in the darkness', live in small, organized gangs, and rumour has it that 'they killed and ate small children almost at will'.[30] As for rats, many humans think they should be killed systematically as they have become too smart and '[s]omeday America may be taken over by rats if we aren't vigilant'.[31] But others maintain that all these 'brilliant animals' (as they are collectively referred to) could instead be an important asset for humans, as helpers or 'servants to us human beings'.[32] Most importantly, mutations have also deeply changed the human species, producing a large number of so-called 'funny people': 'strange and exotic variants on the human life form which flourished now under a much more tolerant – although smokily veiled – sky'.[33] From this perspective, animal freaks are not so different from human freaks. Both are feared and rejected by many (there is also a new US Eugenics Service which is supposed to dispose of 'funny people'), but they were born in this world as well, and they have a right to inhabit it. As Stockstill, Marin County's doctor, realizes: 'There is nothing . . . which is "outside" nature; that is a logical impossibility. In a way there are no freaks, no abnormalities, except in the statistical sense.'[34] Whatever regeneration may be possible for the living world, it needs to make room for all the 'funny' and 'unfunny' creatures now populating it.[35]

This is made even more explicit in *Deus Irae* (1976), which Dick published together with Roger Zelazny and which is in many respects a fantastic and religious rewriting of *Dr Bloodmoney*. Here, the nuclear catastrophe has triggered a general process of genetic mutation and hybridization involving all animal species. The result is quite a wide range of mutants and freaks, a weird bestiary composed especially of grotesque hybrids of human and animal genes. All of them are sentient; some may be very dangerous, such as the huge dark worm who kills every living being who gets too close to its 'possessions', which are a very poor trove of trash from a past civilization.[36] Others are instead well-mannered and benevolent, such as the 'lizards', evolved humanoid reptiles who revere and protect human beings, convinced that humans will be able to repopulate the Earth. The figures composing this diverse population outline a proper hierarchy of living species, a sort of new post-apocalyptic Tree of Life. At the bottom of it are the 'regular' animals, those who have not mutated, such as the cow which pulls the cart of the phocomelic protagonist, Tibor McMasters, or the nice dog the lizards give him to protect him during his pilgrimage. On a higher level are the new hybrid species: the lizards and the worm, but also the disgusting 'bugs', endowed with great loquacity and wit, or the 'runners', humanoid hares who spread 'a kind of peace' wherever they go.[37] Still higher up are the damaged or degenerated humans, including the protagonist Tibor, called 'inc.', that is, 'incomplete', and therefore placed a step below regular humans but still credited with the worth and respect due to those who were once masters of the planet. Above them are the 'complete' humans; and on top of the chain of living beings is the 'God of Wrath', the divine incarnation of the supreme being worshipped by the new post-atomic religion. Tibor's mission is to find Him and reproduce His image in the church mural he is painting for the Servants of Wrath. But when the God of Wrath kills Tibor's dog out of pure wickedness, the inc. kills him. The message is that all creatures who inhabit the Earth are valuable. Even the lowliest living being has its own dignity and right to exist, and if the master of the creation kills it, then He himself deserves to die. In short, interspecies harmony, respect and solidarity among all living beings are the only ways to restore life and heal the planet.

However, the possibility of linguistic exchange is not necessarily a step towards the utopia of an interspecies community. As observed by Sherryl Vint, '[p]erfect knowledge does not immediately and without struggle lead to perfect harmony'.[38] On the contrary, the intellectual evolution of an animal species may be seen as an obvious threat to our leadership on the planet and even to our survival. This dystopian reversal of the theme of humanized animals is typical of popular SF or fantasy, usually grounded in an anthropocentric vision, from the very popular franchise derived from Michael Crichton's *Jurassic Park* (1990) to blockbusters such as *Reign of Fire* (2002). The archetype of these fantasies is definitely the 1963 novel *La Planète des Singes* (*Planet of the Apes*) by the French writer Pierre Boulle, which spawned a rich progeny of intermedial adaptations, sequels and rewritings. Boulle does not deal with the threat of an impending nuclear conflict, although his novel is a clear reflection of Cold War anxieties.[39] As a SF novel of the 1960s, *Planet of the Apes* appears quite naïve in its scientific references and political critique, yet Boulle's novel still arouses our interest in some of its ideas. Foremost among these is the pre-eminent role assigned to linguistic ability. In fact, the apes manifestly hold the right to rule the alien planet on which the terrestrial explorers have landed because they are able to master a complex language; the humans of the planet cannot but be regarded as wild animals because they are not only speechless, but also unable to manage any means of complex communication. The protagonist, Ulysse Merou, manages to attract the attention of the simian scientists simply by showing that he has the cognitive ability to attempt verbal and written communication. Later on, when he has learnt simian language, his public speech at the scientific congress will be enough to grant him the right to be regarded as a 'rational being', and therefore let out of the cage in which he has been held captive and set free. In the end, he will come to be seen as a possible threat to simian civilization, as he may succeed in teaching other humans to think – and to speak. In fact, something similar happened when the apes replaced humans as lords of the planet. The story of the rise of the apes is brought to life by 'awakening the memory of the species' in one of the savage humans. This is how the protagonist and his scientist friends learn that at some point in its civilization humankind suddenly underwent a fast intellectual decline, while primates evolved simultaneously. The reasons for both phenomena are not clarified. All we know is that humans rapidly became intellectually 'lazy' and cowardly and let the apes take over without resistance. It was precisely the acquisition of the ability to use human language that marked the beginning of the apes' rebellion against humans, as one of these memories effectively points out:

> Ça y est ! L'un d'eux a réussi à parler. C'est certain, je l'ai lu dans le Journal de la Femme. Il a sa photographie. C'est un chimpanzé . . . Il y en a d'autres. Le journal en signale tous les jours de nouveaux. Certains savants considèrent cela comme un grand succès scientifique. Ils ne voient pas où cela peut nous mener ? Il parait qu'un de ces chimpanzés a proféré des injures grossières. Le premier usage qu'ils font de la parole, c'est pour protester quand on veut les faire obéir.[40]

> [It's happened! One of them has succeeded in talking. It's certain; I read about it in Woman's Journal. There's a photograph of him, too. He's a chimpanzee . . . There are several others. The papers report fresh cases every day. Certain biologists regard this as a great scientific success. Don't they realize where it may lead? It appears that one of these chimpanzees has uttered some ugly threats. The first use they make of speech is to protest when they are given an order.][41]

Like Shakespeare's Caliban, as soon as the (animal) slave learns the language of his master, he uses it to reject his rule: language is the first step in the process of empowerment of the subordinate subject. The implicit suggestion of Boulle's novel is that we had better beware intelligent (animal) slaves, and especially not let them learn to speak.[42]

Although in relatively more critical terms, the warning of the dangers of letting animals become too smart is reiterated in the latest reboot of the saga, *Rise of the Planet of the Apes* (2011, by Rupert Wyatt), which focuses on the beginning of the progressive 'humanization' of the apes, which will eventually make them the dominant species on the planet. As happened in Boulle's novel, there is a strong connection between the animals' acquisition of linguistic ability and their rebellion against their human masters. The primates will symbolically acquire the right to rebel at the moment the most evolved of them starts to speak human language, and significantly, the first word it utters is 'No'. From this moment on, the revolt appears legitimate, as it does to the protagonist, Dr Rodman, too, who gives up trying to stop the apes as soon as he realizes that they have learned to speak. But it must be noted that, in this updated and more plausible version of the story, the evolutionary leap of the apes is not a natural phenomenon but is produced by foolish humans themselves, through experimentation with a virus which enhances the apes' cognitive abilities. And this brings us to the last and most recent type of SF humanized animals: mutants produced by genetic engineering.

Genetic engineering, or the new Frankensteins of the third millennium

Among twenty-first-century SF works, Margaret Atwood's *MaddAddam* trilogy (2003–13) offers us the richest and most detailed critical reflection of the dangers brought about by the reckless use of new biotechnologies. The first two novels, in which the chronicle of the present day after doomsday alternates with the recollection of the pre-apocalyptic years, outline the scenario of a near future overwhelmed by the combined effect of unrestrained post-industrial capitalism, globalization and the uncontrolled development of biotechnologies. As a result, the Frankensteins of the third millennium have the power to freely manipulate the whole animal species system, modifying or mixing different genetic pools in order to create new species, according to the demands of the ever more careless 'consumerist-corporatist culture'.[43] There are 'wolvogs', an interbred hybrid of wolves and dogs who are used as merciless weapons. The 'ChickieNobs' are living aggregates of edible chicken parts without brains or eyes; they perfectly meet both the need for ever more meat and the ethical scruples of the defenders of animal rights. As explained by the most gifted of these new Frankensteins, Crake, 'the animal-welfare freaks won't be able to say a word, because this thing feels no pain'.[44] The most questionable creation is probably that of the 'pigoon', or '*sus multiorganifer*'. This is a transgenic pig which grows multiple 'organs that would transplant smoothly and avoid rejection', thanks to the use of human genetic material.[45] In this case, though, ethical scruples are unavoidable, as the new creature is literally, unmistakably, a humanized animal.[46] But in a civilization which is already collapsing, where natural resources have been totally exhausted and most people are regarded as worthless and are abused by the elites, moral concerns are easily put aside. As recalled by Jimmy, one of the few survivors of the next apocalypse:

> In the OrganInc brochures . . . to set the queasy at ease, it was claimed that none of the defunct pigoons ended up as bacon and

sausages: no one would want to eat an animal whose cells might be identical with at least some of their own.

Still, as time went on and the coastal aquifers turned salty and the northern permafrost melted and the vast tundra bubbled with methane, and the drought in the midcontinental plains regions went on and on, and the Asian steppes turned to sand dunes, and meat became harder to come by, some people had their doubts. Within OrganInc Farms itself it was noticeable how often back bacon and ham sandwiches and pork pies turned up on the staff café menu. André's Bistro was the official name of the café, but the regulars called it Grunts.[47]

After the almost complete extinction of humankind, caused by a virus engineered by Crake himself, these 'chimeric animals' are the main threat to the small community of survivors. This community comprises a few humans, but also a new species of human hybrids, a perfectly 'eco-sustainable' people whom Crake created with the aim of repopulating the Earth after the Sixth Extinction. The 'Crakers' are vegetarian, immune to illnesses, devoid of aggressive, violent drives, unable to manage complex concepts and abstract language; they naturally seek a balance with the ecosystem and the other species, which they respect and try to understand. Thanks to their mediation, the human community will in fact be able to establish contact with the community of pigoons. In the third volume, a pigoon delegation comes to meet the human people in order to ask for their help in fighting three other human survivors, a criminal gang which has been molesting both communities. The proposal is conveyed to the human leaders, Toby and Zeb, by a Craker translator, as the humans are unable to understand what they perceive as simple 'grunting . . . going on, from pig to pig':[48]

'Then why aren't they talking to us?' says Toby. 'Why are they talking to you?'

Oh, she thinks. Of course. We're too stupid, we don't understand their languages. So there has to be a translator.

'It is easier for them to talk to us,' says Blackbeard simply. 'And in return, if you help them to kill the three bad men, they will never again try to eat your garden. Or any of you,' he adds seriously. 'Even if you are dead, they will not eat you. And they ask that you must no longer make holes in them, with blood, and cook them in a smelly bone soup, or hang them in the smoke, or fry them and then eat them. Not any more.'

'Tell them it's a deal,' says Zeb.[49]

The two communities fight and win the battle together, then agree between them to execute the human criminals, and they celebrate a common funeral for both pigoon and human victims. Significantly, in this rite the pigoons carry the human dead on their backs, 'as a sign of friendship and inter-species co-operation'.[50] This event functions as the establishment of an interspecies pact, which will be kept thereafter and will be recalled in the foundational epics of the new post-human civilization. Together, the former vulnerable subjects – research animals, women, marginalized people – are now empowered not only to survive but also to restore the world to a better place.[51] Maybe the Earth will now be able to heal in peace from all the damage inflicted upon it by human civilization.

As hinted at by *Deus Irae*, and more consciously articulated by Atwood, playing God with the Earth is leading us to destroy the ecosystem, and us with it. Our only chance for survival lies in acknowledging our position, rights and obligations within the necessary ecological balance of all living forms, and in starting to truly respect them. But the first step in this process consists in overcoming anthropocentric prejudice, recognizing ourselves as part of a single although diverse community of living species whose survival on the planet is precarious and fragile. This is the only way to reverse the apocalypse into a true palingenesis – or better, out of the fictional allegory, to avoid it. Yet it is difficult to acquire such an awareness and to cease regarding the world as a set of resources at our complete disposal. Maybe if we could understand what animals say, it would be easier to make up our minds. Let us hope that it will not take an actual apocalypse to do so.

Notes

1. This double implication of anthropomorphic practice has been clearly highlighted by Lorraine Daston and Gregg Mitman: 'humans assume a community of thought and feeling between themselves and a surprisingly wide array of animals; they also recruit animals to symbolize, dramatize, and illuminate aspects of their own experience and fantasies' ('Introduction', 2).
2. Suvin, *Metamorphoses of Science Fiction*.
3. I have discussed in detail the category and phenomenology of the subhuman in speculative imagination in Micali, *Towards a Posthuman Imagination in Literature and Media*, 33–82.
4. Agamben, *The Open*.
5. This discussion was opened by Satz, 'Animals as vulnerable subjects'. See also Thierman, 'The vulnerability of other animals'; Johnson, 'Vulnerable subjects?'; Pick, 'Vulnerability'.

6. For an analysis of the novel in relation to the vivisection controversy, see Dewitt, *Moral Authority, Men of Science, and the Victorian Novel*, 175–81. The cultural context of the anti-vivisection movements in late nineteenth-century Britain has been described by Ritvo, *The Animal Estate*.
7. Wells, *The Island of Doctor Moreau*, 43.
8. Wells, *The Island of Doctor Moreau*, 44, 43.
9. Wells, *The Island of Doctor Moreau*, 101.
10. Wells, *The Island of Doctor Moreau*, 12.
11. Wells, *The Island of Doctor Moreau*, 109.
12. As Moreau obscurely explains: 'And they revert. As soon as my hand is taken from them the beast begins to creep back, begins to assert itself again' (Wells, *The Island of Doctor Moreau*, 106).
13. Wells, *The Island of Doctor Moreau*, 48.
14. Wells, *The Island of Doctor Moreau*, 48.
15. Bulgakov, *The Heart of a Dog*, 5. Written in 1925, the novel was denied publication in the country for more than 60 years, as it was a manifest satire of Bolshevism and easily interpreted 'as an allegory of revolution, the operation of its aftermath paralleling the revolution's misguided attempt to radically transform mankind' (Haber, *Mikhail Bulgakov*, 216–17).
16. The English translation chooses not to modify the protagonist's name, which is a very common Russian name for a dog, meaning 'Little ball'. My gratitude goes to Alessandra Carbone, who helped me to check the original version of the novel.
17. This is clearly stated in the clinical log of the experiment written by Bormenthal: 'Purpose of operation: Experimental observation by Prof. Preobrazhensky of the effect of combined transplantation of the pituitary and testes in order to study both the functional viability in a host-organism and its role in cellular etc. rejuvenation' (Bulgakov, *The Heart of a Dog*, 59).
18. Bulgakov, *The Heart of a Dog*, 61–2.
19. Bulgakov, *The Heart of a Dog*, 67.
20. Bulgakov, *The Heart of a Dog*, 57.
21. Bulgakov, *The Heart of a Dog*, 73–4. The Russian term Sharikov uses, 'папаша' (translated here as 'Dad'), is actually ruder and could be better rendered with 'Pop'.
22. Bulgakov, *The Heart of a Dog*, 126–7.
23. This is made very clear by the reference to '"my dog"' when the policemen are accusing Preobrazhensky of murder (Bulgakov, *The Heart of a Dog*, 126).
24. In the taxonomy of vulnerability proposed by Mackenzie, Rogers and Dodds ('Introduction'), 'situational vulnerability' is a condition deriving from specific situations such as that of domesticated animals, who are completely dependent on the will of humans. As remarked by Ani Satz, '[t]hroughout their lives, domestic animals rely on humans to provide them nourishment, shelter, and other care. The permanent dependency of domestic animals is created and controlled by humans, rendering them uniquely vulnerable to exploitation. Domestic nonhuman animals are, for this reason, perhaps the most vulnerable of all sentient beings' ('Animals as vulnerable subjects', 80). On animals in relation to the taxonomy of vulnerability, and in particular regarding laboratory experimentation, see Johnson, 'Vulnerable subjects?'
25. Bulgakov, *The Heart of a Dog*, 127.
26. The scene of the surgery is the true epiphany of this axiologic inversion between human and animal: while Sharik's body lies 'helplessly' and 'defenceless' on the operating table, the two doctors operate in a hurry and furiously, 'as two murderers working against the clock', with a 'fearsome' expression and a 'savage look', 'like a tiger' or 'a satisfied vampire' (Bulgakov, *The Heart of a Dog*, 53, 55, 56, 57).
27. Steiner, *Anthropocentrism and Its Discontents*, 2.
28. Vint, *Animal Alterity*; McHugh, *Animal Stories*.
29. Dick, *Dr Bloodmoney*, 120.
30. Dick, *Dr Bloodmoney*, 112.
31. Dick, *Dr Bloodmoney*, 115.
32. Dick, *Dr Bloodmoney*, 116.
33. Dick, *Dr Bloodmoney*, 140.
34. Dick, *Dr Bloodmoney*, 142.
35. Fredric Jameson's enlightening study of the ideology conveyed in *Dr Bloodmoney* is based in fact on a narratological analysis of the system of 'freaks or anomalous beings that people this extravagant work': see Jameson, *Archaeologies of the Future*, 349–62, citing from 353.

36. Dick and Zelazny, *Deus Irae*, 95.
37. Dick and Zelazny, *Deus Irae*, 88.
38. Vint, *Animal Alterity*, 69.
39. That the exchange of positions between the former human masters and their simian subordinates was created by a nuclear holocaust was in fact suggested by the 1968 cult film adaptation by Franklin Schaffner.
40. Boulle, *La Planète des Singes*, 166.
41. Boulle, *Planet of the Apes*, 181–2.
42. The novel and its early film adaptations naturally lend themselves to critical readings through the lens of postcolonial theory. For a political analysis of the whole *Planet of the Apes* saga, see Greene, *Planet of the Apes as American Myth*.
43. Moore, *Ecological Literature and the Critique of Anthropocentrism*, 233.
44. Atwood, *MaddAddam*, 203.
45. Atwood, *MaddAddam*, 22.
46. For a discussion of Atwood's novel in the context of recent scientific research into the real possibility of growing human organs in pigs, and the ongoing debate between 'bioliberals' and 'bioconservatives', see Camporesi, 'CRISPR pigs, pigoons and the future of organ transplantation'.
47. Atwood, *MaddAddam*, 23–4.
48. Atwood, *MaddAddam*, 268.
49. Atwood, *MaddAddam*, 270–1.
50. Atwood, *MaddAddam*, 373.
51. On the political message conveyed by Atwood through the account of the post-apocalyptic world, see Weafer, 'Writing from the margin', and Tate, *Apocalyptic Fiction*, 61–82.

Bibliography

Agamben, Giorgio. *The Open: Man and the animal*, translated by Kevin Attell. Stanford, CA: Stanford University Press, 2004.
Atwood, Margaret. *MaddAddam*. New York: Anchor, 2013.
Berger, John. *About Looking*. New York: Pantheon, 1980.
Boulle, Pierre. *La Planète des Singes*. Paris: Julliard, 1971.
Boulle, Pierre. *Planet of the Apes*, translated by Xan Fielding. London: Vintage, 2011.
Bulgakov, Mikhail A. *The Heart of a Dog*, translated by Michael Glenny. London: Vintage, 2009.
Camporesi, Silvia. 'CRISPR pigs, pigoons and the future of organ transplantation'. *Etica & Politica/ Ethics & Politics* 20, no. 3 (2018): 35–52.
Daston, Lorraine, and Gregg Mitman. 'Introduction: The how and why of thinking with animals'. In *Thinking with Animals: New perspectives on anthropomorphism*, edited by Lorraine Daston and Gregg Mitman, 1–14. New York: Columbia University Press, 2005.
Dewitt, Anne. *Moral Authority, Men of Science, and the Victorian Novel*. Cambridge: Cambridge University Press, 2013.
Dick, Philip K. *Dr Bloodmoney, or How We Got Along After the Bomb*. Boston, MA: Mariner, 2012.
Dick, Philip K., and Roger Zelazny. *Deus Irae*. London: Gollacz, 2013.
Greene, Eric. *Planet of the Apes as American Myth: Race and politics in the films and television series*. Jefferson, NC: McFarland, 2006.
Haber, Edythe C. *Mikhail Bulgakov: The early years*. Cambridge, MA: Harvard University Press, 1998.
Jameson, Fredric. *Archaeologies of the Future: The desire called utopia and other science fictions*. London: Verso, 2005.
Johnson, Jane. 'Vulnerable subjects? The case of nonhuman animals in experimentation'. *Journal of Bioethical Inquiry* 10 (2013): 497–504.
Mackenzie, Catriona, Wendy Rogers and Susan Dodds. 'Introduction: What is vulnerability, and why does it matter for moral theory?' In *Vulnerability: New essays in ethics and feminist philosophy*, edited by Catriona Mackenzie, Wendy Rogers and Susan Dodds, 1–30. Oxford: Oxford University Press, 2013.
McHugh, Susan. *Animal Stories: Narrating across species lines*. Minneapolis: University of Minnesota Press, 2011.

Micali, Simona. *Towards a Posthuman Imagination in Literature and Media: Monsters, mutants, aliens, artificial beings*. Oxford: Peter Lang, 2019.
Moore, Bryan L. *Ecological Literature and the Critique of Anthropocentrism*. Houndmills: Palgrave Macmillan, 2017.
Pick, Anat. 'Vulnerability'. In *Critical Terms for Animal Studies*, edited by Lori Gruen, 410–23. Chicago: University of Chicago Press, 2018.
Ritvo, Harriet. *The Animal Estate: The English and other creatures in the Victorian age*. Cambridge, MA: Harvard University Press, 1987.
Satz, Ani B. 'Animals as vulnerable subjects: Beyond interest-convergence, hierarchy, and property'. *Animal Law Review* 16, no. 1 (2009): 65–122.
Steiner, Gary. *Anthropocentrism and Its Discontents: The moral status of animals in the history of Western philosophy*. Pittsburgh, PA: University of Pittsburgh Press, 2010.
Suvin, Darko. *Metamorphoses of Science Fiction: On the poetics and history of a literary genre*. New Haven, CT: Yale University Press, 1979.
Tate, Andrew. *Apocalyptic Fiction*. London: Bloomsbury, 2017.
Thierman, Stephen. 'The vulnerability of other animals'. *Journal for Critical Animal Studies* 9, no. 1 (2011): 182–208.
Vint, Sherryl. *Animal Alterity: Science fiction and the question of the animal*. Liverpool: Liverpool University Press, 2010.
Weafer, Miles. 'Writing from the margin: Victim positions in Atwood's *The Year of the Flood*'. In *Margaret Atwood's Apocalypses*, edited by Karma Waltonen, 57–70. Newcastle: Cambridge Scholars Publishing, 2015.
Wells, Herbert George. *The Island of Doctor Moreau*. London: Gollancz, 2017.

ficial
2
Rewriting the myth: consideration of the Minotaur in Georgi Gospodinov's *The Physics of Sorrow*

Nicole Siri

In his novel *The Physics of Sorrow* (2011), Georgi Gospodinov provides a disruptive interpretation of the myth of the Minotaur, which raises a number of issues with regard to both vulnerability and mediation. Subverting the classical depiction of the Minotaur as a ferocious monster, Gospodinov's postmodern novel portrays the creature as utterly vulnerable, victimized and abandoned by his father. Furthermore, in the novel the narrator's mediation in telling the story of the Minotaur can be opposed to the moments where the Minotaur himself takes the floor and voices his own perspective, thus raising questions about empathy, communication and the understanding of the (non-human) Other. In this chapter, I try to unfold these issues.

'I can't offer a linear story, because no labyrinth and no story is ever linear', declares the narrator-protagonist.[1] In Georgi Gospodinov's second novel, which has been defined as a 'novel-labyrinth', the reader is led through a mesmerizing entanglement of stories which are intertwined with one another.[2] The narration is divided into short paragraphs that are often connected to each other only by an (at times implicit) analogy and it progresses in the form of a disorderly wandering through a labyrinth. As the reader turns the pages of the novel, they encounter stories that are resumed after having been interrupted chapters earlier – and such stories thus acquire new and deeper meanings in the light of other threads that the narrator has explored in the meantime. Within such an architecture, recurrent paragraphs titled 'Side corridors' and 'A place to stop' offer the place for digressions and meta-literary considerations respectively.

There is, however, a linear evolution of the main story – that of the narrator-protagonist – throughout the novel. In the first part (chapters 1–3), as remarked by the Italian translator Giuseppe Dell'Agata, 'the dominant theme consists of an hypertrophic expansion of the I, who, thanks to what is diagnosed by the narrator as a "pathological empathy or obsessive empathetic-somatic syndrome", takes possession of the memories, the joys and the sorrows of his parents, grandparents and acquaintances, as well as of those belonging to mythological creatures'.[3] As someone starts telling their story, the narrator can penetrate into their memories and become them: the reader is thus led from the story of the protagonist to that of his father, from his father's story to that of his grandfather, to the story of the Minotaur, which is one of the most recurrent and richly developed symbols within the novel. The paragraph 'The Aging of an Empath', which opens the fourth chapter ('Time Bomb – To be opened after the end of the world'), marks a turning point: the narrator explains that, as he is growing old, he is progressively losing his empathy, and, to counterbalance his loss, he has become a collector. In the second part of the novel, stories collected by the narrator are thus told one after another, but they remain the stories of strangers. Along with those stories, the second part of the novel is rich with lists, catalogues, excerpts, encyclopaedic knowledge and theoretical meditations.

In this chapter, I will propose a close reading of the two chapters mostly dedicated to the Minotaur, which are the second ('Against an Abandonment: The Case of M.') and the fifth ('The Green Box'). I will argue that the story of the Minotaur has a different function within these two chapters: firstly, it is a way to speak about child abuse in the symbolic language of the unconscious; secondly, while maintaining its symbolic meaning, it becomes the starting point towards blurring the human–animal divide and meditating on the need for an anti-anthropocentric revolution. After providing a psychoanalytical reading of chapter 2, I will question the meaning of the narrator's change of perspective towards the myth in relation to his own evolution as a character within the novel. I will then conclude my chapter by suggesting a possible way to interpret the general sentiment of melancholy that pervades the novel.

'The Case of M.': a story of abuse

The first appearance of the Minotaur in the novel can be found in the first chapter, 'The Bread of Sorrow' (11–57). As the narrator is plunging into the memories of his grandfather (who bears the same name as him,

Georgi), he finds himself at a fair. He has just one coin, so he ponders carefully how it should be spent. Somehow deeply drawn towards it, he eventually chooses to see the Minotaur over all the other available attractions. What he finds inside the tent is a boyish, sad-looking, 'melancholy Minotaur' (14), and he is staggered by his humanity and their similarity. As the chapter unfolds and intertwines the three stories of Georgi the narrator-protagonist, Georgi his grandfather and the Minotaur, several parallels are drawn between the three. Born during the First World War, the protagonist's grandfather was abandoned by his mother and saved by his sister Dana. The paragraph 'I hate you, Ariadne' underlines the contrast between Dana, who saved her brother, and Ariadne, who betrayed him by helping his murderer. The paragraphs 'The Basement' and 'Dad, What's a Minotaur?' tell the story of the young protagonist who, like the Minotaur in the labyrinth, spends most of his afternoons in a dark basement during the years of late socialism. The parallels between the narrator and his grandfather are drawn explicitly throughout the chapter through sentences that remark on continuities in their personalities, such as: 'So that's where I get the indecisiveness that will constantly torment me' (12).

It is in the second chapter, 'Against an Abandonment: The Case of M.', that such parallels are explored in the folds of their symbolic meaning. The whole chapter is dedicated to the Minotaur, and it takes place in the context of a trial. The first part consists of the narrator's arguments. Posing as the Minotaur's lawyer, he tells the jury: 'Over the course of 37 years I have been preparing this case, the case of M. I began at nine ... The first version reads as follows: *The Minotaur is not guilty. He is a boy locked up in a basement. He is frightened. They have abandoned him. I, the Minotaur*' (60; emphasis in the original). He proceeds to argue the Minotaur's case through a long analysis of the occurrences of the myth throughout ancient and modern literature, art and culture – from Ovid's *Metamorphoses* up to the representation of the Minotaur in popular video games such as *World of Warcraft*. An Etruscan vase presenting a rare iconography – Pasiphaë holding the Minotaur just like a madonna holding Jesus in Christian art – leads the narrator to his closing arguments: that there has been a huge erasure throughout history, since the fact that the Minotaur was abandoned as an infant has hardly ever been mentioned.[4] Instead, the Minotaur's story has been unfairly twisted: 'You won't find the youths and maidens devoured by the Minotaur in this list – I don't believe in that part of the myth. Besides, bulls are herbivores' (69).

From a philological point of view, the narrator's use of his sources proves to be deliberately partial; even though his quotations are often literal, he disregards important passages and chooses and cuts his quotations in order to prove his point.[5] However, the philological accuracy of the narrator's dossier and, more generally, of his use of the sources within the novel are not relevant for the purposes of a psychoanalytical reading: as theorized by Francesco Orlando, the object of our analysis must rather be the symbolic coherences internal to the text under consideration.[6]

Two elements in the narrator's arguments appear most relevant for our interpretation. The first is that the narrator's speech is structured as a positivistic dossier that aims at proving a point and is conceptually framed by ideas of lawfulness and normative justice. His speech is filled with juridical terms, and he thinks in terms of rights, crimes and guiltiness:

> We're talking about the *abandonment* and *forcible confinement* of a child, branded by his origins, for which he is not to blame. This is followed by *slander*, *abasement*, and the public circulation of lies . . . the Minotaur's human nature has been recognized. Despite the fact that his *human rights* have been taken away . . . But isn't the Minotaur merely the fruit of such sin, not a *perpetrator*, a *victim*, the most long-suffering victim? A huge mistake and *calumny* lie hidden there, exceptional *injustice*. (62; emphases added)

I will explore the meaning of this mindset in the next section, through a comparison with the attitude of the Minotaur.

The second relevant aspect is that the narrator's argumentative strategy to gain the jurors' empathy is mostly based on pointing out the human nature of the Minotaur: 'The shock comes not from the fact that he looks like a beast, but that he is in some way human' (14); as already cited, 'We're talking about the abandonment and forcible confinement of a *child*' (62; emphasis added); 'Someone dared to recall the obvious, which the myth would quickly forget. We're talking about a baby. Carried and delivered by a woman. We're talking about an infant, not a beast' (67). The narrator is trying, rhetorically, to erase the ontological difference between the Minotaur and the jurors (on an intradiegetic level) and the Minotaur and the readers (on an extradiegetic level). Such a strategy, which is common to the whole first part of the novel, is quite conventional and leaves the human–animal divide unquestioned. In her book *Towards a Posthuman Imagination in Literature and Media*, Simona Micali has theorized this narrative device as one of the most popular for obtaining identification with the non-human. She interestingly underlines how this device functions with empathy:

Such an effect is not necessarily connected to compassion, which properly consists of 'feeling sorry' for another being but which does not always involve identifying with the target of our feeling: this latter is instead what happens in the case of empathy. We can feel sorry for animals, or people we have never met, or enemies, or past and future generations: through compassion we establish with them an emotional connection (we *suffer with* them, according to the Latin etymology of the term, *cum-patior*), which does not affect the ontological or ethical distance existing between Us and Them. Instead, in empathy (from the Greek *empatheia*, i.e. *in-passion*) the identification with the target is the dominant process, which precedes and produces the emotional reaction: we project ourselves *into them*, put ourselves 'in their shoes' (Walton 2015) and therefore share their feelings.[7]

In the second part of this chapter I will argue that there is a (partial) evolution of the narrator's attitude within this issue, and I will question its meaning.

Within the scene of the trial, it is when the Minotaur is given the floor that the narration acquires a more original twist. According to the tradition, the resident judge presiding over the court is Minos. The Minotaur is called to the bar and, in hexameter, defends his case. His argument is very simple and yet utterly disruptive: he points out that, far from being the fruit of adultery, his bovine features are the mark of his legitimate lineage. Minos himself, whom he addresses as father, was born from the union between Zeus, disguised as a bull, and Europa:

> Forsooth! The truth outshines your deepest, darkest fears
>
> Your blood I share – a freak by birth, my lineage's clear.
>
> Your father's likeness true, I'm kin to all you all
>
> The first true bull in our damned house was Zeus; recall
>
> How he seduced the fair Europa, dam to you
>
> From Grandpa Zeus I got my bullish form so true. (71)

Here, fundamental new light is shed on the myth. The Minotaur is no longer a monster; he is a son, abused in that he has been unfairly disowned by his father. One striking element in the Minotaur's speech is that – in opposition to the arguments of the narrator – he does not stress at all the wrongdoings that he has suffered. It may seem surprising that the first concern expressed by the Minotaur, who has so far been depicted as the victim of two millennia of injustice and slander, is to not upset his father. These are the opening verses of his speech:

> Some words I have for you o'er which so long I've mused
>
> In night's embrace, O Minos, Hades' judge most cruel
>
> My tongue has longed to say just once: O father mine!
>
> *Yet I discern your scorn and swallow back my cries.* (71; emphasis added)

The Minotaur's perspective reflects very clearly what is common knowledge about the psychology of the abused: victims often fail to perceive what is being done to them as an injustice. Even when they recognize some behaviours as abusive if they are perpetrated towards other people, when abuse is inflicted upon them the victims often find themselves persuaded – or led to believe – that what they are suffering is to some extent their fault, that they are somehow guilty, that it is their responsibility to avoid it, that they should worry about not upsetting the abuser.

The Minotaur's psychology can be further clarified by the other passage within the novel where he speaks in the first person: the paragraph 'The Minotaur's dream' (in chapter 5, 'The Green Box'): '"I dream that I'm beautiful" he says, "Not exactly beautiful, but inconspicuous. That's what it means to be beautiful, to be like everyone else . . . I walk down the street and no one notices me. Now that's happiness – no one noticing me. It's a happy dream"' (157). In his conceptualization of the mirror stage, Jacques Lacan famously argues that the construction of the self always takes place through the gaze of the Other.[8] The only gaze that the Minotaur has known is disgust, fear, disownment – ever motivated by his difference: hence, his idea of beauty as inconspicuousness, his ideal of happiness as being unnoticed, unperceived.

As the tale of his dream goes on, the reader learns about how he enjoys walking in the street, in the open sunlight, up to the moment when a little accident occurs: 'One woman accidentally bumps into me. I'm afraid she'll scream' (158). Again, as I have remarked interpreting his speech to his father Minos, the Minotaur's concern is not to be a nuisance to the Other. Contemporary psychiatry would probably diagnose this pattern of thinking and behaviour as a trait of the so-called dependent personality disorder.[9] Giving way, traditionally, is a matter of entitlement: walking on the street means, symbolically, having the right to exist in the public space, among others. One of the most famous scenes in one of the masterpieces of the Italian literary tradition, *I Promessi Sposi* (*The Betrothed*), is all about a quarrel that starts with two men bumping into each other: they argue over who is supposed to give way to whom and end up duelling to the death to settle the matter. Gospodinov's Minotaur, on the contrary, is not even for a second thinking about his right to be on the street: to him, it is obvious that his rights are, at best, subordinate to those of the unknown woman who has bumped into him.

The dream goes on, and a little miracle happens: 'She turns around, looks at me from very close up . . . she doesn't recognize me . . . she doesn't scream . . . she smiles . . . and apologizes. *No one has ever apologized to me before*' (158; emphasis added). This is probably the most revealing part of the Minotaur's dream. An apology is what sets the Minotaur at peace: or, to translate the event in Lacanian terms, he dreams of a gaze of the Other that, for the first time, validates him. It is telling that what the woman has done to him – the reason she apologizes – is an accident, not some wrongdoing perpetrated on purpose. The Minotaur's unconscious is not asking for reparation, nor for anyone to own their responsibilities, but merely to be acknowledged.

I conclude this first section by exploring the implications this version of the myth has on the psychology of Minos. There is a consequence to be drawn from the truth revealed by the Minotaur, something that has been neglected through all the readings of the myth, albeit hiding in plain sight: it is that, while the Minotaur is the legitimate son of Minos and Pasiphaë, the son of a woman who has lain with a bull is, instead, Minos himself. When Minos accuses the Minotaur of being a monster, a freak, he is thus projecting (in the Freudian sense of using a defence mechanism) onto his son a characteristic that belongs to him in the first place, and that he cannot accept about himself.

The closing lines of the chapter are enlightening on this matter. After the Minotaur's claim to legitimacy has been voiced, and Minos's nature implicitly revealed, the Minotaur becomes, quite literally, the symbolic incarnation of Minos's repressed. What Minos has done is – literally – to close and imprison the unpleasant content (his son, who incarnates his twofold nature of human and bull and openly reminds him of it) in a dark labyrinth where no one is allowed to go and from where he cannot come out. This is quite an accurate description of the defence mechanism theorized by Freud as repression.[10]

The Minotaur's comeback, his public claims in court, have a disruptive power, and Minos cannot argue against them: he cannot but yield to the faultless logic of the Minotaur. As the Minotaur voices his claims, Minos's repressed is lifted and the king's nudity is revealed: 'The truth outshines your deepest, darkest fears' (71). Yet what Minos can – and does – do is appeal to his powerful position. Finding himself in the paradoxical position of being at once a party in the trial that is being discussed and the resident judge, he can dismiss the Minotaur's claim by refusing to engage with him at all. He does not even respond to the Minotaur; the only words he utters are addressed instead to the police: 'Minos: The court will now break for a recess . . . Take away the defendant' (71).

The Minotaur's reaction closes the chapter. Having up to this moment spoken only in 'heroic hexameter' (70), he loses his ability to speak, and the chapter ends with his unarticulated cry for help: 'Moooooo . . . ooooooooooooooooooooooooooooooooooooooooooooooo oooo ooooooooooooooooooooooooooooooooooooooooooooooooooooo oooooooooooooooooooooooooooooooooo' (71). Any attempt at rational communication with an abuser, who holds a position of psychological (and often structural) power, only translates into further abuse and the silencing of the victim: one of the hardest truths that victims must learn to accept is that it is almost impossible to obtain validation from the abuser himself.

'The Green Box': an anti-anthropocentric revolution

As I have anticipated, there is a linear evolution within the novel, marked by the beginning of the fourth chapter, 'The Aging of an Empath'. As he grows old, the narrator-protagonist progressively loses his empathy and ability to plunge into someone else's mind. The loss of empathy is not complete, yet the totalizing identifications that used to happen to him during his childhood become less and less frequent.

The fifth chapter, 'The Green Box', opens with the transcription of a report from a newspaper: 'Bull leaps into crowd, injuring 40 at a bullfight, the animal is killed' (151). Once again, the narrator identifies with the killed bull: 'for me it turned out to be one of those exceptional events that launched me back into that forgotten "embedding" . . . Something I haven't experienced in years' (151). The narrator thus formulates a triple equivalence: the killed bull = the Minotaur = himself. He can thus tell the readers the story from the bull's perspective: he saw his killer (the matador = Theseus), thought that if his killer was there then his mother must be there too, and therefore started desperately looking for her in the crowd, trying to repair the (Oedipal) loss that is at the origin of the pain of any creature in the world:

> The only word that in all languages – those of humans, animals and monsters – is one and the same:
>
> Mooooooooooom . . .
>
> The labyrinth of the amphitheater catches that cry, ricochets it between the walls of its corridors, diverts it toward the dead-ends, cuts it off, and sends it back slightly distorted to the labyrinth of the human ear like an endless
>
> Mooooooooo . . . (153)

The change of perspective that has occurred is already visible in this passage. Whereas so far the story of the Minotaur has been a way of telling the narrator's story – I, the Minotaur – here it becomes functional to a more generalized claim that might be summarized as: 'Everyone, the Minotaur'.

The bull is eventually shot. This leads the narrator to meditate on murder, and on the difference between face-to-face killing and murder that happens at a distance (154–5). A moral meditation follows, titled 'No animal would do that' (155–7), which eventually leads the narrator to ponder on modern slaughterhouses and the eating of meat.

In this chapter, multiple ideas populate the narrator's discourse, some of which are openly in contrast with one another. The paragraph 'Miriam, or the right to kill' (164–6), for instance, follows paragraphs dedicated to the eating of flesh and the negligent murders of ants and argues instead – as its title summarizes – that 'the right to kill is inviolable' (166). The narrator justifies the presence of both stances within the novel, appealing to his new-found urge to collect: 'I will put Miriam's story in the green box, too, for balance. So we have one of every kind' (166). Other ideas voiced by the narrator appear, instead, as naïve from a rigorously theoretical perspective. When he argues, for instance, that 'the new moral law' should be 'would an animal do that?', he is falling into what contemporary moral philosophy calls the naturalistic fallacy.[11]

The question that thus arises, and that is more interesting, does not concern the content of the narrator's theorizing as much as its timing. Why do ethical concerns and political awareness arise in the protagonist when his empathy diminishes? Why does he start meditating on animal rights, ethics and vegetarianism when his identifications become less frequent? Is this not counter-intuitive? Shouldn't empathy be something that enhances political engagement?

We have so far come to the conclusion that, as long as the narrator-protagonist is endowed with the gift of empathy – or, as he himself puts it, as long as he suffers from the disease of 'pathological empathy' – the Minotaur is a symbol of child abuse and a way to talk about something individual and private. It is perhaps even a way to speak about the unspeakable: in his memories of his father, the narrator-protagonist never mentions or suggests disavowal or neglect, and the reader is left to wonder if the narrator's understanding of the darker parts of the story of the Minotaur depends only on his ability to 'become' someone else or if there is an implicit confession (I, the Minotaur) of something that is unspoken in the explicit story of the protagonist. Why, then, does the Minotaur become, to a certain extent, a symbol of non-human suffering, a symbol that endorses the argument that pain is the same for all creatures when the narrator is losing his empathy?

An answer might be found in Peter Goldie's essay 'Anti-empathy', in the seminal book dedicated to empathy that he also co-edited. In this essay, Goldie distinguishes between two kinds of empathy:

> I am not against what I will call *in-his-shoes perspective-shifting*: consciously and intentionally shifting your perspective in order to imagine what thoughts, feelings, decisions, and so on *you* would arrive at if you were in the other's circumstances. What I am against is what I will call *empathetic perspective-shifting*: consciously and intentionally shifting your perspective in order to imagine *being* the other person, and thereby sharing in his or her thoughts, feelings, decisions, and other aspects of their psychology.[12]

This second kind of empathy seems exactly the kind 'suffered' by the protagonist of *The Physics of Sorrow*. The identification with other beings, in the novel, is total and overwhelming, as revealed already in the 'Prologue':

> I was born at the end of August 1913 as a human being of the male sex . . . I was born two hours before dawn like a fruit fly . . . I was

born on January 1, 1968, as a human being of the male sex . . . I remember being born as a rose bush, a partridge, as ginkgo biloba, a snail, a cloud in June (that memory is brief), a purple autumnal crocus near Halensee, an early-blooming cherry frozen by a late April snow, as snow freezing a hoodwinked cherry tree . . . We am. (7–8)

When Goldie writes 'I might imagine how it is for a mouse caught in a trap but still very much alive, and realize it must be terrifying, but to do this, I don't have to take up the mouse's perspective', he could equally have chosen the example of Gospodinov's protagonist and his plunging into the perspective of the snail eaten by his grandfather to calm his ulcer.[13]

Peter Goldie's argument against *empathetic perspective-shifting* can be summarized in the fact that it does not – it cannot, conceptually, as he argues – take properly into account the individuality of the being with whom the subject empathizes. From this perspective, the emergence of concerns about collective and universal issues in the protagonist's conscience can be explained precisely by his loss of empathy. The 'hypertrophic I' of the beginning of the novel takes up less and less space, leaving room for the Other.

Goldie's essay must be located within the tradition of analytical philosophy. Interestingly, his argument is not very far from the point Derrida makes in *The Animal That Therefore I Am*, when he writes:

Things would be too simple altogether, the anthropo-theomorphic reappropriation would already have begun, there would even be the risk that domestication has already come into effect, if I were to give in to my own melancholy. If, in order to hear it myself, I were to set about overinterpreting what the cat might thus be saying to me, in its own way, what it might be suggesting or simply signifying in a language of mute traces, that is to say without words. If, in a word, *I assigned to it the words* it has no need of.[14]

Derrida's point (and, implicitly, that of Goldie) is to argue for an ethics that is based on the encounter with a radically different Other. Empathy, in the sense of empathetic perspective-shifting, can be interpreted as something that, despite the intentions of one's self, only produces an hypertrophic expansion of the I, the impossibility of really coming to terms with – of coming to know – the Other. From this perspective, one is left to wonder whether the protagonist of *The Physics of Sorrow* ever heals from his 'pathological empathy'.

The answer seems to be in the negative. Even though he seems, over the years, to grow more concerned with the problems of anthropocentrism ('Man needs to shut up for a while and in the ensuing pause to hear the voice of some other storyteller – a fish, dragonfly, weasel, or bamboo, cat, orchid, or pebble'; 166), his doubtful proposal can be interpreted as the admission of his failure: 'I have no idea how to make this happen. Maybe we just need to take the first step. All the world's classics, retold by animals for animals. For example, we could retell *The Old Man and the Sea* through the eyes of the fish, that marlin' (166). The protagonist of the novel seems, ultimately, to remain forever trapped within his I.

This may, in turn, offer an interpretation that can help us understand the universal melancholy that pervades the novel. Having left Bulgaria – 'the saddest place in the world' (202) – to travel, the narrator eventually comes back, concluding that melancholy is everywhere and that 'the saddest place *is* the world' (234; emphasis in the original). The question that should be asked, at this point, is whether the melancholy that the protagonist finds everywhere belongs to the world or, rather, to himself – to a self that cannot find a way to the Other. Is Gospodinov's novel ultimately a novel that – to borrow Derrida's words – depicts a postmodern protagonist who 'gives in to his own melancholy'?

Notes

1. Gospodinov, *The Physics of Sorrow*, 43. All the quotations from the novel, if not otherwise specified, come from this edition. From now on, when quoting the novel, I will indicate the page number in brackets in the main text.
2. Georgi Gospodinov, born in 1968, is currently the most prominent author on the Bulgarian literary scene. His early canonization is testified to by his inclusion, as the last and youngest author, in works that trace the history of Bulgarian literature. See, for instance, Mladenov and Cooper, *An Anthology of Bulgarian Literature*. The anthology starts from the Bulgarian authors of the early eighteenth century. It is to be noted that Gospodinov was included in this anthology even before the publication of *The Physics of Sorrow*. The definition of this novel as a 'roman-labyrinthe' comes from the French translator Vrinat-Nikolov, 'De *Un roman naturel à Physique de la mélancolie*', 174.
3. Dell'Agata, 'Postfazione', 330 (translation my own).
4. The Etruscan vase is the *Childhood of the Minotaur* that J. D. Beazley attributed to the Settecamini Painter and dated to the first quarter of the fourth century BCE: Beazley, *Etruscan Vase-Painting*, 54. It is at present conserved at the Cabinet de Médailles of the Bibliothèque nationale de France. For a commentary on the iconography of the vase, see Bonfante and Swaddling, *Etruscan Myths*, 42: 'This is one of the most charming of Etruscan interpretations of Greek myths, and one befitting their interest in family, children and the affectionate relationship between mother and child; such scenes are not illustrated in Greek art except in situations of terrible, deadly danger.'
5. For instance, in his first quotation, which is from Ovid's *Metamorphoses*, the reference to VIII, 155–6, where the Minotaur is called 'obprobrium generis' [his family's disgrace] and 'monstris . . . biformis' [hybrid monster]: Ovid, *Metamorphoses*, 416–17. Ovid's version of the myth, however, is patently different from that of the narrator: the *Metamorphoses* clearly suggest that the Minotaur's childhood and adolescence are spent in the palace. The very passage cited

by Gospodinov suggests that it is only after the Minotaur has grown up that Minos decides to build the labyrinth: 'destinat hunc Minos thalamo removere pudorem | multiplicique domo caecisque includere tectis' [Minos planned to remove this shame from his house and to hide it away in a labyrinthine enclosure with blind passages]: Ovid, *Metamorphoses*, 416–17 (VIII, 157–8). The meaning of this passage is further clarified by Ovid, *Metamorphoses*, 418–19 (VIII, 169–70): 'Quo postquam geminam tauri iuvenisque figuram | clausit' [In this labyrinth Minos shut up the monster of the bull-man form]. This further passage makes it clear that when the Minotaur is enclosed in the labyrinth he has become a *iuvenis*: since in Latin the terminology to describe the different ages in the life of a man is very rigid (thus the *Oxford Latin Dictionary* on the entry 'iuvenis, iuvenis': 'technically, any adult male up to the age of 45'), one cannot but conclude that, according to Ovid, when the Minotaur is locked up he has completed the process of growing up.
6. See Orlando, *Toward a Freudian Theory of Literature*, 21–2: 'Moreover, this justifies the indifference I shall show toward the literary sources of *Phèdre* (except where a comparison with these can help me prove a point). Whether, in fact, an element of the play was invented by Racine or derived in some way from ancient works by Euripides (*Hippolitus*), Seneca (*Phaedra*), Ovid (*Heroides* IV, *Metamorphoses* VII, XV), or Plutarch (*Life of Theseus*), its true significance comes only from the complex of symbolic coherences belonging exclusively to the work by Racine. The same applies should the element in question be endowed a priori with certain meaning by myth, folklore, or dreams, and perhaps even by the interpretations of psychoanalysis. Freudian psychoanalysis does not ignore recurrent or, so to speak, traditional symbols, but its constant recognition of the predominance of the letter forces it above all to be respectful of anything historically individualized. In this sense the literary scholar may draw from it only a lesson in submissiveness toward the text.'
7. Micali, *Towards a Posthuman Imagination in Literature and Media*, 55. The reference to Walton here is to Walton, *In Other Shoes*.
8. Lacan, 'Le stade du miroir comme formateur de la fonction du Je'.
9. For the criteria defining dependent personality disorder (and personality disorders in general), see the *Diagnostic and Statistical Manual of Mental Disorders*. Dependent personality disorder is, to sum up, characterized by excessive clinginess and the need to please others.
10. As effectively summarized by Orlando, *Toward a Freudian Theory of Literature*, 8: 'In psychoanalysis, repression refers to the operation by means of which an individual attempts to exclude from the conscious ego, or even to keep within the unconscious, a content of images, or thoughts, or memories connected with an instinct.'
11. G. E. Moore was the first to theorize what became known as the 'naturalistic fallacy', in his *Principia Ethica*. Moore defines naturalistic fallacy as wrongly inferring from 'X is' that 'X ought to be'. See Gospodinov, *The Physics of Sorrow*, 155: 'The animal in me. So here's the new moral law – side by side with "the starry sky above me". The basic question, the litmus test, the divider between good and evil – could what I've thought up be done by an animal? Step inside the skin of your favorite animal and find out.'
12. Goldie, 'Anti-empathy', 302 (emphases in the original).
13. Goldie, 'Anti-empathy', 306. See Gospodinov, *The Physics of Sorrow*, 28–9.
14. See Derrida, *The Animal That Therefore I Am*, 18 (emphasis added).

Bibliography

Beazley, J. D. *Etruscan Vase-Painting*. Oxford: Clarendon Press, 1947.
Bonfante, Larissa, and Judith Swaddling. *Etruscan Myths*. London: British Museum Press, 2006.
Dell'Agata, Giuseppe. 'Postfazione'. In Georgi Gospodinov, *Fisica della malinconia*, 329–33. Rome: Voland, 2013.
Derrida, Jacques. *The Animal That Therefore I Am*, edited by Marie-Louise Mallet and translated by David Wills. New York: Fordham University Press, 2008.
Diagnostic and Statistical Manual of Mental Disorders: DSM 5. Washington, DC: American Psychiatric Association, 2013.
Glare, P. G. W., ed. *Oxford Latin Dictionary*. 2nd edition, 2 vols. Oxford: Oxford University Press, 2012.

Goldie, Peter. 'Anti-empathy'. In *Empathy: Philosophical and psychological perspectives*, edited by Amy Coplan and Peter Goldie, 302–17. Oxford: Oxford University Press, 2011.

Gospodinov, Georgi. *The Physics of Sorrow*. Rochester, NY: Open Letter, 2015.

Lacan, Jacques. 'Le stade du miroir comme formateur de la fonction du Je: telle qu'elle nous est révélée dans l'expérience psychanalytique'. *Revue française de psychanalyse* 4 (1949): 449–55.

Micali, Simona. *Towards a Posthuman Imagination in Literature and Media: Monsters, mutants, aliens, artificial beings*. Oxford: Peter Lang, 2019.

Mladenov, Ivan, and Henry R. Cooper, eds. *An Anthology of Bulgarian Literature*. Bloomington, IN: Slavica Publishers, 2007.

Moore, G. E. *Principia Ethica*. Cambridge: Cambridge University Press, 1903.

Orlando, Francesco. *Toward a Freudian Theory of Literature: With an analysis of Racine's 'Phèdre'*. Baltimore, MD: Johns Hopkins University Press, 1978.

Ovid. *Metamorphoses: Volume 1: Books 1–8*, translated by Frank Justus Miller, revised by G. P. Goold. Cambridge, MA: Harvard University Press, 1916.

Vrinat-Nikolov, Marie. 'De *Un roman naturel* à *Physique de la mélancolie* (Gueorgui Gospodinov): de "nous sommes je" à "je sommes nous": à la recherche de la totalité perdue'. *Slovo* 47 (2017): 165–82.

Walton, Kendall L. *In Other Shoes: Music, metaphor, empathy, existence*. New York: Oxford University Press, 2015.

3
A vulnerable predator: the wolf as a symbol of the natural environment in the works of Ernest Thompson Seton, Jack London and Cormac McCarthy

Kateřina Kovářová

Introduction: real vs mythical wolves

The way we as human beings perceive nature changed significantly over the course of the twentieth century. A gradual realization of a phenomenon called the natural environment affected public debate and legislation as well as literature. Equally, culture and literature have influenced and continue to influence our perception of the natural environment as important mediators. This chapter focuses on one species, the wolf (*Canis lupus*), and studies it as a symbol or representative of the natural environment in the works of three American authors: Ernest Thompson Seton (1860–1946), Jack London (1876–1916) and Cormac McCarthy (1933–). The significance of the wolf both as a real animal and as a motif in the American context is apparent from the frequent occurrence of this species in American writings and in the discussion its mere existence has provoked both in the past and nowadays.[1] Literature was crucial in this process as the main medium available at the time of the westward expansion. The wolf is an example of the fact that 'the way we read and write about an animal will affect our behaviour toward that animal, as the way we read and write about anything else does'.[2] Up until the late 1930s, when wolves started to be studied empirically, literature and folklore were in fact the only sources of information about the species and as such formed perceptions of it.³ However, by that time wolves were basically extinct in the American Southwest and the majority of these early studies were conducted on animals in captivity.⁴ As Dana Phillips points out, '[t]here is a considerable irony in the fact that in order to begin to understand nature, we had first to alter it for the worse'.⁵

Many misconceptions and misunderstandings concerning the wolf survive even though these have been disproved by researchers. In his book *Of Wolves and Men*, Barry Lopez notes:

> What wolves do excites men and precipitates strong emotions, especially if men feel their lives or the lives of their domestic animals are threatened. Explanations for the wolf's behavior are rampant. Biologists turn to data. Eskimos and Indians accept natural explanations but also take a wider view, that some things are inexplicable except through the metaphorical language of legend. The owner of a dog team is more righteously concerned with the safety of his animals than with understanding what motivates wolves. And everyone believes to some degree that wolves howl at the moon, or weigh two hundred pounds, or travel in packs of fifty, or are driven crazy by the smell of blood.
>
> None of this is true. The truth is we know little about the wolf. What we know a good deal more about is what we imagine the wolf to be.⁶

Lopez's book aimed to change the widespread negative perception and misunderstanding of wolves not only by presenting research data but also by pointing out the cultural roots of the antipathy which would later be embraced by new emerging media. This chapter demonstrates that the historical development of the American view of this emblematic animal is easily traceable in American literature and that this view corresponds with a change in attitude towards nature itself. The development of lupine imagery is reflected in three significant periods of wolf writing: the period of European settlement, the late nineteenth and early twentieth centuries and the present day.⁷ While the first two periods correspond to a time of war against wolves with the aim of eradicating the species, the discussion of their importance in the ecosystem began in the 1980s and 1990s, when reintroduction programmes were started in the United States. This chapter focuses on literary works from the second and third periods of writing about wolves.

While the 'devil wolf' of the Puritan era evolved into the more recently popular 'sacred wolf', both are anthropocentric and anthropomorphized projections that do not reflect the species as such.[8] Our anthropocentric categories necessarily shape our understanding of non-human categories, in this case the interpretation of territorial behaviour, social structures, predatory instincts and behavioural patterns.[9] Although many myths concerning the dangerousness of wolves have been disproved by research, the 'devil wolf' has never ceased to be an attractive cultural motif. And while such representation may seem harmless, the consequence of anthropomorphization and subsequent misunderstandings may be the extermination of the whole species.

The texts discussed in this chapter are all frequently labelled as 'nature writing'. The analysis focuses, on the one hand, on the way in which wolves are described, with respect to both their physicality and their behaviour, and, on the other hand, on the depiction of nature present in the text, in terms of two (of four) principles of an environmental text based on the work of Lawrence Buell.[10] These principles are, firstly, understanding the natural environment as a process rather than as a constant, and secondly, human accountability to the natural environment as a part of a text's ethical orientation. The analysis is also situated within a theoretical framework of vulnerability, since not only are humans 'vulnerable to the natural environment' but the natural environment and all its inhabitants are vulnerable to human actions.[11]

The centre of this study is Cormac McCarthy's novel *The Crossing*, published in 1994. Reading *The Crossing* alongside Jack London's novels *The Call of the Wild* (1903) and *White Fang* (1906) and Ernest Thompson Seton's short stories 'Lobo the King of Currumpaw', 'Badlands Billy, the Wolf That Won' and 'The Winnipeg Wolf' demonstrates a significant turnabout in perspective, from seeing the wolf and nature as hostile and almost demonic presences towards understanding them as vulnerable and fragile and realizing human accountability for our treatment of the environment. This analysis ultimately points, therefore, to the environmental and ethical orientation of *The Crossing*.

Seton and the trapper story

A trapper story is not an established genre but rather a combination of folk tales, local legends and supposedly true accounts of exceptional trapper-and-wolf combats that were popularized by authors such as Ernest Thompson Seton.[12] As a result of westward expansion and the consequent development of the cattle industry, the wolf became the chief enemy of American society.[13] Once wolves started to attack the herds that replaced their natural prey after the extermination of buffalo, trappers were hired to destroy either a solitary animal or the whole pack. 'No other wolf killing ever achieved either in geographic scope or economic or emotional scale the predator-control war waged against wolves in the nineteenth and early twentieth centuries in the United States and Canada.'[14] Extermination programmes created or supported by the government meant that a trapper or wolfer became an individual and profitable profession. The trappers tended to exaggerate the strength and wit of their enemy in their accounts in order to establish their own reputation as hunters. They were also crusaders in the war against the wilderness, represented by the wolf, and they saw themselves as pioneers and heroes fighting against this villain.[15] 'And as so often accompanies the hubris of doing God's work, wolf hunters were prone to make their adversaries into formidable opponents, even demons, in order to establish their own reputations as effective crusaders or Inquisitors.'[16] They portrayed wolves as almost supernatural creatures of extreme strength and intelligence and with a desire to kill. Such narratives thus describe what S. K. Robisch calls a 'terrible semiotic game' whereby the trapper attempts to find a way to kill the wolf but also expresses his respect for his enemy after its death.[17]

Ernest Thompson Seton was hired as a wolf trapper, and arguably his most famous trapper story, 'Lobo the King of Currampaw', manifests all the characteristics of the 'genre', such as an implausibly huge wolf that kills an incredible number of cattle and an assumption that he destroys the ranchers' livestock simply for the sake of it.[18] Lobo is extreme not only in terms of his size and strength, but also in his ability to hunt and to outwit the trappers. As is the case with Seton's other animal characters, Lobo is constantly anthropomorphized in terms of his behaviour and the motivation for that behaviour.

Seton begins the story with the harmonious image of cattle herds in a valley, which is disturbed by the presence of a predator. Lobo is described as a 'king whose despotic power was felt over [the] entire' region and as a 'gigantic leader of a remarkable pack'.[19] Despite Seton's obvious sympathy for the wolf, Lobo is described as an intruder into the otherwise harmonious coexistence of nature, cattle and farmers. Seton creates an anthropomorphic image of an animal usurping power over the land, as if Lobo did not belong to the environment. Lobo's pack of wolves is anthropomorphized in terms of its behaviour throughout the story: Lobo and his mate Blanca are described as 'laughing at the farmer', Lobo expresses 'his utter contempt' for Seton's poisoned bait and seems to call 'Blanca, Blanca' when the female wolf is destroyed by Seton, an action described as 'the inevitable tragedy'.[20]

Seton's portrayal of Blanca, Lobo's mate, emphasizes her beauty in contrast to Lobo's strength: 'She was the handsomest wolf I had ever seen. Her coat was in perfect condition and nearly white.'[21] While Seton expresses his admiration for Blanca's beauty, the result of it is that the animal undergoes even more suffering. The killing of Blanca, perceived as necessary, was also unnecessarily brutal as a result of Seton's reluctance to spoil the wolf's beautiful hide with a bullet; therefore, she was torn apart by two lassos thrown over her neck and horses sent in opposite directions, a practice that was common at that time.[22] Seton's later remorse for killing Blanca in such a manner anticipates Aldo Leopold's epiphany over the green light of the dying wolf.[23] Both Seton and Leopold lived in times when it was a matter of course to kill every wolf in sight. The ranchers hired trappers to get rid of the predators on their property, and the bounty economy supported by governments turned the whole species into a commodity valuable only in terms of its hide.

In Seton's fiction, wolves are presented as intruders despite the fact that they inhabited the area long before the ranchers and their cattle. The predator is expelled from Seton's picturesque nature. 'Lobo' is an example of the transformation of wilderness from 'a sublime landscape into a series of picturesque scenes' with clear boundaries.[24] Nature is appreciated only in terms of the 'quality of aesthetic experience a landscape provides', without any concern for the processes and relationships involved.[25] In this respect, Seton and other authors clearly reflect the attitude of westward expansion and the desire to control nature. The static character of Seton's natural descriptions allows him to avoid any human responsibility for change in the environment. Animals are evaluated in terms of their utility, which is illustrated in the following passage which takes place after an unsuccessful attempt to destroy the pack by using poisoned baits:

> This is only one of many similar experiences which convinced me that poison would never avail to destroy this robber, and though I continued to use it while awaiting the arrival of the traps, it was only because it was meanwhile a sure means of killing many prairie wolves and other destructive vermin.[26]

Not only is Lobo called a robber – another feature typical of trapper stories, which compare wolves to morally depraved bandits and outlaws – but all other predators are perceived as 'destructive vermin' that must be destroyed as soon as possible. A simple equation of fewer predators means more cattle is put into practice without any concern for its consequences. In this respect Seton represents a reliable source regarding broader attitudes in the late nineteenth and early twentieth centuries. Without much simplification, nature was meant to be controlled and utilized and everything beyond human control, such as predators, was doomed to be destroyed.

Seton's stories 'Badlands Billy' and 'The Winnipeg Wolf' feature similarly mythical figures of wolves reminiscent of supernatural beings. Both eponymous protagonists are giant wolves apt to kill livestock and domestic animals, and they escape the trappers for a significant period of time until the inevitable last battle with man. While Badlands Billy kills 15 dogs that were sent after him and escapes, the Winnipeg Wolf stands up to his enemies in a combat he cannot win:

> He leaped out, knowing now that he had to die, but ready, wishing only to make a worthy fight. . . . He had made his choice. His days were short and crammed with quick events. His tale of many peaceful years was spent in three of daily brunt. He picked his trail, a new trail, high and short. He chose to drink his cup at a single gulp, and break the glass – but he left a deathless name.[27]

Seton's writing conjures up a scene full of pathos, presenting the wolf as desiring to fight against humans. Seton's 'hero' is an anthropomorphized construct onto whom human motivation is projected. While in his 'Notes to the reader' the author declares that his account is accurate, it is not difficult to understand why Seton gained the label 'Nature Faker', a term 'best applied to people whose sentiments about nature blind them to the real living animal in the wild'.[28] None of Seton's wolf characters choose their own fate; the Winnipeg Wolf was not a bandit wishing to inspire folk songs and leave 'a deathless name'. The fate of these animals was determined by the fact that they were born close to human settlement and were considered disposable and useless vermin.

In the story of 'Badlands Billy', Seton presents a more complex vision of the environment and the wolf's habitat:

> In pristine days the Buffalo herds were followed by bands of Wolves that preyed on the sick, the weak, and the wounded. When the Buffalo were exterminated the Wolves were hard put for support, but the Cattle came and solved the question for them by taking the Buffaloes' place. This caused the wolf-war. The ranchmen offered a bounty for each Wolf killed, and every cowboy out of work was supplied with traps and poison for wolf-killing. The very expert made this their sole business and became known as wolvers.[29]

This passage implies the existence of a pastoral past, suggested by the word 'pristine' which evokes both primordiality and purity, and this implication is endorsed by the image of wolves preying only on the sick, weak and wounded, which is similarly inaccurate in describing them as bandits.[30] The slight notion of the extermination of the wolves' natural prey and the arrival of cattle in the area does not question these actions. The single word 'exterminated' is not enough in the context of the stories to be interpreted as a criticism or as an understanding of humankind as responsible for a drastic change in the ecosystem since the transformed land is idealized.

In Seton's short stories, the notion of the wolf as a part of its natural environment is suppressed by the mythical perception of the animal. The author's anthropomorphic image of the wolf-despot has two main effects: the species is presented as a strange element that does not belong to nature and it bears the morally negative reference of an antagonist. Its extermination is perceived in terms of necessity and without any consequences, just like the preceding extermination of buffalo. The species is described with admiration for its physical strength and wit but without any respect for its position in the natural environment.

London's hybrid heroes

While the trapper stories present the wolf as an antagonist, Jack London's novels *The Call of the Wild* and *White Fang* are focalized through the animals, making them the protagonists. In terms of context, London's narratives differ from the trapper narratives since they are set in the north, where the species was neither endangered nor systematically exterminated. Nevertheless, wolves represented a very real threat (like nature itself) in Alaska at the turn of the century.

The opening passage of *White Fang* describes the environment that determines the character of the wolf:

> A vast silence reigned over the land. The land itself was a desolation, lifeless, without movement, so lone and cold that the spirit of it was not even that of sadness. There was a hint in it of laughter, but of a laughter more terrible than any sadness – a laughter that was mirthless as the smile of the sphynx, a laughter cold as the frost and partaking of the grimness of infallibility. It was the masterful and incommunicable wisdom of eternity laughing at the futility

of life and the effort of life. It was the Wild – the savage, frozen-hearted Northern Wild.[31]

The habitat of the wolf is described as a hostile wasteland, an image of wilderness still prevalent at the beginning of the twentieth century. The introductory passage demonstrates a strongly anthropomorphic vision of nature with the motif of 'terrible' and 'mirthless' laughter, a motif which also appeared in Seton, suggesting the evil character of nature and wolf. While Seton's wolves were perceived as strange elements, London's wolf represents its environment perfectly and it is what it has to be in order to survive in such conditions: a merciless killer, a fraud, an animal of extreme strength and aggression without any sign of weakness. It heals extremely well, and both Buck and White Fang seem to be able to survive any hardship, although they are both at some point saved by the superior animal: humans. Not only do they belong to a kind that in London's writings seems to be superior to other species, but they are both exceptional individuals within their species.

The stories are also complicated by the opposition of domesticity and wildness. Buck is a domestic dog that later in life adopts the lifestyle of a wolf in order to become the leader of a pack. He exceeds the timber wolves both in size and strength and gains his wildness by killing 'the noblest game of all', a man.[32] Only then does he complete his transformation and cut off ties with human civilization. He becomes a myth, the father of a new line of wild wolfdogs and a representative of Darwinian theories.

Unlike Buck, White Fang is a wolfdog. However, the emphasis on his origin alters throughout the story: in the first part of the book he is described as a wolf, but in order to make him fit for the domestic environment in the south, his dog ancestry is emphasized after a rather epiphanic moment when he experiences kindness for the first time.[33] While his attachment to his new owner is described in terms of love, White Fang is a subject of 'domestication, which is the elimination, of wildness. We incorporate it, assimilate it, colonize it.'[34] His incorporation means that he is at the mercy of humankind when there are only two options, either to domesticate or to kill him, with both meaning gaining control over the wild creature.

Once the wolfdog is bound to human settlement, he enters a net of social structures that White Fang seems to understand only too well for an animal. He also submits to the anthropocentric hierarchy as he understands that men, and white men in particular, are 'another race of beings, a race of superior gods'.[35] This race negotiates his existence in terms of his value, for instance when Grey Beaver trades White Fang for whiskey.[36] Unlike the wolves from the south, he has a certain value alive, first as a draught animal and then for fighting. Despite the fact that he grew up half wild and underwent trauma from fighting, when it comes to his settling into the new environment, White Fang demonstrates what London calls 'plasticity', an ability to adapt to different conditions and human lifestyles. Buck is similarly able to adapt to the wilderness, a reference to the survival of the fittest that belongs to London's rather rich political and philosophical agenda, an integral part of both novels, including 'Darwinism, atavism, early Marxist socialism, the Nietzschean concept of the over-man, and the tricky relationship between deterministic naturalism and survivalist self-reliance'.[37]

Both London's heroes are anthropomorphic constructs used to exemplify such an agenda rather than realistic representations of their species or the natural environment. Buck is a dog adapting to the life of a wolf, and White Fang is a wolf forced to fit into the lifestyle of a dog. As such, they both represent the tension between the nature–culture relationship, but their character is always subordinate to the anthropocentric aims of the author. However, one aspect of the novels escapes London's mysticism: the fact that once either the animal or the environment is affected by humans, it is changed forever and its fate depends upon human responsibility towards it.

McCarthy's vulnerable predator

'*The Crossing* devotes a third of its volume to a wolf's story, and without didactic intrusion, implying that the wolf's demise is easily as historically and literally significant as anyone else's.'[38] The novel begins as a trapper story, describing Billy Parham and his father obtaining and setting traps to catch a shewolf who came from Mexico to Hidalgo County and started to prey on their cattle.[39] The process of preparing and setting the traps and extensive dialogues focused on the ways to catch the wolf demonstrate the complexity of the craft. The process of trapping is historically accurate, for instance in that they use the No. 4½ Newhouse, the most widely used trap at that time.[40] The first part of the story is set in 1931, when wolves were nearly extinct in the American Southwest, a fact that is reflected several times in the novel. The historical connection to the systematic wolf extermination at the beginning of the twentieth century is emphasized by W. C. Echols, one of the best wolvers in the 1920s.[41] Nevertheless, Echols does not appear as a character in the novel;

he is present only through references and his trapping instruments, as if he had perished with the wolves. However, the Parham family is never judged by the narrator for their intentions to protect their cattle as they – like the shewolf – also struggle to survive in the new country.

In *The Crossing*, the wolf was destined to perish before she came to the country. Unlike Seton, McCarthy emphasizes the role of humankind in altering the region by the systematic exploitation of nature. The state of the wolf's habitat is described as follows:

> Her ancestors had hunted camels and primitive toy horses on these grounds. She found little to eat. Most of the game was slaughtered out of the country. Most of the forests cut to feed the boilers of the stampmills at the mines. . . . She was moving out of the country not because the game was gone but because the wolves were and she needed them.[42]

This concise passage describes a ruined ecosystem with the notion of the mutual dependence of various species. Unlike other species that usually 'become extinct through the destruction of habitat', wolves and buffaloes were exterminated by a targeted effort.[43] The excerpt also demonstrates the impact of human actions on the whole area: humans are held to be directly responsible for the change in the environment through the presence of stampmills and mines, as well as through the slaughtering of the game. The wolf does not move to Hidalgo County deliberately but rather is forced there by human-made conditions, including the trapping of her mate. The wolf did not choose her own fate, as was the case in both Seton and London; instead, her fate is forced upon her by external factors and by changes in her environment.

While Seton and London focus mainly on the extreme strength of their wolf representatives and exaggerate the aggression and predatory instinct of the species, McCarthy's description of the shewolf's first encounter with Billy emphasizes her vulnerability:

> She was caught by the right forefoot . . . The wolf crouched slowly. As if she'd try to hide. Then she stood again and looked at him and looked off toward the mountains . . . When he approached her she bared her teeth but she did not growl and she kept her yellow eyes from off his person. White bone showed in the bloody wound between the jaws of the trap. He could see her teats through the thin fur of her underbelly and she kept her tail tucked and pulled at the trap and stood.[44]

Though a predator, the shewolf is described in an extremely vulnerable state: trapped, pregnant, wounded and at the mercy of humans in an environment where she is undesirable. Her most prominent feature is not her strong white teeth, a common image in wolf literature, but an exposed white bone surrounded by blood and the metal jaws of the trap, putting the man in the position of the merciless predator. In her book *The Body in Pain*, Elaine Scarry does not focus on the pain inflicted on animals, but since she claims that the experience of pain is not transmittable even from one human to another,[45] the following observation may serve as a means of understanding McCarthy's method:

> Both weapon (whether actual or imagined) and wound (whether actual or imagined) may be used associatively to express pain. To some extent the inner workings of the two metaphors, as well as the perceptual complications that attend their use, overlap because the second (bodily damage) sometimes occurs as a version of the first (agency).[46]

Like every living creature, the shewolf is inherently vulnerable to 'hunger, thirst . . . and physical harm'.[47] McCarthy's descriptions of the wolf enhance both her mythical and mystical qualities, but at the same time they insist on her physicality. 'The creature, then, is first and foremost a living body – material, temporal, and vulnerable.'[48] However, her situation also relates to a social or contextual form of vulnerability which we do not often associate with animals. Standing there, trapped, she is a true representative of both the reality and the history of her species, suffering from physical pain inflicted by humans with the clear purpose of destroying her as her ancestors had been destroyed for centuries. Deprived of her own kind and of her natural prey, she is vulnerable from the beginning of the story, and when she is bound and muzzled by Billy, she becomes wholly defenceless. In a scene strongly reminiscent of Blanca's death in Seton's 'Lobo', Billy throws a lasso over her neck, but with the opposite motivation. This trapper decides to save his adversary and attempt to lead her back to Mexico, where she might live and raise her puppies.

The Crossing is an outstanding literary representation of the wolf, as McCarthy describes the species in a more sophisticated way than the preceding wolf literature had done.[49] The seemingly objective third-person narrator addresses the physical characteristics and behavioural responses of the animal in precise detail, usually without further interpretation of their meaning and carefully avoiding anthropomorphism, which is used only when a particular scene is focalized through Billy or another character.⁵⁰ The wolf's physicality and frequent remarks about her body language such as flattening her ears, baring her teeth and tucking her tail underneath her warn us against understanding her only as a symbol. She is neither a devil nor a sacred wolf but rather a truthful representative of a critically endangered species. This does not mean that McCarthy demystifies the wolf completely. He offers a new, harmless mythology of the species based on respect for the deeper knowledge of the world that the wolf seems to possess and that is inaccessible to humans, meaning that the wolf is interconnected with the world in a way that humankind cannot be. The wolf's eyes become a symbol of the impenetrability of this world and of the crossing over into another one: 'When the flames came up her eyes burned out there like gatelamps to another world. A world burning on the shore of an unknowable void.'⁵¹

The shewolf never ceases to resist Billy's attempts to caress her.⁵² Although she responds to Billy in the end, she remains wild and – in accordance with McCarthy's nature in general – indifferent and inaccessible, not only to Billy but also to the reader, since the narrator does not interpret her behaviour. There is no epiphany of human kindness as in *White Fang*. Where Seton and London created anthropomorphized animals that think and behave in quite a human manner, the mind of McCarthy's shewolf remains obscure. And yet Billy never abandons the ethical responsibility he feels for the shewolf and identifies with her and her species. He is able, borrowing a phrase from Timothy Morton, to 'love the nature nonidentical with us'.⁵³ In this respect, Billy is a remarkable character considering his upbringing and his cultural context, in which wolves are destroyed without a second thought.⁵⁴ However, Billy, being a lone figure in his effort, faces the dire consequences of society's hatred of wolves, and his mission fails.

The wolf and its absence become 'a metaphor for man's careless appetite for control over the natural world', meaning that man 'controls the animals he can, and he kills those animals he cannot'.⁵⁵ Billy's attempt to save the wolf may, though noble, be considered as the manifestation of a similar desire for control. Yet there is a great difference between Billy's actions and 'the federal government's methodical wolf-eradication program . . . base[d] on the bounty-value of a dead wolf'.⁵⁶ Billy attempts to return the shewolf to 'her' home, not to bring her to his home and possess her. Throughout the journey, Billy faces danger and discomfort because of a promise he made to the animal. He fights to save the wolf until the end and even lets her off her chain without a muzzle in the fighting pit without any idea whether she will attack him or not. And although his mission utterly fails, and he kills the wolf out of mercy, he keeps his promise, trades his rifle for her body and buries her in the mountains.

Billy's reluctance to conform to society's demand for the death of the wolf emphasizes the societal lack of responsibility or sympathy for nature. In Seton's stories, the wolves are valuable only if dead. White Fang's existence is negotiated several times in the novel and he is valued as a draught animal, a fighting dog or a pet. Billy's motivation is based on attachment to the animal and does not show any trace of ecological awareness, but the mere fact that he does not treat the shewolf as a commodity and refuses to sell her several times is exceptional in its historical context. Trading his rifle for her body is a last hopeless gesture, one last act of resistance.

Conclusion: the endangered wolf

In *The Crossing*, McCarthy not only creates a more complex and truthful image of the wolf but also challenges his literary predecessors by using similar motifs and images. Instead of following Seton and London in creating anthropomorphized animal heroes possessing human qualities and demonstrating humankind's supremacy over nature, he focuses on a faithful rendering of the representative of a species that might easily vanish forever and emphasizes humankind's responsibility for its survival. Describing the predator as beautiful and vulnerable is crucial for changing the way in which the wolf is imagined. As Anat Pick states in *Creaturely Poetics*, '[i]f fragility and finitude possess a special kind of beauty, this conception of beauty is already inherently ethical. It implies a sort of sacred recognition of life's value as material and temporal.'[57] If humankind perceives the predator in different terms, there may be a chance to save it and literature can either assist or prevent any change in perception.

McCarthy's novels are often interpreted in terms of nostalgia for a more harmonious human–nature relationship in the past; for instance, Dianne C. Luce reads *The Crossing* in terms of a vanishing world. However, McCarthy worked on *The Crossing* in the late 1980s and early 1990s, when a plan for wolf reintroduction in Yellowstone was presented to the American public. The programme started in 1995 and still has many opponents. There is evidence that McCarthy was aware of the programme and discussed it with Edward Abbey.[58] Instead of reading *The Crossing* as a lamentation for the extermination of the wolf in the 1930s and for a lost cowboy lifestyle, I suggest reading it as a novel concerned with its current situation and as a warning against repeating the same mistake. The ending of the first part of *The Crossing*, which is quite similar to the ending of McCarthy's last novel *The Road* (2006), supports this reading by emphasizing what the world would lose were the wolf to disappear forever. *The Crossing* is a novel emphasizing man's responsibility for the natural environment and suggesting that we 'reconsider our position and role in the natural world'.[59] By using the wolf as a representative of both its species and the natural environment more broadly, the novel represents a thorough critique of an anthropocentric worldview which perceives nature as a commodity. *The Crossing* is not an elegy; it is a powerful text with a powerful ethical message.

Notes

1. Robisch, *Wolves and the Wolf Myth*, 7.
2. Robisch, *Wolves and the Wolf Myth*, xii.
3. Robisch, *Wolves and the Wolf Myth*, 28.
4. Lopez, *Of Wolves and Men*, 32.
5. Phillips, 'Ecocriticism, literary history, and the truth of ecology', 598.
6. Lopez, *Of Wolves and Men*, 2–3.
7. Robisch, *Wolves and the Wolf Myth*, 28.
8. Robisch, *Wolves and the Wolf Myth*, 20.
9. This fact applies not only to literature but also to zoological research. Lopez discusses the problem of perception that even zoologists face when studying the species and the questionable objectivity of the observer.
10. Buell, *The Environmental Imagination*, 7–8.
11. Mackenzie, Rogers and Dodds, 'Introduction', 1.
12. Robisch, *Wolves and the Wolf Myth*, 398–400.
13. The strong antipathy towards wolves travelled with the settlers from their European background. Lopez discusses in detail the medieval obsession with wolves based on a real threat (both of actual attack and of the possible transmission of rabies) and how they were associated with the devil. See the chapter 'Out of a medieval mind' in *Of Wolves and Men*.
14. Lopez, *Of Wolves and Men*, 169.
15. Nash, *Wilderness and the American Mind*, 24.
16. Robisch, *Wolves and the Wolf Myth*, 399.
17. Robisch, *Wolves and the Wolf Myth*, 398, 400.
18. Robisch, *Wolves and the Wolf Myth*, 400.
19. Seton, *Wild Animals I Have Known*, 17.
20. Seton, *Wild Animals I Have Known*, 30, 35, 46.
21. Seton, *Wild Animals I Have Known*, 45. In comparison with Seton's photograph of Blanca, the emphasis on her white coat seems a bit exaggerated and more symbolic than based on reality.
22. Not only were wolves hunted down, they were frequently killed in a particularly brutal manner for no apparent reason. See Lopez, *Of Wolves and Men*, 169.
23. Luce, 'The vanishing world of Cormac McCarthy's Border Trilogy', 168.
24. Byerly, 'The uses of landscape', 53.
25. Byerly, 'The uses of landscape', 53.
26. Seton, *Wild Animals I Have Known*, 35.
27. Seton, *Animal Heroes*, 318–20.
28. Lutts, *The Nature Fakers*, 176.
29. Seton, *Animal Heroes*, 112–13.
30. Robisch, *Wolves and the Wolf Myth*, 400.
31. London, *The Call of the Wild* and *White Fang*, 113.

32. London, *The Call of the Wild* and *White Fang*, 105.
33. Robisch, *Wolves and the Wolf Myth*, 312, 321.
34. Robisch, *Wolves and the Wolf Myth*, 327.
35. London, *The Call of the Wild* and *White Fang*, 238.
36. Robisch, *Wolves and the Wolf Myth*, 311.
37. Robisch, *Wolves and the Wolf Myth*, 290.
38. Robisch, *Wolves and the Wolf Myth*, 375.
39. I keep McCarthy's version of the spelling of 'shewolf' without the hyphen.
40. Brown, *The Wolf in the Southwest*, 33.
41. Brown, *The Wolf in the Southwest*, 73–6, 83.
42. McCarthy, *The Crossing*, 25–6.
43. Robisch, *Wolves and the Wolf Myth*, 68.
44. McCarthy, *The Crossing*, 54.
45. Scarry, *The Body in Pain*, 3.
46. Scarry, *The Body in Pain*, 16.
47. Mackenzie, Rogers and Dodds, 'Introduction', 7.
48. Pick, *Creaturely Poetics*, 5.
49. Robisch, *Wolves and the Wolf Myth*, 376.
50. Robisch, *Wolves and the Wolf Myth*, 383–5, 373.
51. McCarthy, *The Crossing*, 75.
52. Robisch, *Wolves and the Wolf Myth*, 379.
53. Morton, *Ecology without Nature*, 185.
54. Luce, 'The vanishing world of Cormac McCarthy's Border Trilogy', 181.
55. Sanborn, *Animals in the Fiction of Cormac McCarthy*, 131, 134.
56. Sanborn, *Animals in the Fiction of Cormac McCarthy*, 142.
57. Pick, *Creaturely Poetics*, 3.
58. Woodward, 'Cormac McCarthy's venomous fiction', 30.
59. Arnold, 'McCarthy and the sacred', 216.

Bibliography

Arnold, Edwin T. 'McCarthy and the sacred: A reading of *The Crossing*'. In *Cormac McCarthy: New directions*, edited by James D. Lilley, 215–38. Albuquerque: University of New Mexico Press, 2002.

Brown, David E., ed. *The Wolf in the Southwest: The making of an endangered species*. Tucson: University of Arizona Press, 1988.

Buell, Lawrence. *The Environmental Imagination: Thoreau, nature writing, and the formation of American culture*. Cambridge, MA: Harvard University Press, 1995.

Byerly, Alison. 'The uses of landscape: The picturesque aesthetic and the national park system'. In *The Ecocriticism Reader*, edited by Cheryll Glotfelty and Harold Fromm, 52–68. Athens: University of Georgia Press, 1996.

London, Jack. *The Call of the Wild* and *White Fang*. London: Wordsworth Editions, 1992.

Lopez, Barry Holstun. *Of Wolves and Men*. With Photographs by John Bauguess. New York: Charles Scribner's Sons, 1978.

Luce, Dianne C. 'The vanishing world of Cormac McCarthy's Border Trilogy'. In *A Cormac McCarthy Companion: The Border Trilogy*, edited by Edwin T. Arnold and Dianne C. Luce, 161–97. Jackson: University Press of Mississippi, 2001.

Lutts, Ralph H. *The Nature Fakers: Wildlife, science, and sentiment*. Charlottesville: University of Virginia Press, 2001.

Mackenzie, Catriona, Wendy Rogers and Susan Dodds. 'Introduction: What is vulnerability, and why does it matter for moral theory?' In *Vulnerability: New essays in ethics and feminist philosophy*, edited by Catriona Mackenzie, Wendy Rogers and Susan Dodds, 1–30. Oxford: Oxford University Press, 2013.

McCarthy, Cormac. *The Crossing*. London: Picador, 2010.

Morton, Timothy. *Ecology without Nature: Rethinking environmental aesthetics*. Cambridge, MA: Harvard University Press, 2007.

Nash, Roderick. *Wilderness and the American Mind*. Revised Edition. New Haven, CT: Yale University Press, 1979.
Phillips, Dana. 'Ecocriticism, literary theory, and the truth of ecology'. *New Literary History* 3 (1999): 577–602.
Pick, Anat. *Creaturely Poetics: Animality and vulnerability in literature and film*. New York: Columbia University Press, 2011.
Robisch, S. K. *Wolves and the Wolf Myth in American Literature*. Reno and Las Vegas: University of Nevada Press, 2009.
Sanborn, Wallis R. *Animals in the Fiction of Cormac McCarthy*. Jefferson, NC: McFarland & Company, 2006.
Scarry, Elaine. *The Body in Pain: The making and unmaking of the world*. Oxford: Oxford University Press, 1985.
Seton, Ernest Thompson. *Animal Heroes*. New York: Constable & Company, 1911.
Seton, Ernest Thompson. *Wild Animals I Have Known*. New York: Charles Scribner's Sons, 1912.
Woodward, Richard B. 'Cormac McCarthy's venomous fiction'. *The New York Times Magazine*, 19 April 1992.

Part 2:
Violence/Resistance

4
Retelling the Parsley Massacre: vulnerability and resistance in Danticat's *The Farming of Bones*

Eleonora Rapisardi

Narratives of vulnerability and trauma constitute a paradigm that enables us to reconsider and, ultimately, rewrite issues of race, nationhood and belonging. Indeed, these narratives could help change the ready-made categories that constitute the frame through which we understand reality.[1] Echoing the claim of Susana Onega and Jean-Michel Ganteau in their introduction to *Victimhood and Vulnerability in 21st Century Fiction*, this chapter focuses on 'the way in which victimhood and vulnerability are constructed by reference to the perception and literary representation of such notions as race or nationhood'.[2]

To this end, I will analyse *The Farming of Bones* (1998) by the Haitian American writer Edwidge Danticat.[3] This novel represents the events surrounding the Parsley Massacre (*la masacre del perejil*), in which between 15,000 and 20,000 Haitians were killed on behalf of the regime of the Dominican dictator Rafael Leonidas Trujillo. Through fictional narratives, official historical accounts can be challenged and the voices of the most vulnerable subjects can be heard. This chapter focuses on the possibilities that the literary medium affords to those groups who have been silenced by the dominant historical discourse.

The vulnerable subjects, who have been dispossessed of history, are in this case Haitians under Trujillo's dictatorship, hence Black and poor people, who constitute an obstacle to the regime's design of national unity and cohesion. This chapter is about race inasmuch as I consider Black Haitian subjects and examine the question of how their cultural and social group has been represented in Dominican propaganda. In addition, this chapter is also concerned with nationhood and the question of how it has been constructed through physical violence against the most vulnerable groups.

In the first part of this chapter, I read *The Farming of Bones* and analyse how narratives are employed to represent testimonials of the events immediately preceding the slaughter. In the second part, I connect this trauma to the dispossessed (in this case Haitians) and their quest to find their own voice(s) and repossess their own narratives. Thus, vulnerability becomes a powerful paradigm by means of which vulnerable groups can reclaim their own existence and rewrite their own epistemology, referring 'as much to collective imaginaries as to an objective historical reality', as Guillermina De Ferrari writes in *Vulnerable States: Bodies of memory in contemporary Caribbean fiction*.[4]

The massacre and its context

The Caribbean island of Hispaniola has become a terrain where race and nationhood have been extensively discussed and fought over, both in respect of its colonial and its recent history. Between 1791 and 1804, Haiti, or Saint Domingue, as it was named in those days, was the setting of the Black slaves' revolution. This was led by Toussaint Louverture and Jean-Jacques Dessalines, among others, and it would give birth to the Haitian Republic, the first Black republic in the world and the second nation to gain independence from the colonizers in the western hemisphere. As the Haitian historian Michel-Rolph Trouillot argues in *Silencing the Past* (1995), this revolution was not understandable to its contemporaries because it disrupted most of their epistemological categorizations. As Trouillot writes, '[t]hey could read the news only with their ready-made categories, and these categories were incompatible with the idea of a slave revolution'.[5]

In those days, colonialism was justified by the belief that African slaves were less than human. In the words of Trouillot once more, 'non-European groups were forced to enter into various philosophical, ideological, and practical schemes', all of which 'recognized degrees of humanity . . . [U]ltimately, some humans were more so than others.'[6] Humiliation, violence, slaughter, slavery, torture and death were inflicted on Black slaves and on the indigenous population alike within larger schemata, which were justified by the colonial epistemology. De Ferrari writes: 'That colonial agents felt compelled to find in the physical body a justification for their political position reveals that colonial domination was effectively based on the vulnerability of the material body to the forces of symbolic power.'[7] Bodies of colour were considered entities upon which meaning could be inscribed, which constitutes a paradigm of conquest and domination. As such, Black slaves, the indigenous population and their descendants were vulnerable not only to bodily pain and torture, but also to the symbolic power of colonial epistemology.

The Parsley Massacre (frequently known as *El corte* in Spanish, *koutkout-a* in Haitian creole) was committed in 1937 by the regime of the Dominican dictator Trujillo in the context of a larger operation of national unification. Estimates of the number of people killed range between 15,000 and 20,000; many others were wounded and displaced. The victims were people of Haitian origin who had lived in the Dominican Republic for two or more generations. The massacre was committed at the north-western border between Haiti and the Dominican Republic and in the adjacent region of El Cibao.[8]

This massacre was motivated by the will to make the nation more cohesive and to rewrite it as consisting of mulatto, Hispanic, Catholic subjects. There was no space in Trujillo's political design for Black subjects who believed in voodoo rather than in Catholicism, and who were culturally closer to Africa, while Dominicans felt closer to Spain. In *The Farming of Bones*, Father Romain, a priest who was imprisoned during the massacre, mindlessly repeats what he has been instructed to say when captured:

> 'Our motherland is Spain; theirs is darkest Africa, you understand? They once came here only to cut sugarcane, but now there are more of them than there will ever be cane to cut, you understand? Our problem is one of dominion . . . Those of us who love our country are taking measures to keep it our own.' (260)

Since then, this anti-Haitian sentiment has not disappeared; rather, it has increased and evolved into institutionalized racism. Both in the era of colonialism and in the twentieth century, Black lives were made vulnerable in order to exploit them for political and economic purposes. As Paul Gilroy writes in *The Black Atlantic* (1993), 'the ideas of nation, nationality, national belonging, and nationalism are paramount' and supply an 'absolute sense of ethnic difference' which 'is maximised so that it distinguishes people from one another and at the same time acquires an incontestable priority over all other dimensions of their social and historical experience, cultures, and identities.'[9] The Parsley Massacre should be seen as epistemologically coherent with the colonial enterprise, even if it was committed by the Dominican government. Gilroy writes that 'racial terror is not merely compatible with occidental rationality but cheerfully complicit with it'.[10]

In *The Farming of Bones*, a confused and babbling Father Romain also says:

> 'Sometimes I cannot believe that this one island produced two such different peoples . . . We, as Dominicans, must have our separate traditions and our own ways of living. If not, in less than three generations, we will all be Haitians. In three generations, our children and grandchildren will have their blood completely tainted unless we defend ourselves now, you understand?' (261)

Migrants are vulnerable as soon as they are transformed into the problem of society. Indeed, not everybody is regarded as containing life, but rather some are condemned to be lifeless, to be captured or left abandoned. In other words, whatever form of life is left in them must be transformed into death. As Achille Mbembe and Libby Meintjes write in 'Necropolitics', the Black migrant 'truly becomes a subject – that is, separated from the animal – in the struggle and the work through which he or she confronts death (understood as the violence of negativity). It is through this confrontation with death that he or she is cast into the incessant movement of history.'[11]

Regarding the inherent importance of the revolution, I argue that, in murdering Haitians, Trujillo attempted to kill a whole set of meanings that the Haitian Revolution had created. In *Caribbean Discourse*, Édouard Glissant defines Haiti (or Saint-Domingue) as '[p]ossibly the new "motherland"'.[12] He adds that 'there (and only there) could be found the conditions for organized survival and the political (revolutionary) self-affirmation that emerged . . . Haiti retains a strength derived from *historical memory*, which all Caribbean people will one day need.'[13] In *The Farming of Bones*, Danticat describes the following scene taking place after the massacre:

> A woman was singing, calling on the old dead fathers of our independence. Papa Dessalines, where have you left us? Papa Toussaint, what have you left us to? Papa Henry, have you forsaken us?
>
> 'Freedom is a passing thing' a man said. 'Someone can always come and snatch it away.' (212)

The collective memory of the Haitian Revolution is still present, even in the aftermath of the massacre. According to Gilroy, '[i]n periodising modern black politics it will require fresh thinking about the importance of Haiti and its revolution for the development of African American political thought and movements of resistance'.[14] In this sense, Danticat mobilizes these meanings of the Haitian Revolution through her narration, so that they can be remembered and pave the way for a new approach to this momentous historical event.

Narrating the massacre

The Farming of Bones retells the story of the massacre through the diegetic voice of Amabelle. Amabelle is a Haitian servant working for a Dominican family in the Dominican Republic. She was found by Don Ignacio after her parents drowned in the Massacre River and has been living with his family ever since.[15] The novel opens with Señora Valencia, Don Ignacio's daughter, giving birth to twins. She goes into labour early, so Amabelle, whose mother was a midwife in Haiti, must help her give birth. The two babies, born to the same mother, have completely different appearances. Indeed, Danticat is, in an act of counter-epistemology, using this event as a metaphor. The twins are a boy and a girl: the son, like Señora Valencia, 'was coconut-cream colored, his cheeks and forehead the blush pink of water lilies' (9). The girl was born second and came as a surprise to Señora Valencia and Amabelle. Her face was covered by a caul, 'a thin brown veil, like layers of spiderwebs' (10), and the umbilical cord was wrapped dangerously around her neck. For Señora Valencia, these signs are a curse. She is smaller than her brother and her skin is darker, 'a deep bronze, between the colors of tan Brazil nut shells and black salsify' (11). The girl, Rosalinda, was completely unexpected, and her birth is surrounded by signs of bad luck. When the doctor later comes and hears about the umbilical cord, he says: 'Badly placed, around her neck? It's as if the other one tried to strangle her' (19).

With her description of the newborns, Danticat shows in a symbolic way how meanings are assigned to bodies of colour from the moment they come into the world. This becomes even more evident in the following passage, when Señora Valencia asks: 'Amabelle do you think my daughter will always be the color she is now? . . . My poor love, what if she is mistaken for one of your people?' (12). When the doctor makes a comment on the colour of her skin, Don Ignacio reacts in an irritated way, saying that her complexion must come from the father's family and highlighting his own family's Spanish descent.

Birth and death thus give the writer many opportunities for the renegotiation of meaning. When driving home to see his newborn children, Señor Pico kills Joël, a Haitian sugarcane worker. He was walking together with two other workers, Sebastien and Yves, when the car ran over him and sent him into the ravine. Death is also a moment where corporeal vulnerability is accentuated, and the meanings attributed to bodies are more visible. Joël is killed by Señor Pico, a Dominican who works in Trujillo's army and who will be one of the material executors of the Parsley Massacre. For Señor Pico, Joël was not even human.

Amabelle describes Joël as 'taller and larger-boned, the kind of man who was called upon to pull an oxcart full of cane when the oxen were too tired to do the job' (54). On the one hand, she is pointing out his corporeal presence. On the other hand, she is showing what type of jobs he usually accomplishes, how his corporeal strength has not only been taken advantage of but also symbolically appropriated. Amabelle is sent by Don Ignacio, Señor Pico's father-in-law, to Kongo, Joël's father, to relay Don Ignacio's offer to pay for the funeral. Kongo refuses the offer, saying that his son would not want ceremonies. He wants to bury him where he was killed, in the ground. When Amabelle asks him what she should say to Don Ignacio then, Kongo answers: 'Tell him I am a man . . . He was a man, too, my son' (109).

Here, the cane worker is treated 'as if he or she no longer existed except as a mere tool and instrument of production'.[16] Nevertheless, she or he can draw from experience to break with 'uprootedness and the pure world of things of which he or she is but a fragment' and 'to demonstrate the protean capabilities of the human bond through . . . [the] very body that was supposedly possessed by another', through the remembrance and the retelling of vulnerabilities that enable group-forming narratives to come about.[17]

Before the massacre, the shock of his imprisonment and the violence inflicted upon him, Father Romain would encourage the cane workers to remember the ties that held their community together. Danticat writes: 'In his sermons to the Haitian congregants of the valley he often reminded everyone of common ties: language, foods, history, carnival, songs, tales and prayers. His creed was one of memory, how remembering – though sometimes painful – can make you stronger' (73).

Vulnerability can be regarded not only as the capacity to be hurt, but also as the possibility of self-awareness, as the beginning of strength that is transformed into resistance. Onega and Ganteau point out that 'more encompassing considerations taking such notions as susceptibility to the wound, exposure, and victimhood as potentialities or general characteristics [are] helping define what it is to be human'.[18] In this sense, narratives of vulnerability are capable of breaking what Trouillot calls 'the iron bonds of the philosophical milieu' in which they originated.[19]

While building the narrative towards the tragic violent climax of the massacre, Danticat, through the narrating voice of Amabelle, shows how such a violent episode is not an exception, but rather the peak of a long tradition of racist rhetoric. Black bodies are vulnerable to the assignation of symbolic meanings from the moment they are born, and, throughout their lives, they keep on being perceived by means of such epistemological categories until their death and even beyond. Narration and remembering are a way of subverting the symbolic meanings assigned to their bodies. Remembering and retelling vulnerabilities is key to the process of rethinking them.

Conclusion: narration and community

In this sense, I want to highlight how Danticat's novel, through storytelling about trauma and vulnerability, enables group-forming narratives to come about. In *Wounded Heroes* (2013), Marina McCoy writes that 'vulnerability, or the capacity to be hurt, is distinct from the state of actually being harmed or suffering pain. Instead of communicating the actual experience of pain or harm, the term communicates the possibility of such experience, and self-awareness of its possibility'.[20] Talking about these experiences also means finding your own voice, a narrative voice that escapes the symbolic web of meanings to which you have been assigned.

In the following passage from *The Farming of Bones*, Amabelle is talking to other victims after the massacre:

> 'Will you go yourself to see these priests?' I asked.
>
> 'I know what will happen,' he said. 'You tell the story and then it's retold as they wish, written in words you do not understand, in a language that is theirs, and not yours.' (246)

The memories of the survivors of the massacre are deeply vulnerable to the hegemonic account of history, which is imbued with colonial epistemology and thus leaves unheard the stories of the most vulnerable groups. Kelli Lyon Johnson, in 'Both sides of the massacre' (2003), writes:

> On the Haitian side of the Massacre River, there are no markers. The official silence about the trujillato and its aftermath have created in the Haitian imagination the sense that their history must be made salient and available not only for Haitians but also for the world. Danticat breaks that official silence, creating from her own research and the collective memory of those to whom she spoke a narrative of the history of the victims and the survivors of the Haitian massacre.[21]

In this sense, fiction is instrumental in making those voices heard. Danticat's novel embraces a style that is deeply influenced by the Haitian tradition of oral storytelling. The first-person narration is often interrupted by oneiric pages. While they are still narrated from Amabelle's perspective, they incorporate remembrances and dreams. The layout of the pages mirrors this change of register; those parts are printed in bold in the text. Onega and Ganteau write that 'the narratives of victimhood and vulnerability flaunt their own vulnerable form and become exposed to the reader's consideration by having recourse to a range of specific devices'.[22] Turning to the oneiric scenes, I would like to emphasize how they undoubtedly represent a creative way of renegotiating what is being said and how, by altering its form. This is exemplified by the following passage:

> It is perhaps the great discomfort of those trying to silence the world to discover that we have voices sealed inside our heads, voices that with each passing day, grow even louder than the clamor of the world outside.
>   The slaughter is the only thing that is mine enough to pass on. All I want to do is find a place to lay it down now and again, a safe nest where it will neither be scattered by the winds, nor remain forever buried beneath the sod.
>   I just need to lay down sometimes. Even in the rare silence of the night, with no faces around. (266)

Through a passage rich in metaphors, included in one of the dreamlike passages, Danticat expresses the vulnerability of those stories that are, nevertheless, necessary and must be saved. She adopts a multiplicity of narrative experiments, including the choral pattern of the novel, which produces an account that is fragmented and, in this way, makes sense of the complexity of the event. Danticat incorporates orality into her writing, voicing both the memories of a vulnerable community and the vulnerability of cultural transmission itself. Literary fiction thus tells these stories to a large readership while underlying their intrinsic vulnerability.

As Onega and Ganteau point out, 'such strategies as generic hybridization and/or narrative experimentation are aimed at fighting the unrepresentability of trauma'.[23] Moreover, Danticat integrates these strategies into the most representative Western form of (creative) writing, the novel. For these reasons, the following passage is significant for both its content and its form. Amabelle is remembering Sebastien, with whom she was in love and who has been killed during the massacre:

> This past is more like flesh than air; our stories testimonials like the ones never heard by the justice of the peace or the Generalissimo himself . . .
>
> His name is Sebastien Onius. Sometimes this is all I know. My back aches now in all the places that he claimed for himself, arches of bare skin that belonged to him, pockets where the flesh remains fragile, seared like unhealed burns where each fallen scab uncovers a deeper wound . . .
>
> Men with names never truly die. It is only the nameless and faceless who vanish like smoke into the early morning air.
>
> His name is Sebastien Onius. (282)

The body retains the memory not only of the violence inflicted upon it during the massacre but also of Sebastien's loving touch. Amabelle wants these stories ('our stories') to be heard, to be included in the public discourse, as she keeps repeating Sebastien's name and says '[m]en with names never truly die'. Onega and Ganteau write: 'By putting together all individual vulnerabilities and securing the ascendance of a collective "we", empowerment becomes possible without negating the powers of interconnectedness and solidarity, and by banking on them, precisely.'[24] The 'collective "we"' is easily traceable in Danticat's words, for instance in the phrase cited above, 'our stories [are] testimonials'. It is this collective we that allows this 'narrative community' to keep existing.[25] In *The Farming of Bones*, the novel is used to construct a discourse that avoids reiterating neo-colonial and hegemonic stances, a discourse that gives space to the subjects that have not been heard.

Notes

1. See Trouillot, *Silencing the Past*, 73.
2. Onega and Ganteau, 'Introduction', 10.
3. References to quotations from this text will be given in the main body in parentheses, citing from Danticat, *The Farming of Bones*.
4. De Ferrari, *Vulnerable States*, 216.
5. Trouillot, *Silencing the Past*, 73.
6. Trouillot, *Silencing the Past*, 76.
7. De Ferrari, *Vulnerable States*, 2.
8. For more detailed information on the massacre and its causes, see the following sources: Derby, 'Haitians, magic, and money'; Derby and Turits, 'Historias de terror y los terrores de la Historia'; Martinez, 'Not a cockfight'; Turits, 'A world destroyed, a nation imposed'.
9. Gilroy, *The Black Atlantic*, 3.
10. Gilroy, *The Black Atlantic*, 56.
11. Mbembe and Meintjes, 'Necropolitics', 14.
12. Glissant, *Caribbean Discourse*, 265.
13. Glissant, *Caribbean Discourse*, 265–6 (emphasis in the original).
14. Gilroy, *The Black Atlantic*, 17.
15. The Dajabón is a river in the north of the Dominican Republic, at the border with Haiti. It got the name Massacre River well before the Parsley Massacre, in 1728. For more information, see Matibag, *Haitian–Dominican Counterpoint*, 139.
16. Mbembe and Meintjes, 'Necropolitics', 22.
17. Mbembe and Meintjes, 'Necropolitics', 22.
18. Onega and Ganteau, 'Introduction', 7.
19. Trouillot, *Silencing the Past*, 74.
20. McCoy, *Wounded Heroes*, vii.
21. Johnson, 'Both sides of the massacre', 89.
22. Onega and Ganteau, 'Introduction', 10.
23. Onega and Ganteau, 'Introduction', 4.
24. Onega and Ganteau, 'Introduction', 9.
25. Nünning, 'Making events – making stories – making worlds', 208.

Bibliography

Danticat, Edwidge. *The Farming of Bones*. New York: Penguin, 1999.
De Ferrari, Guillermina. *Vulnerable States: Bodies of memory in contemporary Caribbean fiction*. Charlottesville: University of Virginia Press, 2012.
Derby, Lauren. 'Haitians, magic, and money: Raza and society in the Haitian–Dominican borderlands, 1900 to 1937'. *Comparative Studies in Society and History* 36, no. 3 (1994): 488–526.
Derby, Lauren, and Richard Turits. 'Historias de terror y los terrores de la Historia: La masacre haitiana de 1937 en la República Dominicana'. *Estudios Sociales* 26, no. 92 (1993): 65–76.
Gilroy, Paul. *The Black Atlantic: Modernity and double consciousness*. London: Verso, 1993.
Glissant, Édouard. *Caribbean Discourse: Selected essays*, translated by J. Michael Dash. Charlottesville: University Press of Virginia, 1989.
Johnson, Kelli Lyon. 'Both sides of the massacre: Collective memory and narrative on Hispaniola'. *Mosaic: A journal for the interdisciplinary study of literature* 36, no. 2 (2003): 75–91.
Martinez, Samuel. 'Not a cockfight: Rethinking Haitian–Dominican relations'. *Latin American Perspectives* 30, no. 3 (2003): 80–101.
Matibag, Eugenio. *Haitian–Dominican Counterpoint: Nation, state, and race on Hispaniola*. Basingstoke: Palgrave Macmillan, 2003.
Mbembe, J.-A., and Libby Meintjes. 'Necropolitics'. *Public Culture* 15, no. 1 (2003): 11–40.
McCoy, Marina. *Wounded Heroes: Vulnerability as a virtue in ancient Greek literature and philosophy*. Oxford: Oxford University Press, 2013.
Nünning, Ansgar. 'Making events – making stories – making worlds: Ways of worldmaking from a narratological point of view'. In *Cultural Ways of Worldmaking: Media and narratives*,

edited by Vera Nünning, Ansgar Nünning and Birgit Neumann, 191–214. Berlin: Walter de Gruyter, 2010.

Onega, Susana, and Jean-Michel Ganteau. 'Introduction'. In *Victimhood and Vulnerability in 21st Century Fiction*, edited by Jean-Michel Ganteau and Susana Onega, 1–18. New York: Routledge, 2017.

Trouillot, Michel-Rolph. *Silencing the Past: Power and the production of history*. Boston: Beacon Press, 1995.

Turits, Richard Lee. 'A world destroyed, a nation imposed: The 1937 Haitian Massacre in the Dominican Republic', *Hispanic American Historical Review* 82, no. 3 (2002): 589–635.

5
Toni Cade Bambara's vulnerable men

Tuula Kolehmainen

In her 1970 anthology *The Black Woman*, Toni Cade Bambara writes, 'if a woman is tough, she's a rough mamma, a strident bitch, a ballbreaker, a castrator. But if a man is at all sensitive, tender, spiritual, he's a faggot'.[1] While in her essay Bambara criticizes stereotypical gender roles in capitalist society in general, with the images in this quotation she refers to the attitudes in the African American community. In this chapter, I analyse how Bambara portrays and challenges these still pervasive stereotypes in two short stories, 'The Hammer Man' and 'Raymond's Run'. The stories were published in the short story collection *Gorilla, My Love* (1972) only two years after Bambara's essay 'On the issue of roles' appeared in *The Black Woman*.[2] As an activist in the Civil Rights Movement, the Black Arts Movement and Black feminism, Bambara concerned herself with gendered and racist stereotypes. Indeed, she suggests in the same essay that '[p]erhaps we need to let go of all notions of manhood and femininity and concentrate on Blackhood'.[3] In my view, this concern is present in her short fiction.

Having written stories since she was a young girl, the short story genre was the most familiar to Bambara. Of course, the author called herself a 'cultural worker', which meant 'using the arts – literary works, film, theater, music, dance, and the visual arts – as instruments of self-renewal and transformation'.[4] Despite her clear talent in multiple media forms, she is, however, most known for her short stories. Bambara's first collection, *Gorilla, My Love*, features 15 stories about life in African American communities, most clearly in New York. As even the covers of different editions of the collection illustrate, the stories are usually seen as representations of either the female narrators or the all-Black neighbourhoods. In an interview, the author says she compiled the stories for her first collection because her agent knew a woman named Toni Morrison 'who was really interested in [her] work'.[5] Personally, Bambara recounts elsewhere, she preferred the short story genre because the 'short story is far more effective in terms of teaching us lessons'.[6] Even though she did not think writing was 'a perfectly legitimate way to participate in struggle' before 1973,[7] I believe that Bambara set out to teach her readers some lessons in these early short stories as well. And she typically did so using the voices of African American girls and women.

Overall, critics of *Gorilla, My Love* have paid most attention to its female narrators. Elizabeth Muther argues that the narrators 'are not diminutive characters, to be outgrown with the coming of age of the movement. Rather, through their precocious insight they anticipate the resistance strategies and forms of collective self-affirmation that will be essential to the survival of community.'[8] In other words, even though the narrators are children, they express powerful visions that can benefit their whole community. More often than not, Bambara's stories describe a coming-of-age of the female narrator. I would not consider them to be examples of the Bildungsroman genre as such because the stories end leaving the narrator a child, but with a lesson learned. That is, they are more about an individual epiphany than a whole-hearted character change. Whatever the lesson they learn may be, the narrators are clearly exceptional. They resist expectations of what a girl should be like, say what they think and, even if you cannot always trust what they say, seem to fight for what is best for the whole community. In this way, the narrators seem to be on a mission to challenge gendered stereotypes in order to find the essence of 'Blackhood'.

The focus of this chapter is on the male characters of Bambara's stories, which is an area less covered by critics. The selected stories are unique in that they introduce young, Black, male characters with unspecified but apparently non-physical disabilities. Even though the titles of the stories refer to males, Manny in 'The Hammer Man' and Raymond in 'Raymond's Run', these two male characters are nevertheless seen less in their own right and more as supporting the female narrators' growth. The male characters are juxtaposed with the female narrators, who are gutsy, sassy and bright, while manhood is represented as infantile, dependent and vulnerable. The male characters can be seen as props, as assistants to the female characters, thus reversing the sexist notion of male power and female dependency. I argue that here Black male vulnerability is represented in order to challenge certain stereotypical images and, thus, that in these stories vulnerability works as resistance.

For the purposes of this approach, vulnerability must first be understood on a basic level. In short, vulnerability is in essence the openness to being hurt and being dependent (on others). However, within the context of the lives of many African Americans, the term vulnerability carries another, overlapping connotation. According to Tommy J. Curry, Black male vulnerability refers to 'the material disadvantages Black males face due to incarceration, unemployment, police brutality, homicide, domestic and sexual abuse throughout society, or their victimhood'.[9] Curry discusses the history of Black male vulnerability and its manifestations today and refers to 'the vulnerable condition' of Black males. Being seen as 'a living terror', they are liable to be 'killed, raped, or dehumanized at any moment'.[10] This aspect of vulnerability is largely due to persisting racist stereotypes of the Black male, which, in my view, are being identified and questioned in Bambara's stories.

As supporting fictional characters that do not take part in any dialogue, Raymond and Manny are dependent on the female narrators to tell their stories. They are thus vulnerable to unreliable representation of themselves and can be seen as experiencing 'linguistic vulnerability'.[11] Butler explains the term thus: 'who we are, even our ability to survive, depends on the language that sustains us'.[12] Manny and Raymond's linguistic vulnerability lies in that they are silenced in the stories: Raymond is only described as 'hollering' and Manny is only reported to speak in his imaginary world, and what he says is of no importance to either the narrator or the other characters. If what Frantz Fanon argues is true and 'it is implicit that to speak is to exist absolutely for the other',[13] Manny and Raymond hardly exist in the stories and are dependent on others to speak for them.

On a textual level, however, a more complex progression concerning the male characters can be traced. Following David T. Mitchell's notion, I will show that the disabled male characters can be seen as serving a 'narrative prosthetic' function, which means that in order to portray certain issues and tell important stories, narratives use disabled characters as 'crutches'.[14] In my view, Raymond's and Manny's 'crutch-like' roles would seem to lie in foregrounding the female narrators' strong characters and supporting their growth, as well as making it possible to tell the story of vulnerability.

Indeed, narratives need characters with disabilities even though the stories are not about people with disabilities per se. The need arises from the assumption that the able body, for its apparent normativity, cannot stand for non-normative experiences. For this purpose, Mitchell has coined another term, the 'materiality of metaphor'. It means that disabled characters lend to the narrative something it cannot otherwise possess: materiality. Disabled characters provide tangible metaphors and thus create a 'symbolic effect' that 'the healthy corporeal surface fails to achieve ... without its disabled counterpart'.[15] I claim that Raymond and Manny serve as corporeal metaphors and thus symbolize the 'vulnerable condition' of African American men, which can be seen as a 'nonnormative' experience. In other words, while the experiences of people with disabilities in these stories are represented quite narrowly, important issues about the condition of African American men are discussed through their representations. Acknowledging that the characters with disabilities have been used in their narrative prosthetic function and that they stand for something else – or more – than the life experiences of the people they represent, I argue that the vulnerable characters in these stories assist in challenging racist gendered stereotypes. Next, I start the analysis of the stories by discussing the juxtapositions through which the characters are represented.

Juxtaposing the deviant: representations of vulnerability

The thread of this chapter finds its focus in the intersections of diverse subject positions. In terms of the representations of African Americans, Toni Morrison argues that, in the works of the white canon, African Americans have often been stock characters, surrogate bodies through which it was easier for white people to discuss issues that were frightening to them and to help define themselves as superior. Morrison argues that 'Africanism is the vehicle by which the American self knows itself not as enslaved, but free; not repulsive, but desirable; not helpless but licensed and powerful; not history-less, but historical; not damned, but innocent; not a blind accident of evolution, but a progressive fulfillment of destiny'.[16] That is, Africanist bodies have often been seen in literature through polarities. According to Morrison, they have typically been portrayed through these dichotomies, having little further value but to stand for the 'not-me' for the white characters and readers.

As for the representation of disability, Rosemarie Garland-Thomson has investigated the portrayals of people with disabilities in American literature, and she claims that narrating disability has engendered the subject position of the 'normate'. She argues that the 'normate subject position emerges, however, only when we scrutinize the social processes and discourses that constitute physical and cultural otherness. Because figures of otherness are highly marked in power relations, even as they are marginalized, their cultural visibility as deviant obscures and neutralizes the normative figure that they legitimize'.[17] That is, paradoxically, the figures of otherness create and legitimize the normate subject position, that is, the 'cultural self',[18] which finds its counterparts in the figures of (cultural) otherness: women, people with disabilities, racialized people and the Africanist personae, for example. Created by the figures of otherness, the normate subject position reproduces and reinforces the marginalized position of the other. Moreover, in line with Morrison's argument, the disabled body is used to contemplate negative or otherwise troublesome or intimidating themes. As Garland-Thomson notes, '[c]onstructed as the embodiment of corporeal insufficiency and deviance, the physically disabled body becomes a repository for social anxieties about such troubling concerns as vulnerability, control, and identity'.[19] In my view, this also relates to people with cognitive impairment, such as Manny and Raymond appear to be.

The perspectives provided by Morrison and Garland-Thomson are useful in scrutinizing Bambara's stories because all the main characters in 'The Hammer Man' and 'Raymond's Run' are relational, and they are represented through polarities such as male/female and strong/vulnerable. What is of interest to me lies in the intersections of these representations. Alice Hall states that '[s]ocial oppression is constructed through a complex web of these intersecting identities and cultural conditions', meaning power relations and forms of social stratification such as gender, class, race and sexuality.[20] To better understand social oppression, my aim is to find out how the doubly othered subject positions of characters that are both racialized and disabled are portrayed and what kinds of issues they stand for. It is important to note that these male characters are not shown in relation to their parents, teachers or other children, only to the strong female narrators, who at first seem to take on the position of the 'normate'.

However, the image of the strong Black woman is also a common stereotype in literature and pervasive in other contemporary discourses as well. While it is associated with seemingly positive attributes such as resilience, independence and self-sufficiency, the position is problematic. Melissa Harris-Perry states that '[t]he brash, independent, hostile black woman rarely shows vulnerability or empathy'.[21] Tracing the roots of '[t]he myth of black women's emasculating anger' in the image of the Sapphire, Harris-Perry claims that this stereotype has often been unacknowledged because it has been considered as a natural trait of African American women.[22] Moreover, Trudier Harris criticizes the tendency of African American fiction to reinforce the stereotype of 'black women who are almost too strong for their own good, whether that strength be moral or physical, or both'.[23] This means that being strong may lead to the inability to share loving feelings with children, for example. Harris also argues that the strong female characters have been 'praised . . . for exhibiting traits that Western culture has traditionally designated more masculine than feminine', suggesting that strength is considered as a more masculine trait.[24] I would also argue that in Bambara's stories, these stereotypical images are seen in that the girls perform character traits that are, quite generally, considered as masculine. The male characters, by contrast, are represented as dependent and vulnerable, which are traits more often than not connected with femininity in Western culture.

We can see how the juxtapositions of the male and female characters operate by examining the plots of the two stories. In 'The Hammer Man', the unnamed narrator is a young girl from New York City who lives in a 'deviant family' (38). She struggles with the imbalance between the gender roles imposed on her by society and the kind of identity she herself wants to perform. The girl says, for example, that she was playing pool when she should have been sewing (39). Prone to dishonesty, she is at least verbally abusive, 'a big-mouth', in her own words (41). She expresses her gutsiness by continuously fighting with Manny, a potentially violent boy from the same neighbourhood who is, according to the narrator, 'supposed to be crazy' (35). Manny is likely to suffer from a kind of emotional or cognitive impairment, signalled by his problems in interacting with others, as well as his reputation in the neighbourhood as different. The narrator says that being crazy was 'his story' (35), but as becomes clear, Manny lives, at least partly, in his own imaginary world. After a fight, when the girl had verbally attacked Manny and his mother, Manny had climbed onto the roof of her house (35). Knowing that Manny is a 'sucker for sick animals and things like that' (36), which the narrator believes is how he had been tricked by other children to climb onto the roof, she spreads the word that Manny had gotten mad at her and threatened to kill her. The adults of both families start fighting each other, but as Manny falls off the roof, everything seems to return to normal in the neighbourhood.

The final encounter between Manny and the narrator is different, taking place at a basketball court where the girl finds Manny focusing on an imaginary ball game and talking to himself. Two white police officers come to the court, asking the children questions. Since Manny does not answer, one of the police officers slaps him and calls him a 'black boy' (40). Until this point, the racial identities of the characters have not been mentioned but after the remark, the narrator expresses a new-found feeling of fellowship with Manny in her own sassy manner: 'Now when somebody says that word like that, I gets warm. And crazy or no crazy, Manny was my brother at that moment and the cop was the enemy' (40). The fact that the police officer's slur carries a meaning that is recognized as heavily offensive even by a child can be deduced from the way the girl is more offended by what the cop said ('black boy') than what he did (violence). The slur is twofold. Firstly, a white person calling another person black is an act of trying to put the other person 'in their place', in this case, reminding Manny that he is of an 'inferior' race. Secondly, calling somebody a 'boy' infantilizes the other person, putting him into a vulnerable social category by representing him as smaller, more dependent and more ignorant than the one uttering the word.[25]

Confronted in this way, Manny appears unable to defend himself and is even more vulnerable when placed in juxtaposition with the girl, who is fully aware of the criticalness of the situation. However, she loses her temper and tries to help Manny by saying: '"You better give him back his ball . . . Manny don't take no mess from no cops. He ain't bothering nobody"' (40). Manny's vulnerable situation makes his antagonist resist the police officers in order to save him. Manny continues playing and the girl thinks he moves with the basketball 'damn near like he was some kind of very beautiful bird' (41). Using similar diction to Bambara in her essay, she describes Manny's lay-up as being 'about the most beautiful thing a man can do and not be a fag' (42). By defending Manny, she surrenders to vulnerability, that is, to the risk of being hurt, knowing 'how frantic things can get with a big-mouth like me, a couple of wise cops, and a crazy boy too' (41). However, the officers do not even acknowledge the girl's comments and, taking Manny with them, leave the girl on the court. Doubly marginalized, both by his race and by his disability, Manny has become a victim of racist police officers and is liable to face violence, oppression and imprisonment. As an African American male, he is more likely to be incarcerated than others.[26] The short story ends with the narrator recounting how Manny had, indeed, been institutionalized, to 'some kind of big house for people who lose their marbles' (42), but not killed by the officers as she had feared. After the incident, the narrator takes part in a fashion show in her first corsage instead of her dungarees, thus suddenly yielding to her mother's wish and performing a more 'feminine' role (43).

The narrator of 'Raymond's Run' confronts similar issues. Called 'Squeaky' for her squeaky voice, the narrator does not get along with other girls and, even if her mother wishes she would 'act like a girl for a change' (27), favours running over pole dancing. Squeaky is a good runner and reflects throughout the story on her competence in the sport compared with other girls. She is suspicious of and reacts quite aggressively to anyone but her father and her disabled older brother Raymond, who conversely is depicted as well meaning in an extremely childish way. If confronted, Squeaky prefers 'to just knock you down right from the jump and save everybody a lotta precious time' (26). However, Squeaky's gutsiness also includes her willingness to stand by and protect Raymond from bullies, even with physical violence. This is how she depicts the situation:

> But a lot of people call him my little brother cause he needs looking after cause he's not quite right. And a lot of smart mouths got lots to say about that too, especially when George [the brother of Squeaky and Raymond] was minding him. But now, if anybody has anything to say to Raymond, anything to say about his big head, they have to come by me. (23)

Here, Squeaky appears gutsier than either of her brothers and Raymond is represented through established images of disability: a big head, an inability to take care of himself and not being 'quite right'. Raymond is called Squeaky's little brother because, even though he must be a teenager and is bigger in size, he acts more like a child. For example, he is 'subject to fits of fantasy' and sometimes thinks 'he's a circus performer' (24), and he likes to go on the swing even though he is almost too big to fit in it (28).

The most important part of Squeaky's description, however, is the fundamental dependence of Raymond: he is a child with a disability, dependent on the care of his little sister. Dependence and vulnerability – while not always synonymous – can be seen as interrelated. People with disabilities are often viewed as vulnerable because of this tendency to be dependent on others and thus face infantilization.[27] Examples of infantilization due to dependence in 'Raymond's Run' include Squeaky's comment, cited above, that 'a lot of people call him my little brother cause he needs looking after' (23), as well as the way that Squeaky underrates Raymond's capacity to understand the meaning of words and actions. For example, she does not let him speak for himself although Raymond seems to understand even the man on the loudspeaker, although, according to Squeaky, 'you can hardly make out what he's saying for the static' (30). Squeaky takes care of Raymond because she believes that he will become a victim of robbery, bullying and violence if left behind (25).

The story's climactic scene is the May Day race, where Squeaky competes with her new rival, Gretchen. She has asked Raymond to wait on the other side of a fence, but to her astonishment she sees him running on the other side 'in his very own style' (31). The scene marks the beginning of Squeaky's moving away from her strong and somewhat masculine role. After the run, Raymond starts 'rattling the fence like a gorilla in a cage' and then climbs up the fence 'like a dancer or something' (31). Impressed by Raymond's first run and later understanding that Raymond does not have anything 'to call his own' (32), Squeaky comes to view Raymond and other children more empathetically. Like the narrator of 'The Hammer Man', Squeaky suddenly breaks free from the stereotypical role of the strong woman.

As we have seen, in both 'The Hammer Man' and 'Raymond's Run' many aspects of vulnerability are present: the openness to attack, dependence, disability and age.[28] Bambara's stories juxtapose strong, even aggressive, girls who perform traits that are more often than not thought of as 'masculine' and vulnerable men who are infantilized and dependent. In the course of the stories, each girl goes through a character change while the male characters seem to remain static.

Narrating disability, narrating ideology?

As discussed above, 'The Hammer Man' and 'Raymond's Run' can be seen as coming-of-age stories of the young female protagonists, and the male characters can be seen as supporting their growth. We do not know exactly what happens to them after the climactic moments, since the stories end soon after the males achieve agency. Thus, the narrative seems to focus on the change experienced by the female characters, leaving the male characters as other to the readers and as mere vehicles for the narrative. In this way, the disabled male characters can be seen as serving a 'narrative prosthetic' function, which refers to 'the pervasive dependency of literary narratives on the trope of disability'.[29]

In this context, another term by Mitchell, the 'materiality of metaphor', becomes even more useful. Manny and Raymond's relational vulnerability lies in the fact that they are constructed as others and stigmatized in a community inhabited by apparently able-bodied – or 'able-minded' – people. To me, this is reminiscent of the subject position of many African Americans in a racist society. Of course, rather than drawing any equivalence between the experiences of people in different groups, I view them as sharing common concerns, their experiences often 'intersecting' or 'conflating'.[30] Morrison argues that the white literary canon has sometimes used African American characters as 'surrogate selves' through which to contemplate issues such as 'powerlessness . . . internal aggression . . . evil' and 'sin'.[31] One way of looking at Bambara's vulnerable male characters is that they serve as tools to meditate on the marginalization and oppression of African American men. I will now describe the metaphorical function of the disabled male characters in 'The Hammer Man' and 'Raymond's Run'.

The social, political and historical vulnerabilities of African American men had been a topic of discussion long before Bambara's time. According to David J. Leonard, Richard Wright, the author of a memoir called *Black Boy* (1945), believed that Black men:

> were emasculated and infantilized, both by whites' racism and by their own responses to it. Wright maintained that black men – relegated to 'boy' status and forced to depend on their wives, mothers, and daughters for financial support – responded through regressive actions that only underscored and reinforced their boyishness, whether it be by killing their white father (literally or symbolically), embracing black nationalism, or remaining submissive.[32]

To Wright, slavery and racism had caused not only the social, economic and political adversities of African American men, but also the survival strategies that only reinforced their vulnerability. Infantilization, emasculation and submission – all these factors are present in Bambara's short stories, including Manny's boy status, Raymond's infantile boyishness and their dependence on the female characters, to name but a few. Michael Gellert states that '[t]o be a slave in the South meant remaining a permanent child, dependent forever', thus emphasizing that the association of infantilization with dependence is connected to the history of American slavery.[33] This connection is also acknowledged by the narrator of 'The Hammer Man', when she tells the police: 'You must think you're in the South, mister' (41), after he has called Manny a boy.

However, these vulnerabilities have anything but vanished from contemporary discourses. According to Tommy J. Curry, for example, Black men are feminized in relation to white men due to their powerlessness: 'Because *maleness* has come to be understood as synonymous with power and patriarchy, and racially codified as white, it has no similar existential content for the Black male, who in an anti-Black world is denied maleness and is ascribed as feminine in relation to white masculinity'.[34] Curry argues that while Black men cannot achieve power or hegemonic masculinity because of this process of feminization, they are nevertheless categorized as hypermasculine. This means that Black men are infantilized and feminized, but at the same time, they are constructed as violent brutes and sexual predators, and thus threats to both white masculinity and femininity, in order to construct and maintain white supremacy. In my view, this paradox constructs the core of Black male vulnerability. In the case of the disabled Black subject, the process of feminization is twofold, because according to Garland-Thomson, 'the non-normate status accorded disability feminizes all disabled figures'.[35] In this way, Manny and Raymond can be seen as being feminized both due to their status as Black males and as people with disabilities, while the female protagonists perform more masculine character traits.

Thus, instead of leaning on hypermasculinity as a way of coping with belittlement and infantilization, these men are dependent on strong women. As Harris notes, '[t]his strength we celebrate has sometimes crippled black men',[36] and it might at first seem that Bambara's ideology lies in portraying strong women beside weak men, whose only hope for survival is to count on the women. Nevertheless, in my view these stories resist stereotypes concerning female strength and male vulnerability, and thus Bambara's agenda is more subtle than merely inverting the representations for the benefit of the female characters.

Challenging (in)vulnerability

> I have always, I think, opposed the stereotypic definitions of 'masculine' and 'feminine', not only because I thought it was a lot of merchandising nonsense, but rather because I always found the either/or implicit in those definitions antithetical to what I was all about – and what revolution for self is all about – the whole person.[37]

In both these stories, Bambara has sketched a strong girl and a vulnerable boy in a highly relational way, even though it was not what she was 'all about'. The question could be raised: how much does relationality impact on presuppositions about the vulnerability and/or invulnerability of the characters? Do we just assume that when the one (in this case, the male character) is vulnerable, then the other one (the female narrator) is without exception invulnerable? Or do we assume – from the textual clues presented in the narrative – that when the relational female character is strong, the male character has to be vulnerable? Butler, Gambetti and Sabsay argue:

> When vulnerability is projected onto another, it seems as if the first subject is fully divested of vulnerability, having expelled it externally onto the other. When vulnerability is owned as an exclusive predicate of one subject and invulnerability attributed to another, a different kind of disavowal takes place. Indeed, asymmetry and disavowal work together.[38]

In other words, as one subject is deemed completely vulnerable, and, in this case, juxtaposed with another subject, the other is denied vulnerability. Then again, if a subject is deemed fully invulnerable (for example, the strong Black woman), it may lead to the denial of their vulnerability. Following the argument of Butler, Gambetti and Sabsay, it could be stated that the representations of vulnerability in Bambara's stories are asymmetrical, meaning that the other subject's extreme vulnerability overshadows the other's vulnerability. The disavowal that takes place, then, concerns both genders: the strong girls seem to be denied vulnerability and the male characters remain as boys and are thus denied manhood.

However, the narrators' potential unreliability makes the representation more complex. Manny is, I believe, portrayed by the female narrator as less vulnerable than he actually is. For instance, she calls him a variety of condescending names, such as 'old Hammer Head' (38), 'ole Manny' (39), 'Crazy Manny' (36) and 'a crazy boy' (41), but he is only referred to as a man in the title of the story. In addition to naming him, she is in control of telling Manny's story, thus reinforcing her own strong character. According to Butler, Gambetti and Sabsay, '[p]sychoanalytic feminists have remarked that the masculine positions are effectively built through a denial of their own vulnerability. This denial or disavowal requires one to forget one's own vulnerability and project, displace, and localize it elsewhere.'[39] As discussed earlier, the narrator and Manny are polarized, and Manny is feminized due to being a Black male with a disability, which would render the girl's position as masculine.

I view Manny's hammer as a symbol of power and masculinity, which the narrator claims to have taken away from him (38). The statement is obviously a lie, since at the end of the story Manny still has his hammer. Due to his inability or reluctance to use it – or the power it may symbolize – the hammer does not help him. Neither does it work as a threat to anyone's safety. According to Curry, 'Man-Not-ness names the vulnerability that Black men and boys have to having their selves substituted/determined by the fears and desires of other individuals'.[40] Racist stereotypes are often constructed upon the fear of Black masculinity, and this fear, I believe, is the key to Manny's isolation and eventual institutionalization. It is clearly a displaced fear, because Manny is only represented as violent by the narrator, and perhaps stereotypically profiled as such by the white police officers. In truth, Manny is submissive; he is taken away by the police without resistance.

Because of this fear, it is difficult to notice that the narrator is, and is allowed to be, violent. She is also institutionalized for a while as she is sent to a community house by her mother. There she finds out information about herself:

> I looked into one of those not-quite-white folders and saw that I was from a deviant family in a deviant neighborhood. I showed my mother the word in the dictionary, but she didn't pay me no mind. It was my favorite word after that. I ran it in the ground till one day my father got the strap just to show how deviant he could get. (38)

Not taken care of by her mother, and being beaten by her father, the narrator seems to be replicating the behavioural patterns of her family. What is important here is that in reality not only Manny is deviant. The stigma is carried by the whole neighbourhood. The question remains: if everybody is deviant, from whom is Manny deviant? Perhaps the narrator's mother has the answer: Manny is the 'craziest one' (35). It is his disability that allows such a categorization.

Similarly, Raymond's extreme vulnerability dissolves Squeaky's vulnerability. In fact, I believe that Squeaky represents Raymond as more vulnerable than he actually is in order to strengthen her own character. The fact that she is vulnerable to the violent behaviour of adults is not as marked when juxtaposed with Raymond's vulnerability. She is 'a poor Black girl' (27) who was beaten at home because Raymond had wet his clothes while playing (24), but she nevertheless underlines her own reputation as the 'baddest' (30) and Raymond's vulnerability and dependency. Furthermore, placing a little girl in the 'strong Black woman' role can be seen as a way of challenging the notion of African American women as heads of the family, and their almost 'suprahuman' strength.[41]

Raymond's disability, on the other hand, enables his stigmatization. The stigmatizers are childish, dependent and vulnerable, too, because Raymond is (allegedly) bullied by other children. Then again, only Squeaky appears as a bully in this story. Calling other girls names such as 'fatso' (27), she has a way of boasting about her violent behaviour: 'I have whupped her behind many times for less salt than that' (26). After deciding that she will 'give' Raymond running lessons and start coaching him, she is able to give in to the expectations of being a girl who is a friend of other girls:

> We stand there with this big smile of respect between us. It's about as real a smile as girls can do for each other, considering we don't practice real smiling every day, you know, cause maybe we too busy being flowers or fairies or strawberries instead of something honest and worthy of respect . . . you know . . . like being people. (32)

It is interesting how Squeaky juxtaposes performing 'feminine' roles and humanization. This happens right after Raymond's run, which I see as a replica of their father's running style and thus an attempt by Raymond to embrace masculinity. Squeaky reports that her father 'can beat me to Amsterdam Avenue with me having a two fire-hydrant headstart and him running with his hands in his pockets and whistling' (24). Even though the narrator says that Raymond is 'running his arms down to his side and the palms tucked up behind him' and thus 'running in his very own style' (31), it appears as if Raymond is actually trying to mimic his father's running style. Squeaky says that the fact that she cannot beat her father at running is 'private information' (24), but it is clear that Raymond has seen them running.

As we have seen, images of vulnerability and invulnerability are being questioned in these stories by seemingly polarized representations. However, the fact that the narrators' reliability is not clear functions to subvert any strict notions of femininity and masculinity in these stories.

Towards 'Blackhood': conclusion

Toni Cade Bambara's vulnerable men and sassy women offer a juxtaposition through which various issues can be investigated. Raymond and Manny serve a narrative prosthetic function in that they support the growth of the female narrators and also provide corporeal metaphors which enable critical discussion of gendered and racist stereotypes. Butler, Gambetti and Sabsay argue that:

> vulnerability is part of resistance, made manifest by new forms of embodied political interventions and modes of alliance that are characterized by interdependency and public action. These hold the promise of developing new modes of collective agency that do not deny vulnerability as a resource and that aspire to equality, freedom, and justice as their political aims.[42]

Bambara's short stories are good examples of the aspiration for 'collective agency' and the desire for 'equality, freedom, and justice,' in that they persuade readers to take part in the deconstruction of gendered racist stereotypes. Ideally, that would lead to deconstructing and challenging those images in real-life discourses as well.

Weak is not a synonym for vulnerability, and invulnerability is only a fantasy. The resistance to the gendered stereotypes can be seen as foregrounding the importance of African American men to connect with African American women and how vulnerable they are without that connection. In this sense, through writing these stories, Bambara would have joined the '[w]ise progressive black women' who, according to bell hooks, 'have understood that any coming together of free, whole, decolonized black males and females would constitute a formidable challenge to imperialist white-supremacist capitalist patriarchy'.[43] For hooks, one of the causes for the adversities of African American men is their acceptance of patriarchy, and the only way to freedom would be to embrace feminism. Instead of feminist propaganda that would work against males generally, I argue that these stories take part in challenging patriarchy and emphasize the importance of unity in African American communities.

In her short stories, Bambara takes notions such as femininity/masculinity and vulnerability/strength and dismantles them in order to perhaps steer the focus towards other issues. In her essay 'On the issue of roles', she connects her insights on maleness and femaleness to politics and society at large: 'What are we talking about when we speak of revolution if not a free society made up of whole individuals? I'm not arguing for the denial of manhood or womanhood, but rather a shifting of priorities, a call for Selfhood, Blackhood.'[44] I view the representations of vulnerable male characters in these stories as 'embodied political interventions' and, consequently, see vulnerability as resistance.

Notes

1. Bambara, 'On the issue of roles', 102.
2. 'The Hammer Man' was originally published in *Negro Digest* in 1966 and 'Raymond's Run' in a 1971 anthology edited by Bambara, *Tales and Stories for Black Folks*. Both texts are cited from Bambara, *Gorilla, My Love*, with page references given in the main text in parentheses.
3. Bambara, 'On the issue of roles', 102.
4. Holmes, *A Joyous Revolt*, xviii.
5. Lewis, *Conversations with Toni Cade Bambara*, 129.
6. Lewis, *Conversations with Toni Cade Bambara*, 12.
7. Lewis, *Conversations with Toni Cade Bambara*, 4.
8. Muther, 'Bambara's feisty girls', 449.
9. Curry, *The Man-Not*, 29.
10. Curry, *The Man-Not*, 29.
11. Butler, 'Rethinking vulnerability and resistance', 16.

12. Butler, 'Rethinking vulnerability and resistance', 16.
13. Fanon, *Black Skin, White Masks*, 17.
14. Mitchell, 'Narrative prosthesis and the materiality of metaphor', 17.
15. Mitchell, 'Narrative prosthesis and the materiality of metaphor', 28.
16. Morrison, *Playing in the Dark*, 52.
17. Garland-Thomson, *Extraordinary Bodies*, 8–9.
18. Garland-Thomson, *Extraordinary Bodies*, 8.
19. Garland-Thomson, *Extraordinary Bodies*, 6.
20. Hall, *Literature and Disability*, 39.
21. Harris-Perry, *Sister Citizen*, 88.
22. Harris-Perry, *Sister Citizen*, 88–9.
23. Harris, 'This disease called strength', 110.
24. Harris, 'This disease called strength', 114–15.
25. The use of the term 'boy' dates back to slavery in the United States and was still widely used during the Jim Crow and Civil Rights Movement eras. Even though it has lost some of its power through lesser use, the word 'boy' still has racist echoes in today's language. Although it is normal to call male children boys, calling somebody a boy, not to mention a 'black boy', in this historical context is an act of disregarding their humanity and manhood.
26. Butler points out that in the United States today, 'two-thirds of prisoners are black men' (Butler, 'Rethinking vulnerability and resistance', 20).
27. Kari Krogh and Jon Johnson argue that '[i]nfantilizing people with disabilities is a common form of symbolic violence that forces adults with disabilities to enact dependent roles' (Krogh and Johnson, 'A life without living', 166).
28. With 'age' as an aspect of vulnerability, I refer to the fact that all the main characters in the stories are children.
29. Mitchell, 'Narrative prosthesis and the materiality of metaphor', 21.
30. Hall, *Literature and Disability*, 40.
31. Morrison, *Playing in the Dark*, 37–8.
32. Leonard, 'Wright, Richard', 509.
33. Gellert, *The Fate of America*, 245.
34. Curry, *The Man-Not*, 6 (emphasis original).
35. Garland-Thomson, *Extraordinary Bodies*, 9.
36. Harris, 'This disease called strength', 116.
37. Bambara, 'On the issue of roles', 101.
38. Butler, Gambetti and Sabsay, 'Introduction', 4.
39. Butler, Gambetti and Sabsay, 'Introduction', 3–4.
40. Curry, *The Man-Not*, 34.
41. Harris, 'This disease called strength', 111.
42. Butler, Gambetti and Sabsay, 'Introduction', 4.
43. hooks, *We Real Cool*, 134.
44. Bambara, 'On the issue of roles', 105.

Bibliography

Bambara, Toni Cade. *Gorilla, My Love*. New York: Random House, 1981.
Bambara, Toni Cade. 'On the issue of roles'. In *The Black Woman: An anthology*, edited by Toni Cade Bambara, 101–10. New York: Penguin, 1970.
Bambara, Toni Cade, ed. *Tales and Stories for Black Folks*. Garden City, NY: Zenith Books, 1971.
Barrett, Lindon. 'Identities and identity studies: Reading Toni Cade Bambara's "The Hammer Man"'. *Cultural Critique* 39 (1998): 5–29.
Butler, Judith. 'Rethinking vulnerability and resistance'. In *Vulnerability in Resistance*, edited by Judith Butler, Zeynep Gambetti and Leticia Sabsay, 12–27. Durham, NC: Duke University Press, 2016.
Butler, Judith, Zeynep Gambetti and Leticia Sabsay. 'Introduction'. In *Vulnerability in Resistance*, edited by Judith Butler, Zeynep Gambetti and Leticia Sabsay, 1–11. Durham, NC: Duke University Press, 2016.

Curry, Tommy J. *The Man-Not: Race, class, genre, and the dilemmas of Black manhood*. Philadelphia: Temple University Press, 2017.

Fanon, Frantz. *Black Skin, White Masks*. New York: Grove Press, 1967.

Fields, Claude, ed. *Stereotypes and Stereotyping: Misperceptions, perspectives and role of social media*. New York: Nova Publishers, 2016.

Garland-Thomson, Rosemarie. *Extraordinary Bodies: Figuring physical disability in American culture and literature*. New York: Columbia University Press, 1997.

Gellert, Michael. *The Fate of America: An inquiry into national character*. Washington, DC: University of Nebraska Press, 2002.

Hall, Alice. *Literature and Disability*. London: Routledge, 2016.

Harris, Trudier. 'This disease called strength: Some observations on the compensating construction of Black female character'. *Literature and Medicine* 14, no. 1 (1995): 109–26.

Harris-Perry, Melissa V. *Sister Citizen: Shame, stereotypes, and Black women in America*. New Haven, CT: Yale University Press, 2011.

Holmes, Linda Janet. *A Joyous Revolt*. Westport, CT: ABC-CLIO, LLC, 2014.

hooks, bell. *We Real Cool: Black men and masculinity*. New York: Routledge, 2004.

Krogh, Kari, and Jon Johnson. 'A life without living: Challenging medical and economic reductionism in home support policy for people with disabilities'. In *Critical Disability Theory: Essays in philosophy, politics, policy, and law*, edited by Richard F. Devlin and Dianne Pothier, 151–76. Vancouver: University of British Columbia Press, 2006.

Leonard, David J. 'Wright, Richard'. In *American Masculinities: A historical encyclopedia*, edited by Bret E. Carroll, 509–10. New York: The Moschovitis Group, 2003.

Lewis, Thabiti, ed. *Conversations with Toni Cade Bambara*. Jackson: University Press of Mississippi, 2012.

Mitchell, David T. 'Narrative prosthesis and the materiality of metaphor'. In *Disability Studies: Enabling the humanities*, edited by Sharon L. Snyder, Brenda Jo Brueggemann and Rosemarie Garland-Thomson, 15–29. New York: The Modern Language Association of America, 2002.

Morrison, Toni. *Playing in the Dark: Whiteness and the literary imagination*. Cambridge, MA: Harvard University Press, 1992.

Muther, Elizabeth. 'Bambara's feisty girls: Resistance narratives in *Gorilla, My Love*'. *African American Review* 36, no. 3 (2002): 447–59.

Pickering, Michael. *Stereotyping: The politics of representation*. London: Palgrave, 2001.

Wright, Richard. *Black Boy: A record of childhood and youth*. New York: Harper, 1945.

6
The Secret Agent – fictionalizing history: Joseph Conrad and Stan Douglas

Sandra Camacho

Can reality be documented through fiction? Can history be interpreted through a novel, through a film installation, through the convergence of multiple temporalities and genres? In 1907 Joseph Conrad published *The Secret Agent*; here a senseless terrorist act becomes central to the construction of a plot that ponders not only the power states hold over individuals, but also the social and familial transformations occurring in late nineteenth-century Britain. Transposed to Lisbon *circa* 1975, Stan Douglas's film adaptation (2015) explores post-revolutionary upheavals and Cold War tensions by following a group of lethargic anarchists and an ineffectual attempt to attack 'modernity itself' by exploding a centre of transatlantic communications: the Marconi installation in Sesimbra, Portugal.[1]

Taking the shape of a six-screen film installation, Douglas's *The Secret Agent* creates a fictional world that nonetheless investigates historical realities – the Portuguese 'Hot Summer' of 1975 and the concerns of the United States over a potential power grab by communists – while illustrating multiple possibilities and pathways in moments of transition. Such multiple 'realities' are only augmented by the use of the multiscreen environment, thus calling attention to both the viewer's implicated role and the potentialities of the media involved. Editing is not established, as in traditional film, through interchanging shots and reverse shots, but by the physical movement of the spectator and her alternating gaze.

Such a use of the multiscreen may hark back to notions of expanded cinema;[2] however, it may also reflect the constant presence of screens in contemporary everyday life, revealing concerns of a panoptical view of the city, particularly of a city under threat. In the following pages, the importance of factual incidents in the development of *The Secret Agent* both as a novel and as a film installation will be examined. We will consider how, in both works, the collapsing of historical events into a fictional account may call forth the atmosphere of a society in transition, bringing readers closer to a historical 'truth'. But we shall also consider how the choice of the multiscreen conveys the tension present in the multi-layered plot and how it determines its reading.

We will begin by looking at the historical and political upheavals that influenced Conrad's development of his novel, as well as the historical position of Douglas's adaptation. In the reading of Douglas's work, we will introduce other adaptations of Conrad's text that will assist us in demonstrating the way adaptations reflect and converse with the societies and the time in which they are produced. Moreover, by considering other adaptations, the uniqueness of Douglas's piece in tackling the non-linear chronology of the novel will come to the fore. Here the use of the film loop, in which a moving image work is presented continuously, will be of particular significance. Furthermore, we will examine how the use of the multiscreen may evoke the control room, where information from multiple sources can be monitored simultaneously, a situation that may also lead to the dispersion of one's attention due to the sheer volume of information available. The concept of information overload will appear in Douglas's adaptation not solely by its use of the multiscreen, but also through the very positioning of the spectator in relation to the work, and in the necessity of her physical participation in its 'editing'. It will be here that the notion of suture, as defined by Jean-Pierre Oudart, will come into play.

A Simple Tale of the Nineteenth Century

In 1894, a bomb went off near the Greenwich Observatory; it was being carried by Martial Bourdin when it exploded, by some mishap or blunder, killing only the French anarchist himself. It is this moment of senseless, of failed violence that served as inspiration for Joseph Conrad's 1907 book *The Secret Agent*. Set in London, in or around 1886,[3] the book follows the actions – or inactions – of a group of anarchists led by Mr Verloc, who has grown accustomed to a certain lifestyle – a shop whose goods hint 'at impropriety',[4] leisure time and, most importantly, a wife – financed by an unnamed foreign embassy, possibly Russia, in exchange for inconsequential information. Adolf Verloc's lifestyle is threatened by the death of his contact, the First Secretary Baron Stott-Wartenheim, and the arrival of Mr Vladimir, who requires a less passive approach. Mr Vladimir requires an explosion, an attack that is 'purely destructive':[5]

> something outside of the ordinary passions of humanity . . . A bomb in the National Gallery would make some noise. But it would not be serious enough . . . There would be some screaming of course, but from whom? Artists – art critics and such like – people of no account. Nobody minds what they say. But there is learning – science. Any imbecile that has got an income believes in that. . . . Yes . . . the blowing up of the first meridian is bound to raise a howl of execration.[6]

The setting of the novel in the dates surrounding 1886 is key to the reading of Conrad's *A Simple Tale of the Nineteenth Century* – as *The Secret Agent* was subtitled in its earlier editions.[7] The book becomes a reflection on the anxieties assailing London in the period of transition from the nineteenth to the twentieth century. From the 1860s to the 1910s the population living in London more than doubled, accounting for over seven million inhabitants.[8] Such a dramatic influx was not generated by internal migrations alone: a significant part of London's population was composed of European immigrants. Under the Extradition Act (1870) Britain granted asylum to political fugitives, a legislative act that, while introducing limitations to the admission of foreign nationals into the country, was reinforced by the 1905 Aliens Act:

> An immigrant who proves that he is seeking admission to this country solely to avoid prosecution or punishment on religious or political grounds or for an offence of a political character, or persecution, involving danger of imprisonment or danger to life or limb on account of religious belief, leave to land shall not be refused.[9]

Nevertheless, the sudden increase in revolutionary thinkers,[10] political fugitives (anarchists among them) and religious asylum seekers (mostly Jews fleeing pogroms in Eastern Europe) was met with discontent, both inside and outside Britain. 'As far as many European nations were concerned, Britain's asylum policy simply helped terrorists, and undermined the stricter European legislative measures'[11] – a concern that is raised early on in the novel by State Councillor Wurmt: 'The general leniency of the judicial procedure here, and the utter absence of all repressive measures, are a scandal to Europe.'[12]

Such were not the only anxieties gripping Europe or Great Britain. The period 1881–5 saw the Irish Republican Brotherhood implementing a Fenian dynamite campaign 'planned, organized and funded by Irish-Americans using advances in modern science, technology and the increasing globalization of Victorian society'.[13] What the Fenians brought to the stage of terrorism was the technological ability, inherited from American bomb-makers,[14] to home-produce increasingly sophisticated detonators and to quickly divulge such methods through the Brooklyn Dynamite School, led by O'Donovan Rossa and a man known as Professor Mezzeroff.[15] Conrad, too, would employ a professor in his motley crew, one whose sole ambition is to create a 'perfect detonator',[16] a character displaying the detachment expected of an anarchist. Mr Verloc, with his marital status, does not seem to possess this trait in the eyes of Mr Vladimir: 'Anarchists don't marry. It's well known. They can't. It would be apostasy.'[17]

In his author's notes to the 1920 publication of *The Secret Agent*, Conrad observes that, in truth, it is Winnie Verloc's story that he was writing, the 'figures grouped about Mrs Verloc and related directly or indirectly to her tragic suspicion that "life doesn't stand much looking into"'.[18] It is her brother Stevie, an impressionable young man who seems to possess some sort of developmental disability, who will be led into Greenwich Park by Mr Verloc and given a bomb. It is Stevie who will stumble against the root of a tree and fall, the bomb going off right under his chest.[19] However, it was not the sacrifice of an innocent man that caused the most outrage at the time of the book's publication in 1907. The damnable act that Conrad felt the need to defend 13 years later in his notes was the death of Mr Verloc at the hands of his wife. It would be her stabbing of the man she had married in the hope that some comfort and protection might be extended to her brother and mother – the man who would cause the death of her beloved Stevie – that would damn her in the eyes of Conrad's readers. In this condemnation, one might read the influence of the founding of the Women's Social and Political Union in 1903 by Emmeline Pankhurst, the rise of the women's suffrage movement in the following years and the public disapproval these women met; it is a setting that, arguably, may have informed Conrad's writing. Occurring in the public sphere, such political upheavals would nevertheless be transported into the private sphere, into the household – a permeable separation that, as we shall see, will echo in Douglas's multi-screen adaptation.

A moment in flux

For his film installation Stan Douglas transposed the action of *The Secret Agent* to post-revolutionary Lisbon. After Portugal had been under fascist dictatorial rule for 48 years, the regime was brought down on 25 April 1974 by a coup organized by the Armed Forces Movement, which was met with enthusiastic popular support. The Ongoing Revolutionary Process (PREC – Processo Revolucionário em Curso) was established and election dates were set, firstly for the creation of a constitutional assembly on 25 April 1975, followed by the legislative elections on 25 April 1976. However, factions emerged both outside and inside the military. Workers' movements sprang up across the country, occupying factories, farmlands, radio stations and other sites. The possibility that a power grab by communists might take place began to raise concerns, not least in the United States; such events were, after all, taking place during the Cold War.

The period between 11 March and 25 November 1975 came to be known as the 'Hot Summer' of 1975. A series of upheavals and bombings ensued throughout the country, culminating in the attempt, and failure, of a coup on 25 November by left-wing radicals in the military. Of these bombings, one stands out as an attack on the media itself. Earlier in the year, a station of Rádio Renascença – a radio channel with links to the Catholic Church – had been occupied by its left-leaning workers, who proceeded to broadcast communist propaganda. Despite several attempts to remove the workers, it was only on 6 November that radical action was ordered. That evening marked the first televised political debate in Portugal; it was a face-off between moderate socialist leader Mário Soares and communist leader Álvaro Cunhal. Growing tired of the media attention given to the radical left and the use of Rádio Renascença as a propaganda hub, the provisional government, led by José Pinheiro de Azevedo, ordered that a bomb be parachuted in, finally silencing the station on 7 November.[20]

Such an attack on communications finds echoes in Douglas's adaptation. Mr Vladimir, now a US embassy official, demands the bombing of the Marconi installation in Sesimbra:

> The only thing the Portuguese care about now is the future. They never want to be a backward country again. You anarchists hate the status quo and since bombs are your means of expression why

not bomb modernity itself? What do you think about an assault on communication?

...

Blow up the Marconi installation at Sesimbra Mr Verloc. Sever the umbilical cord between Europe and the New World. All European telecommunications with America would be disrupted for months. What makes Portugal a modern nation? The colonies it couldn't afford? Its useless industry? No, it's that braid of copper under the Atlantic Mr Verloc. Why do you think a gang of fascists was welcomed by NATO for the last twenty-five years? Before the first free election in half a century we want a strategy of tension that will make the middle classes think twice before they vote.[21]

Thus, in Conrad, Mr Vladimir's aim is to raise public outcry against revolutionaries and anarchists in London, in the hope that they will not be able to continue to use the city as a haven, and as such will not continue to organize attacks on their countries of origin. In Douglas's work, Mr Vladimir hopes that the threat of isolation, and the fear of being pushed out of NATO, as Henry Kissinger was suggesting at the time,[22] will influence voters in Portugal against the Communist Party. What one finds in Douglas, as in Conrad, is the representation of a society in 'flux', where:

> things have been put in suspension and so a choice can be made of what the future is going to look like. And by looking at those moments we can see that the world we live in is not necessarily the only world we could have realised for ourselves. To realise that what we have now is not the only reality that is possible.[23]

By employing the multiscreen in his adaptation, Douglas is bringing to the fore the possibility of multiple pathways for every given moment. He is emphasizing the existence of multiple points of view, something that might mirror Conrad's shift in time and narrator throughout the narrative. But the multiscreen also offers a level of instability to the viewers' relation to the work that, arguably, cannot be found in single-screen adaptations, a tension present at the very core of the novel and of these societies.

Conrad's novel has seen multiple film, television and radio adaptations since its publication, from Conrad's own adaptation of the work into a three-act stage drama in 1922 to a recent BBC adaptation, its fourth, starring Toby Jones. Conrad's fidelity to his own work in adapting it to the stage received great criticism at the time.[24] As Richard J. Hand points out, for the *Daily Mirror* the play felt 'like portions of a book read out by characters in costume'.[25] However, the main issue Conrad and subsequent adaptors had to tackle was the non-linear chronology of the novel. It is understandable that mainstream films and television shows might tend to avoid turning what is already a challenging work, with its intricate characters and plots, into a visual representation that is even more convoluted by temporal jumps. However, there is one technique associated with expanded cinema that enabled Douglas to overcome such difficulties: the film loop.

Looping time

Expanded cinema first emerged as an artistic practice in the 1970s, having been conceptualized by Gene Youngblood in his 1970 book *Expanded Cinema*. Such terminology is less centred on classifying a specific artistic genre than it is on encompassing a variety of cinematic interpretations. Nonetheless, as Karen Mirza and Brad Butler point out, the corporeal interaction of the viewer with the work is key: 'expanded cinema . . . explores and allows different kinds of performative action or ways of engaging with the body', in opposition to the 'single-screen format of cinema' where 'you have only one, relatively fixed, ocular experience'.[26] The movement necessary to interpret most expanded cinema pieces is provided by the breaking out of the cinema theatre onto the streets, as with VALIE EXPORT in *Tapp und Tastkino (Touch Cinema)* (1968),[27] or more commonly into the gallery or museum space. Such freedom in space also provided for freedom in time, with few artists and galleries implementing fixed viewing schedules. The loop served as a practical device, but it also offered additional viewer participation as the 'respective beginning and end' of the work was set 'simply by entering the story at a certain point and departing at another'.[28]

Separated by two intertitles, Douglas's *The Secret Agent* is composed of two sections. Depending on the time she enters the gallery, the viewer may find the words 'Two Weeks Earlier' written across three of the six screens, which may induce her to believe she has come across a flashback – to what exactly is not known. What she will witness are in fact the events that will lead up to the bombing – Verloc's and Vladimir's meeting; the anarchist group assembled in the projection room of Verloc's cinema; the professor and his interactions with Ossipon and Inspector

Heat – but the viewer will not see the attack; instead, she will find another intertitle: 'Two Weeks After'. Thus, time has jumped forward and the viewer is now faced with the fallout – Stevie's death and the political implications it carries for the provisional government; Verloc's anxieties and Winnie's reaction; and the consequences of such a reaction – only to be once again confronted with 'Two Weeks Earlier'. Through these intertitles Douglas plays with the temporal jumps of the novel. Furthermore, like Conrad, he refuses the viewer access to the plot's central event, the bombing. The advantage of the intertitles for a museum-going audience is that one is allowed to enter a closed circuit, a film whose reading is not conditioned by beginnings or endings, an endless loop that lasts until one decides to leave.

The loop certainly has another presence in Douglas's adaptation: as mentioned previously, Verloc's shop has been transformed into a cinema, and the old backroom from the book is now a projection room. The spooling and re-spooling of the projected film – Bertolucci's *Last Tango in Paris*, which we will discuss below –, a '"wheeling" motion that is the material base of filmic motion', causes spectral inverted images to be projected onto the ceiling, ghostly figures that remind us 'that the wheel of memory constitutes the very materiality of film'.[29] As Giuliana Bruno reminds us, back 'in the thirteenth century, Ramon Lull introduced movement into memory by experimenting with circular motion and creating an art of memory based on setting figures on revolving wheels'.[30] Such 'circular mechanics, together with the automated motion that includes repetition, constitutes the essential "wheel" that drives our imaginative processes and forges representational history'.[31] History repeats itself; historical events recur.

One of the criticisms Conrad received of his 1922 stage adaptation was that anarchist bombers were outdated and thus were unconvincing as characters. As the *Manchester Guardian* put it in its 3 November 1922 issue, '[n]ow that violent revolution has become a reality of armies and republics, these droppers of sporadic bombs seem remote and futile creatures, so futile as to be incredible'.[32] Today, sporadic bomb attacks no longer seem to be the product of futile creators; they've become part of everyday life, once again. For the most part adaptations serve the purpose of entertainment, but they also hold out a mirror to the societies in which they are created. As Linda Hutcheon has asserted, '[t]here is a kind of dialogue between the society in which the works, both the adapted text and adaptation, are produced and that in which they are received, and both are in dialogue with the works themselves'.[33] The political and economic turmoil represented in Douglas's adaptation – its setting in

1970s Portugal – may, apparently, position the work outside contemporary events. Still, the artist's long fascination with the 1970s has been his method of apprehending some contemporary issues: the question of terrorism, but also the role of media in government and the threat of isolation, through its disruption, of a young democracy. 'Douglas is invested in understanding the seeming blandness of this historical period in-between "the utopias of the sixties" and the "protectionist greed of the 1980s" as actively setting the stage for new global dominance of financial markets.'[34] Other adaptations have focused on different topics; the 2016 BBC adaptation transformed Inspector Heat into an empathetic, self-sacrificing member of the British police force – conflicted over the use of torture to obtain information but willing to accept it as a method of preventing further casualties. Such a promotion of British national security services through televised fictional series raises a number of questions, all outside the scope of the present chapter; however, there is an adaptation that is relevant for the issues at hand, not just for the mastery of its production but also for the impact it would have on Douglas's work: Alfred Hitchcock's 1936 thriller *Sabotage*.

From Hitchcock to the multiscreen

Starting with the title itself, one finds that Hitchcock took several artistic liberties in adapting *The Secret Agent*.[35] The action continued to take place in London but was moved to 1936 – another moment when anxieties were beginning to bubble under the surface – following the Great Depression. This was the justification for having an American actress, Sylvia Sidney, play Mrs Verloc, a young woman forced to change her country of residence as '[b]usiness wasn't too good over there'. Mr Verloc – now renamed Karl Verloc – is revealed to be part of a terrorist group from an unnamed European country, operating from the living quarters of his cinema. Placed undercover as the next-door greengrocer, Detective Sergeant Ted Spencer – a merging of Ossipon and Inspector Heat – attempts to gain access to information by eavesdropping behind the film screen. By transforming Verloc's shop into a cinema, Douglas makes a clear reference to the 1936 film, just as the inverted film projection Spencer sees is mirrored in the images playing across the ceiling in Verloc's 1970s projection room. Additionally, if in *Sabotage* one may already find the suggestion that racy films may have been on show – at one point another grocer says to Verloc: 'You must have been showing some funny sort of films, I daresay. You know, perhaps a bit too hot' – in

Douglas it is clear from the start that the films Alex Verloc plays are films with more than just a hint of suggestion.

At the time the action takes place in Douglas's adaptation, Verloc is showing Bertolucci's *Last Tango in Paris* (1972). Up until the revolution Bertolucci's film had been censored in Portugal, as had any films featuring or suggesting sex. The instant the revolution took place these restrictions were lifted, and on 30 April 1974 – only five days after the revolution – the film premiered to huge crowds, including numerous visitors from Spain, where the film would be unavailable until 1978. Douglas's characters mention an address throughout the film, that of Verloc's cinema: Rua do Loreto. Any person familiar with the Chiado area in Lisbon will recognize the street and will recognize the presence of a cinema. It is a presence that has existed, in one form or another, since 1904. And, although in the 1970s it was showing westerns rather than Bertolucci's film, from the early 1990s until 2014 Cine Paraíso, as it was then named, specialized in erotic films. What one finds in Douglas is that factual and fictional events, and diverse temporalities, bleed into one another; 'the sheer number of references, allusions, and shifts inherent in all of his works do not precisely certify anything but instead liberate interpretation, thus producing a recombinant narrative that always permits – if not demands – new and contradictory varieties of readings and conclusions'.[36]

The use of the multiscreen simply adds to these varieties of readings; the instability of the viewers' relationship to the medium stresses the instability of the events being represented. But the multiscreen does more than facilitate the transmission of multiple layers of information, or even emphasize the multiple pathways an event may take. Douglas's use of the multiscreen is a projection of a 'proliferation of technology' that, having reached 'a certain level of saturation in the environment', viewers cease to be separate from.[37] Douglas's film installation is an environment composed of six large-screen projections. Upon entering the darkened exhibition space, the viewer finds two walls with three screens facing each other; in the middle of the room, small backless benches invite the visitor to a position in which she is surrounded by the images. This is an enclosed space that today evokes more familiarity than oddity: 'We are surrounded today, everywhere, all the time, by arrays of multiple, simultaneous images ... The idea of a single image commanding our attention has faded away. It seems as if we need to be distracted in order to concentrate.'[38] In a culture 'where screens displaying moving images have proliferated, cinematic space has become dispersed and activated in the ubiquitous forms of media existing in public, domestic and personal space'.[39] However, information overload does not necessarily occur by simultaneous activation of screens. It may happen, as in Douglas, by the constant shifting of position necessary to capture the "whole" picture and the disquietedness it produces in the viewer: 'In turning around, I've perhaps missed some detail, perhaps something crucial for the unfolding of the narrative.'[40]

Although there are six screens in place, very rarely are they all in use simultaneously. The viewer might find the occasional panorama of Lisbon rooftops when three screens are in play concurrently; these might then display events that are taking place in parallel, or they might feature adjoining spaces; characters might walk from one screen to another. But much more commonly these screens are grouped into pairs: one on each wall facing the other. These pairs are not random; rather the artist has assigned them as representations of 'governance', of 'private space' and of the 'street'. However this 'street' – the central pair – is more about shared space than an actual exterior space; for Douglas, '[t]he street is the interface between governance and private space'.[41] Some characters never leave their assigned screen pair, while others move between all three: Inspector Heat, for instance, interacts with the assistant commissioner in the 'governance' pair, but when he shadows the latter's actions or when he trades tense exchanges with the professor he moves into the 'street'; similarly, when he confronts Verloc on Stevie's death in the cinema lobby, he has moved into the 'private space' pair. Douglas's separation between the political sphere and the home is a permeable one, even in the way it has been shot. Steven Jacobs has suggested that the spatial visualization of the cinema lobby, which 'is rendered on two screens by cameras positioned perpendicular to one another . . . references the images filmed by CCTV-cameras'.[42] It is little wonder that such a hypothesis has been put forward: the very notion of the multiscreen harks back to the control room, and few artists have explored this medium as extensively as Charles and Ray Eames.

In 1959 two national exhibitions made headlines: the United States and the Soviet Union had agreed to exchange national exhibits on 'science, technology and culture'.[43] The Soviet exhibition was held in New York, whereas the American exhibits were shown in Sokolniki Park in Moscow. It was a propaganda tool for both sides, but while the Soviets focused on displaying their scientific and industrial achievements, the Americans promoted their lifestyle, their new and shiny items for mass consumption: 'You have lots of dolls, furniture, dishes, but where are your technical exhibits?', asked a Russian teacher in a *Wall Street Journal* article.[44] Charles and Ray Eames's *Glimpses of the USA* – a multiscreen presentation consisting of seven suspended screens inside a dome-shaped building – played a key part in advertising an idyllic vision of American life. A stereotypical day in the lives of American families – early morning sceneries, suburban neighbourhoods, men heading to work in the morning traffic, children being sent off to school, women doing their daily supermarket shopping – was projected simultaneously over the seven screens, tiny glimpses that overwhelmed their viewers in an unrelenting torrent. The model of the situation room or the mission control room is one that is impossible to separate from the works of the Eameses, not least for their relationship with some of the men involved in the war rooms military project.[45] As Charles Eames himself pointed out in his second Norton Lecture at Harvard University in 1970, the war room could be used for multiple actions, including those of controlling a city:

> In the management of a city, linear discourse certainly can't cope. We imagine a City Room or a World Health Room (rather like a War Room) where all the information from satellite monitors and other sources could be monitored . . . The city problem involves conflicting interests and points of view. So the place where information is correlated also has to be a place where each group can try out plans for its own changing needs.[46]

But the model of a room containing multiple screens is one that we have seen applied to purposes other than military and citizen control: it is a model that can easily be associated with media rooms. It can be found in television studios, 'with their walls of monitors from which the director chooses the camera angle that will be presented to the viewer', or it can be linked to the multiple screens of the devices we operate daily.[47] It might be linked to the propagation of black boxes anticipated by Henry Jenkins: 'There will be no single black box that controls the flow of media into our homes. Thanks to the proliferation of channels and the portability of new computing and telecommunications technologies, we are entering an era when media will be everywhere.'[48] Of course the collation of information derived from multiple platforms relies on one's ability to associate, to read. It relies on the viewers' capacity to connect unrelated images into one flowing whole; it relies on suture.

The process of suture

Developed by Jacques-Alain Miller as an intervention in Lacan's 24 February 1965 seminar 'Crucial Problems for Psychoanalysis', the notion of suture was first applied to film by Jean-Pierre Oudart in his seminal essay 'Cinema and suture' (1969). According to Miller, '[s]uture names the relation of the subject to the chain of its discourse'.[49] In film, suture is what allows the spectator to suspend her disbelief and become absorbed by the film as a realistic and believable depiction. For Oudart, suture is founded in the shot/reverse shot model; the first shot might feature a character looking or speaking to an unknown, who is designated as an 'Absent One', breaking the viewer's immersion in the film – 'Who is at the other side of the gaze?' – while the second shot, that which corresponds to what is being looked at or addressed, sutures this rupture and answers the question.

In *The Secret Agent*, Douglas uses the multiscreen to play with the shot/reverse shot model. In various dialogue sequences – the ones pertaining to the 'governance' pair – characters face each other in opposing screens. It is up to the viewer to decide which will have the attention of her gaze; it is up to the viewer to participate in the editing of the work. Suture occurs not through directorial decisions but through the visitor's corporeal movements: 'Having a tactile relationship with the images and physically intervening with the screen space, the structure of the montage is ultimately theirs.'[50] It is up to the visitor to move around the installation space in order to interpret, to complete the work. This experience will be completely individualized; no two people will ever 'see' the exact same film, nor will one individual be able to repeat precisely a previous viewing. Independent of how many visits the spectator makes to the work, she will not be able to repeat or to reproduce the exact instant of her shifting gaze. Each viewing will produce a new 'editing', a new, even if only slightly different, version. Thus, it will be the spectator who will hold control over the narrative construction, even if the use of the multiscreen stands for a totalizing view of the same. The multiscreen points to a 'wish for a historical panopticism in the relationship of the characters with the revolution, even if, in their capacity as characters, they are always submitted to the general determinations of a narrative that they cannot control, just as they cannot control the revolution'.[51] The medium does more than reflect the instability of the narrative. It tackles historical instabilities in moments of transition, and anxieties much closer to the present time. Arguably, one might read Douglas's choice to adapt Conrad's novel and to place it in a period and location that was in the grip of terrorism and political upheaval as a concern with a new rise in terrorism. Likewise, the choice of an attack on communications was not a random one, as Douglas points out: 'The cable is the first manifestation of the network, the thing that now defines us.'[52] The proliferation of screens demanding one's attention, the propagation of technologies of control – that is, CCTV – and even the mediatization of terrorism itself might be read in Douglas's film installation, in a merging of temporalities that, just as in Conrad's fiction, brings its viewers/readers closer to the grasp of a historical 'truth' than a mere signalling of chronological events might. Here one might consider fiction to be 'the lie that tells the truth'.[53] Furthermore, the use of the multiscreen emphasizes the vulnerability of the spectator in the face of the oppressive presence of generalized screens in her day-to-day existence. Just as the themes explored in Conrad's and Douglas's pieces cannot but be associated with the vulnerability of societies in transition and moments in flux, the boundaries between the personal, the political and the public are always susceptible to being broken down.

What we have tried to put forward with this chapter is that, even without the presence of historical accuracy, *The Secret Agent*, in the various mediums it has inhabited, is nonetheless capable of evoking the atmosphere of the tensions lived in moments of transition. Although both Conrad's and Douglas's pieces are placed at an earlier date than that of its creation, one might easily read concerns and anxieties much closer to their present. Conrad's novel calls attention to the disquieting events that gripped turn-of-the-century London – the bombings and attacks – but with its focus on Winnie it also highlights some apprehensions about transformations occurring in the private sphere. Similarly, Douglas's adaptation can be seen as establishing parallels between a moment and a society in flux in the 1970s and present tensions – tensions related not only to the rise and mediatization of terrorism, but also to the propagation of technologies of control and to an ever-present screen.

Notes

1. Douglas, *The Secret Agent*, 86.
2. Youngblood, *Expanded Cinema*.
3. For a discussion of the precise dating of *The Secret Agent*, see Schanuder, *Free Will and Determinism in Joseph Conrad's Major Novels*, 206–7.
4. Conrad, *The Secret Agent*, 13.
5. Conrad, *The Secret Agent*, 35.
6. Conrad, *The Secret Agent*, 35–7.
7. Early editions of *The Secret Agent* also carried Conrad's dedication to H. G. Wells: 'TO H.G. WELLS. THE CHRONICLER OF MR LEWISHAM'S LOVE, THE BIOGRAPHER OF KIPPS AND THE HISTORIAN OF THE AGES TO COME. THIS SIMPLE TALE OF THE XIX CENTURY IS AFFECTIONATELY OFFERED.'
8. Emsley, Hitchcock and Shoemaker, 'London history'.
9. Aliens Act 1905 (5 Edw. VII. c. 13), s. 1(3)(d).
10. Karl Marx had arrived in London in 1849 and attracted a number of communist and socialist supporters in the following decades.

11. Houen, *Terrorism and Modern Literature*, 35.
12. Conrad, *The Secret Agent*, 24.
13. Kenna, 'The Fenian dynamite campaign'.
14. 'An infernal machine explodes in a railway car', referenced in Kenna, 'The Fenian dynamite campaign'.
15. 'In order to give the Dynamite School a semblance of revolutionary credibility, Rossa apparently had entered into a five-year contract with a Russian explosives expert theatrically known as Professor Mezzeroff . . . Mezzeroff, however, rather than being a Russian expert, was an Irishman identified variously as either Smith or Rodgers' (Kenna, 'The Fenian dynamite campaign', n.p.).
16. Conrad, *The Secret Agent*, 64.
17. Conrad, *The Secret Agent*, 38.
18. Conrad, *The Secret Agent*, 10–11.
19. Conrad, *The Secret Agent*, 79.
20. 'Contagem decrescente para uma guerra civil'.
21. Douglas, *The Secret Agent*, 86.
22. Burr, 'Document Friday'. https://unredacted.com/2010/11/19/document-friday-the-us-military-had-a-contingincy-plan-to-take-over-portugal/.
23. Hasselblad Foundation, 'Announcement'.
24. See Hand, 'Conrad and the reviewers'.
25. Hand, 'Conrad and the reviewers', 5.
26. Mirza and Butler, 'On expanded cinema', 258.
27. VALIE EXPORT's *Tapp und Tastkino (Touch Cinema)* (1968) was an examination of 'breasts as a central theme within the film industry'. Participants were invited to feel rather than see the work: 'The *Tapp und Tast* film is a street film, a mobile film and the first real women's film. The performance takes place as usual, in the dark. Only the movie theatre has become somewhat smaller, there is room in it only for two hands. In order, to see the film, which means in this case to sense and feel it, the "viewer" must put both hands through the entranceway to the theatre. Thus the curtains which previously had been drawn up only for the eyes is [sic] also finally raised for the hands' (EXPORT, 'Expanded cinema', 296).
28. Dressler, 'Specters of Douglas', 24.
29. Bruno, *Public Intimacy*, 13, 15.
30. Bruno, *Public Intimacy*, 15.
31. Bruno, *Public Intimacy*, 15.
32. See Hand, 'Conrad and the reviewers', 31.
33. Hutcheon, *A Theory of Adaptation*, 149.
34. Margulies, 'Stan Douglas's clear and present strangeness', 163.
35. It is thought that Alfred Hitchcock drew inspiration not from the book but from Conrad's stage adaptation: 'the twenty-three-year-old Alfred Hitchcock went to see the play at the Ambassadors. Apparently, it "made so strong an impression on [him] that he persuaded [the film producer Michael] Balcon to let him film it, in 1936, as *Sabotage*"' (Hand, 'Conrad and the reviewers', 10).
36. Dressler, 'Specters of Douglas', 13.
37. Youngblood, *Expanded Cinema*, 128.
38. Colomina, 'Enclosed by images', 7.
39. Ball, 'Conditions of music', 273.
40. Lapa, *History and Interregnum*, 38.
41. Compton, 'Eye spy'.
42. Jacobs, 'From scene to screen', 12.
43. Colomina, 'Enclosed by images', 8.
44. Colomina, 'Enclosed by images', 9.
45. As Beatriz Colomina ('Enclosed by images', 16) points out, the Eameses were friends with Buckminster Fuller, Eero Saarinen and Henry Dreyfuss, and, although they may not have had knowledge of the war room project during the war years, it is very likely that soon after they would have learnt about it.
46. Colomina, 'Enclosed by images', 16.
47. Colomina, 'Enclosed by images', 7.
48. Jenkins, *Convergence Culture*, 16.
49. Miller, 'Suture (elements of the logic of the signifier)'.

50. Hatfield, 'Expanded cinema', 264.
51. Lapa, *History and Interregnum*, 44–5.
52. Kennedy, 'Stan Douglas's "The Secret Agent" offers a refracted vision of history and terrorism'.
53. Gaiman, *The View from the Cheap Seats*, 13.

Bibliography

'An infernal machine explodes in a railway car'. *New York Times*, 28 October 1876. Accessed 16 June 2021. https://www.nytimes.com/1876/10/28/archives/an-infernal-machine-explodes-in-a-railway-car.html.

Ball, Steven. 'Conditions of music: Contemporary audio-visual spatial performance practice'. In *Expanded Cinema: Art, performance, film*, edited by A. L. Rees et al., 267–75. London: Tate Publishing, 2011.

Bruno, Giuliana. *Public Intimacy: Architecture and the visual arts*. Cambridge, MA: MIT Press, 2007.

Burr, William. 'Document Friday: The US military had "a contingency plan to take over" Portuguese islands!?'. Unredacted, 19 November 2010. Accessed 20 June 2021. https://unredacted.com/2010/11/19/document-friday-the-us-military-had-a-contingincy-plan-to-take-over-portugal/.

Colomina, Beatriz. 'Enclosed by images: The Eameses' multimedia architecture'. *Grey Room* 2 (Winter 2001): 5–29.

Compton, Nick. 'Eye spy: Stan Douglas goes undercover at London's Victoria Miro'. *Wallpaper*, 5 February 2016. Accessed 25 May 2021. http://www.wallpaper.com/art/stan-douglas-the-secret-agent-victoria-miro.

Conrad, Joseph. *The Secret Agent*. London: Penguin Popular Classics, 1994.

'Contagem decrescente para uma guerra civil'. *Público*, 22 November 2009. Accessed 25 May 2021. https://www.publico.pt/temas/jornal/contagem-decrescente-para-uma-guerra-civil-18261109.

Douglas, Stan. *The Secret Agent*. Antwerp: Ludion, 2015.

Dressler, Iris. 'Specters of Douglas'. In *Stan Douglas: Past imperfect: Works 1986–2007*, edited by Hans D. Christ and Iris Dressler, 8–24. Ostfildern: Hatje Cantz, 2008.

Emsley, Clive, Tim Hitchcock and Robert Shoemaker. 'London history – a population history of London'. *Old Bailey Proceedings Online*, version 7.0. Accessed 16 June 2021. https://www.oldbaileyonline.org/static/Population-history-of-london.jsp.

EXPORT, VALIE. 'Expanded cinema: Expanded reality'. In *Expanded Cinema: Art, performance, film*, edited by A. L. Rees et al., 288–98. London: Tate Publishing, 2011.

Gaiman, Neil. *The View from the Cheap Seats*. New York: William Morrow & Company, 2016.

Hand, Richard J. 'Conrad and the reviewers: "The Secret Agent" on stage'. *The Conradian* 26, no. 2 (Autumn 2001): 1–67.

Hasselblad Foundation. 'Announcement: "Stan Douglas, Hasselblad Award Winner 2016"', 7 March 2016. Accessed 25 May 2021. https://www.youtube.com/watch?v=fVB31bSnh9M.

Hatfield, Jackie. 'Expanded cinema: Proto-, photo and post-photo cinema'. In *Expanded Cinema: Art, performance, film*, edited by A. L. Rees et al., 262–6. London: Tate Publishing, 2011.

Hitchcock, Alfred, director. *Sabotage*. General Film Distributors (GFD) Ltd., 1936.

Houen, Alex. *Terrorism and Modern Literature, from Joseph Conrad to Ciaran Carson*. Oxford: Oxford University Press, 2002.

Hutcheon, Linda. *A Theory of Adaptation*. New York: Routledge, 2006.

Jacobs, Steven. 'From scene to screen: *The Secret Agent* by Stan Douglas'. *Millennium Film Journal* 63 (Spring 2016): 12–15.

Jenkins, Henry. *Convergence Culture: Where old and new media collide*. New York: New York University Press, 2006.

Kenna, Shane. 'The Fenian dynamite campaign and the Irish American impetus for dynamite terror, 1881–1885'. *Inquiries Journal/Student Pulse* 3, no. 12 (2011). Accessed 25 May 2021. http://www.inquiriesjournal.com/a?id=602.

Kennedy, Randy. 'Stan Douglas's "The Secret Agent" offers a refracted vision of history and terrorism'. *New York Times*, 11 April 2016. Accessed 25 May 2021. http://nyti.ms/1qk0r9r.

Lapa, Pedro. *History and Interregnum: Three works by Stan Douglas*. Lisbon: Archive Books, 2015.

Margulies, Ivone. 'Stan Douglas's clear and present strangeness'. In *Stan Douglas: Past imperfect: Works 1986–2007*, edited by Hans D. Christ and Iris Dressler, 154–70. Ostfildern: Hatje Cantz, 2008.
Miller, Jacques-Alain. 'Suture (elements of the logic of the signifier)'. *The Symptom: Online Journal* 8 (Winter 2007). Accessed 25 May 2021. http://www.lacan.com/symptom8_articles/miller8.html.
Mirza, Karen, and Brad Butler. 'On expanded cinema'. In *Expanded Cinema: Art, performance, film*, edited by A. L. Rees et al., 258–61. London: Tate Publishing, 2011.
Oudart, Jean-Pierre. 'Cinema and suture'. *The Symptom: Online Journal* 8 (Winter 2007). Accessed 25 May 2021. http://www.lacan.com/symptom8_articles/oudart8.html.
Schanuder, Ludwig. *Free Will and Determinism in Joseph Conrad's Major Novels*. Amsterdam: Rodopi, 2009.
Youngblood, Gene. *Expanded Cinema*. New York: P. Dutton, 1970.

7
New worlds: violent intersections in graphic novels
Jessica Gross

Introduction: new worlds and contrapuntal readings

Although European colonizers called the Americas a 'new world', they set out almost immediately to transform this new world into the old one with which they were familiar. Transformations can take place in many ways, but there is perhaps no swifter and surer way to change a social and physical landscape than through violence. This violence creates a new world and makes a return to the 'old' world, the world as it was before the violence, an impossibility. Of course, in the colonial sense in which I invoked the phrase 'new world' in the opening sentence, there was no true 'new world'. The so-called new world had been there all along; what was truly new was Europeans' contact with it, and their attempt to reproduce *their* world in this, for them, new territory.[1] Both of the graphic novels analysed in this chapter address this issue: what happens when one culture or group of people attempts to make a society in its own image? These graphic texts demonstrate that such attempts lead to great suffering for all – for the powerless, the powerful and even the physical landscape.

On the one hand, 'The Rabbits' by Shaun Tan and John Marsden (first published in Australia in 1998) tells the tale of the violent encounters between British imperialists and indigenous peoples in Australia while picturing these two groups of people as animals fighting over the same territory. The rabbits, colonizing creatures who arrive in large ships to spread across this new land, attempt to transform the land into something more directly resembling their homeland. On the other hand, *Déogratias* (first published in French in 2000) by J. P. Stassen is the story of the Rwandan genocide, focusing on a young Hutu man named

Déogratias who ends up taking part in the killing of Tutsis. *Déogratias* shows that the genocide was more than a simple Hutu–Tutsi conflict, but that European colonization helped to create the conditions that led to the Rwandan genocide. The genocide ultimately creates a new world in Rwanda that killers as well as survivors must now struggle to live in.[2]

These texts show that one people imposing their will upon another creates violence that hurts all involved, and at the narrative level these texts show this through a process that in *Culture and Imperialism* Edward Said calls 'contrapuntal reading'. Contrapuntal reading, Said writes, takes 'account of both processes, that of imperialism and that of resistance to it, which can be done by extending our reading of the texts to include what was once forcibly excluded'.[3] As in Said's definition above, that which is 'forcibly excluded' on a historical level in 'The Rabbits' is resistance to imperialism. The text itself performs a contrapuntal reading, however, which makes visible both imperialism and the resistance against it. While *Déogratias* also has a colonial backdrop, the causes of violence in the story it tells are not solely engendered by imperial occupation, as was the violence in 'The Rabbits'. Nonetheless, *Déogratias* also performs a contrapuntal reading by showing what was 'forcibly excluded' during and immediately after the Rwandan genocide: an acknowledgement, on the part of a perpetrator, of the injustice that was committed, and a realization of how many stakeholders were responsible for the deaths that took place. In the case of *Déogratias*, this forcible exclusion is so strong on the societal level that an acknowledgement of the crimes committed surfaces only through the psychotic episodes of one of the genocide's perpetrators, Déogratias. This suggests that the forcible exclusion of what happened during the genocide has become so pervasive that it is perhaps only a madman, not bound by normal social conventions, who can speak the truth and bring to light what has been forcibly excluded from public discourse. Déogratias, as a madman existing outside societal norms, is able to exhibit a vulnerability absent from other characters that allows the reader to feel the full import of the violence committed in Rwanda. Post-genocide, the other characters in this comic do not speak of what has happened, either because they were sheltered from it by privilege or because they are still secretly harbouring the racist sentiments that led to the genocide. Déogratias, in the vulnerable role of madman, frequently weeps and is frightened by his psychotic episodes in which he relives the genocide. A contrapuntal reading of *Déogratias* shows Déogratias to be both a violent perpetrator and a vulnerable figure whose poor self-image made him an easy target for manipulation during the genocide. As the indigenous animals' vulnerability in 'The Rabbits' makes plain to the reader the power imbalance between indigenous peoples and European colonizers, so too Déogratias's vulnerability makes clear to the reader the hierarchical power structure in Rwanda that not only fuelled the genocide but obfuscated its existence afterwards.

Together, these graphic narratives and the contrapuntal readings they perform show that violent conflict alters physical landscapes, social patterns and even the human psyche. Violence here creates a new world both for the recipient of violence and for the one who caused the violence. Ultimately, these works show that living together is unavoidable, even when violence has been used in the attempt to exterminate the other.

A world before violence

'The Rabbits' is a largely pictorial narrative, with short sentences accompanying each full-page image. The story begins with several expansive and tranquil images of nature that indicate what this world was like before the arrival of the Europeans. In the edition of this story published for the American market, which is included in a volume of three of Shaun Tan's works, there is an opening two-page spread of the night sky before the title page.[4] The title page depicts much the same image, except that it portrays a lower view of the same scene that reveals a large ship sailing on the ocean. Although the colonizers (the rabbits) are present here in the image of the ship, nature nonetheless still dominates this image.[5]

The next two-page spread establishes the pre-rabbit norm and is a scene that is remembered nostalgically at the end of the story.[6] This two-page spread depicts a tranquil lake in which flowers grow and in which several varieties of birds are standing or swimming. Large rock formations, depicted in other images in the story, are reflected in the lake. The world as it is depicted here is unrestricted, spontaneous and peaceful. That is, there is no mathematical symmetry between the left and right sides of the page, depicting different parts of the lake. Instead, the scene depicts an unordered ease found in nature; different varieties of birds peacefully share this space.

As depicted in this image, the world before the rabbits was tranquil, plentiful and not ordered by the governing principles of production and industrialization. Different kinds of animals are able to peacefully share the same resources – and these resources are abundant for all. The first text in the story comes on the next two-page spread, and this text reads simply: 'The rabbits came many grandparents ago.'[7] Because the narration begins at a time long after the arrival of the rabbits, the image of the lake is a flashback, a reminder of how things were long ago, before a violent, traumatic event.

Déogratias also mentions a time before the arrival of the Europeans and also traces the seeds of violence (in this case, of the Rwandan genocide) back to the arrival of the Europeans. In a flashback scene, Déogratias, a Hutu, is in class with his Tutsi friends Benina and Apollinaria when the teacher explains the differences between the three major ethnic groups in Rwanda: the Hutu, the Tutsi and the Twa.[8] This scene is a flashback to the life pre-genocide of Déogratias, the book's protagonist. The book then returns to the present, post-genocide, when Déogratias, who has gone mad after the genocide, is talking with a Hutu leader named Bosco. Bosco says:

> Hutu, Tutsi . . . ce sont les blancs qui ont inventé ces différences entre nous ! Ils ont inscrit ces mots sur nos cartes d'identité ! . . . Avant leur arrivée, avant qu'ils ne sèment le germe de la division, avant qu'ils ne nous réduisent en esclavage, nous vivions paisiblement ici.
>
> [Hutu, Tutsi . . . The whites made up those differences between us! They wrote those words on our ID cards! Before they came, before they sowed the seeds of division, before they enslaved us, we lived peacefully here.][9]

Déogratias's ironic rejoinder, 'Le lait et le miel coulaient alors' [in a land of milk and honey],[10] undercuts the rosy picture Bosco paints of Rwanda's pre-colonial days, but this and other passages in the book nonetheless show how European intervention created a world in which Hutu and Tutsi saw themselves as separate peoples. As the book continues, the tensions between the two groups continue to grow until the Hutu are referring to the Tutsi as cockroaches and view them as subhuman.

Both 'The Rabbits' and *Déogratias* show that there was a world before the violent clash between cultures, but that this world has been completely remade through violence. Significantly, in both books this world before great violence was a world in which different kinds of people (or, in the case of 'The Rabbits', different species of animal) could live together peacefully. These were worlds in which differences between people or animals were not cause for alarm, and there was enough land and resources for everybody. In both 'The Rabbits' and *Déogratias* the arrival of Europeans was an event that set in motion changes that would eventually lead to large-scale violence. What the arrival of the Europeans changed, in both cases, was the ability for all to share the same social and physical resources. Instead, the Europeans (in this case pictured as rabbits) in 'The Rabbits' insist on dividing up and farming the land, forcing different species to compete for resources. The Europeans in *Déogratias* divided up and categorized different ethnic groups and created quotas that pitted one group against another in a competition for scarce jobs and other resources.

First encounters

The initial encounter between the colonizing rabbits and the indigenous animals in 'The Rabbits' is cautiously friendly, but the indigenous animals come to realize how different the rabbits are from them and how intent they are on transforming this new world into the old one whence they came. Although 'The Rabbits' depicts several kinds of animals (such as the birds in the depiction of the pre-rabbit norm), the story centres on the interaction between the rabbits and small brown tree-dwelling animals whose collective voice narrates the story. Although these animals bear a visual resemblance to animals that actually inhabit Australia, they are never named in the story, whereas the narrator consistently refers to the rabbits as 'the rabbits'.[11] The rabbits must be named because they do not belong to this landscape; they are simply not a part of this ecosystem as are the other animals in the story. In this chapter, I will refer to the small brown animals who narrate the story as 'indigenous animals'.[12]

At the first meeting between the indigenous animals and the rabbits, three indigenous animals stand to the left, while a carriage with three rabbits is on the right. In the centre of the page, one indigenous animal and one rabbit cautiously approach one another. The image is dominated by the ground, which shows the wheel marks from the rabbits' carriage. Already there is the sense that the rabbits are altering the physical landscape, even in this first seemingly innocent encounter.[13] The text accompanying the image reads: 'At first we didn't know what to think. They looked a bit like us. There weren't many of them. Some were friendly.'[14] While cautious, this initial assessment by the indigenous animals attempts to find commonalities with this new species, rather than reasons to fear it.

Just as many Hutu and Tutsi begin the story of *Déogratias* as close friends rather than as enemies, here too the rabbits and the indigenous animals have no inherent reason to do one another harm. This begins to change, however, when the rabbits start to transform the landscape into an entirely new world. As previously mentioned, the rabbits first start to alter the landscape through small actions, such as leaving tyre marks on the ground. Their first interventions into the landscape are through their looking glasses, which turn the land into an area to be systematically mapped and divided into economically productive plots. In *Seeing the First Australians*, Ian Donaldson and Tamsin Donaldson explain how collecting measurements, as the rabbits do throughout 'The Rabbits', is itself an exercise of power:

> To shoot or poison the local people and appropriate their land is to exercise one kind of power. To measure their heads, cover their loins, record their tongues, sketch their faces, or film their ceremonies is to exercise quite another kind of power, milder, subtler, often benign in its intentions, yet possessed none the less of its own significance, implying a relationship of subject to object, observer to observed.[15]

This 'observer to observed' relationship, set up already in this first encounter between the rabbits and the indigenous animals in 'The Rabbits', eventually leads to the violence that nearly destroys the land, the indigenous animals and even the rabbits themselves. This observer to observed relationship established by colonialism forces the indigenous animals into a vulnerable position that is then exploited by the colonizing rabbits, who view themselves as indestructible. The end of 'The Rabbits' will demonstrate, however, that the colonizing rabbits themselves are also ultimately vulnerable to their own destruction of the land.

Just as the possibility for peace between the rabbits and the indigenous animals existed at the beginning of 'The Rabbits', the possibility for peace between all ethnic groups in Rwanda exists at the beginning of *Déogratias*. When the story begins, the Hutu Déogratias is close friends with his Tutsi classmates Benina and Apollinaria. Anti-Tutsi rhetoric becomes increasingly violent as the story progresses, however, and by the time the genocide begins Déogratias is referring to the Hutu as his 'brethren' despite the fact that he is in a romantic relationship with Benina, a Tutsi. The outbreak of violence, and the pressure from the other Hutu men to join it, causes Déogratias to view the world in a new way and to make divisions where he had seen none before.[16] Once he becomes involved in the violence, Déogratias's present is irrevocably severed from his past; violence has changed everything.[17]

In *Déogratias*, the divisions between ethnic groups are accomplished first at a linguistic level, differentiating between the Hutu and

Tutsi in oral and written speech and then referring to the Tutsi as cockroaches. These divisions finally manifest themselves in physical violence when the genocide begins. In 'The Rabbits', as in *Déogratias*, there is initial recognition between those who are different: the indigenous animals see something of themselves in the rabbits, and the Hutu and Tutsi do not see each other as being so different from one another. Once this recognition has broken down, however, there is a steady decline until conditions are created that allow for – even encourage – the most barbaric acts of violence and aggression.

Violent intersections

When overt violence breaks out in 'The Rabbits' it quickly transforms the physical and social landscapes. The transformation of the world by violence is starkly shown by the change in colour palette and the page structure.[18] The bright, vivid colours that marked the beginning of the book are replaced by sepia tones, and the large, expansive page spread is broken into small snapshots of the violence. The physical landscape has been transformed; the rivers are drying up and the land is devoid of vegetation. Although the indigenous animals make several attempts to destroy the rabbits' machinery on these pages, it is clear that machinery has replaced wildlife in this landscape. A new world has already been made in terms of the natural landscape. Here, this change is presented as a great violence against the land; all that is natural and organic has been killed to make way for machinery and efficiency. As is evidenced on these pages, the change in the physical landscape has also altered the social landscape. Previously practised communal activities, such as gathering water (pictured in the images in the top left of page 97), are now made impossible by violence, for the indigenous animals are attacked by the rabbits while they are filling their water bowls. This leads the indigenous animals to retaliate against the rabbits, creating a cycle of violence that eventually ends in the rabbits' superior firepower annihilating the indigenous animals' resistance.

In *Déogratias*, the violence of the genocide also sharply ruptures the social ties in human society and affects how one reads the physical landscape. Déogratias, swept up in the killings by his Hutu friends, ends up killing his classmates Apollinaria and Benina, as well as their mother, Venetia. But later, as he is in the neutral turquoise zone, protected by French troops and about to flee the country, Déogratias decides he wants to go back into Rwanda to the scene of his killings. When he returns, he sees a pile of bodies being eaten by dogs, with his friends Apollinaria and Benina on top.[19] Bosco, a Hutu military man, walks over to Déogratias and comments, 'Un fou . . . encore un. Il ne reste que des cadavres, des fous et des chiens' [Another madman . . . All that's left are corpses, madmen and dogs].[20] This comment is indicative of the ways the old world has been supplanted by a new, horrifying world. The previously vibrant social landscape has been transformed into one in which society is composed of corpses, madmen and dogs (and Déogratias is both a madman *and* a dog, since when he goes mad he believes himself to be a dog). A fourth category could perhaps be added: killers who, unlike Déogratias, do not come to understand what they have done and so do not become mad like Déogratias. These killers are, returning to Said's language, a part of the system that is forcibly repressing discussion of what has really happened. By allowing the reader to see Déogratias's psychotic episodes, however, the text itself engages in a contrapuntal reading that brings these forcibly repressed topics to the surface. It also shows that Déogratias, in showing vulnerability brought on by sorrow and madness in the wake of the genocide, is portraying a more honest response to the genocide than are the killers who seem to be unaffected by the events that they witnessed – and caused.

New worlds

In *Déogratias,* post-genocide the world is populated by the increasingly insane Déogratias; Hutu leaders who are varyingly frustrated by their inability to exterminate all the Tutsi and somewhat troubled by what they have done;[21] and Europeans who fled during the genocide but who are now returning post-genocide, ignorant as to how irrevocably Rwanda has been changed by the violence. In short, the genocide has ruptured all relationships, even between those who took part in the killings. For Déogratias, the rupture is so sharp that he goes mad upon seeing his friends' dead bodies. From that point on he has frequent psychotic episodes in which he believes himself to be a dog, because, like the dogs, he has destroyed the bodies of Benina, Apollinaria and Venetia. The new world created by violence is a world in which Déogratias can no longer think of himself as human; he can only be a dog, a predator who consumes the corpses of the innocent.

As previously mentioned, the violence creates rifts even between those who were united during the killings. Déogratias is now so disturbed by what he has seen and done, and so unable to live in the new world created by the genocide, that after the genocide he sets out to poison anyone whom he associates with the killings – both Hutu and Tutsi leaders, as well as a French soldier who has returned to Rwanda as a tourist. One of the final scenes in the story depicts Déogratias, mad and seemingly incoherent, rambling to Brother Philip, a Belgian priest who has returned to Rwanda to see what has happened to his friends. After mentioning some of the men whom he has just poisoned, Déogratias mutters, 'Je devais les tuer . . . ils savaient ce que font les chiens . . . Vedette, Bénigne, Apollinaire' [I had to kill them . . . They knew what the dogs do . . . Venetia, Benina, Apollinaria].[22] Déogratias was so traumatized by seeing the dogs eat his friends' bodies that he is now systematically setting out to poison anyone who 'knew what the dogs do'. Thus, even in his attempt to right the wrongs of the past, Déogratias can find no way to do it other than through violence. The cycle of violence begun in the genocide continues, and the violence he began to perform during the genocide now continues throughout Déogratias's madness. Although it was violence that originally scarred him, Déogratias can find no other way to live than to continue to kill. This suggests that the new world created in Rwanda through violence is, at the book's closing, still a world where violence and various forms of injustice can continue to thrive.

In *Testimony: Crises of witnessing in literature, psychoanalysis, and history*, Shoshana Felman and Dori Laub explain that, for the traumatized person, the traumatizing event continues into the present. Because it is part not just of the traumatized person's past but of their present as well, it alters the world in which they live daily. Felman and Laub explain that chronological time does not apply to the way trauma is experienced:

> While the trauma uncannily returns in actual life, its reality continues to elude the subject who lives in its grip and unwittingly undergoes its ceaseless repetitions and reenactments. The traumatic event, although real, took place outside the parameters of 'normal' reality, such as causality, sequence, place and time. The trauma is thus an event that has no beginning, no ending, no before, no during and no after. This absence of categories that define it lends it a quality of 'otherness,' a salience, a timelessness and a ubiquity that puts it outside the range of associatively linked experiences, outside the range of comprehension, of recounting and of mastery. Trauma survivors live not with memories of the past, but with an event that could not and did not proceed through to its completion, has no ending, attained no closure, and therefore, as far as its survivors are concerned, continues into the present and is current in

every respect. The survivor, indeed, is not truly in touch either with the core of his traumatic reality or with the fatedness of its reenactments, and thereby remains entrapped in both.[23]

Although my discussion here focuses on the experience of just one character, Déogratias (and *Déogratias* itself, as the title suggests, also focuses on this same character), Déogratias's experience is a part of the wider Rwandan experience, and the fact that Déogratias continues to relive the events of the genocide makes a point about the enduring trauma Rwanda is facing. The events of the genocide are, from the vantage point of trauma, still ongoing, and therefore still present in quotidian Rwandan life. As Felman and Laub point out, for those who are traumatized, there is nothing about the traumatizing event that is in the past: the traumatizing event is continuously present and continuously being experienced.

Both 'The Rabbits' and *Déogratias* indicate that in the wake of great violence, everyone – both perpetrator and victim alike – is left to live in the new world created by violence. One ever-present reminder of this in *Déogratias* is the recurring image of the night sky, which ends three of the four narrative sections of the book and is the final image in the book.[24] The significance of this image is explained early on by Apollinaria in a scene in a Rwandan museum, when she explains that ancient Rwandans believed that 'Les Esprits des morts peuplaient le royaume de sous la terre où ils complotaient avec malice contre les vivants; la nuit, ils éclairaient le ciel du Rwanda' [the spirits of the dead filled the underworld, where they schemed spitefully against the living: and at night they lit up the sky over Rwanda].[25] This recurrent image of the stars throughout the book, then, shows that even the physical landscape comments on the violence done in human society, and this same night sky covers all the current residents of Rwanda, whether they be Hutu, Tutsi, Twa or European. As in 'The Rabbits', even the natural world is affected by the violence done by human society (or, in the case of 'The Rabbits', by anthropomorphized animals), and the changes to the physical landscape in both 'The Rabbits' and *Déogratias* demonstrate that violence has created a new world that looks very different from the one that came before it.

The landscape in 'The Rabbits' is altered even more drastically than that of *Déogratias*. A two-page spread towards the end of the story shows a dismal brown landscape dominated by large pipes spewing out some sort of waste. This image is accompanied by the words: 'The land is bare and brown and the wind blows empty across the plains'.[26] A single rabbit opens a small door in the wall underneath the pipes and looks out at a curled-up indigenous animal on the ground. This image shows that this new world created by violence – so different from the one before – is now home to both the indigenous animal *and* the rabbit, and this is a world in which both must now figure out how to survive.

The parallel between this and the initial meeting between a single rabbit and a single indigenous animal is striking.[27] In that image, the landscape was still abundant, with plenty of resources for all, and there was a moment of recognition wherein the indigenous animals seemed to think they might be able to cohabit peacefully with the rabbits. The image here is far different, however.[28] The bright colours of the earlier images are replaced entirely by browns and greys, and unlike most of the earlier images, in this image the rabbit and the indigenous animal are roughly on the same scale. In many of the previous images the rabbits loomed large over the indigenous animals, and their brightly coloured clothing set them even further apart from the brown indigenous animals. Misery is a great equalizer, however, and in this image both the rabbit and the indigenous animal are small, dwarfed by the huge pipes that spill waste onto the ground. And both here are depicted with drab colours, fading into the equally drab landscape. The violence the rabbits have enacted upon the landscape seems to have been returned here to them, for this rabbit, too, must live in this landscape that appears to provide no means for survival.

The final words in 'The Rabbits' are contained under a small image set against two black pages. The text reads: 'Who will save us from the rabbits?'[29] An inset contains a rabbit and an indigenous animal who sit on either side of a pool of water that reflects the night sky.[30] They are surrounded by trash and industrial waste on the ground. The 'us' of the narrative voice shifts here from the indigenous animals to include also, I believe, the rabbits themselves, because they too must now survive in this new world they have created. And here the indigenous animal and the rabbit resemble each other in a way, since they are roughly the same size and the same bluish-grey colour that blends with the other colours in this image. The fact that there is only one indigenous animal, but also only one rabbit, suggests that the rabbits, along with the indigenous animals, have been largely killed off as a result of the rabbits' destruction of the land and the subsequent scarcity of resources.

Glimmers of hope: a new new world?

Although there has been so much destruction, and this destruction is present in this image, the night sky above the animals and the reflection of the sky in the pool into which the animals are looking hark back to the opening images of the expansive night sky. The Earth seems to have been destroyed, but the sky remains. The last two pages of this story are a spread of the night sky filled with stars.[31] This image presents some hope for the future, since some of the beauty present at the beginning of the story is present even in the final, sad image of the animals. The story seems to suggest, through the image of the stars, that a future world is possible for the indigenous animal *and* for the rabbit if they can find a way to survive, together, this post-violence landscape. Although the Earth seems to have been largely destroyed, the reflection of the stars in the pool of water is a reminder that all is not lost. There is still a remnant of the idyllic beauty from before the rabbits arrived present even in this seemingly apocalyptic landscape. And because both the rabbit and the indigenous animal are looking at this pool that reflects the stars, there is the suggestion that both are contemplating how to preserve – and even share – what is left.

Another new world that has somewhat recovered from this new post-violence world is possible, but a return to the previous world – a world before the rabbits – is impossible. A future world of peace, rather than the world created here through violence, must be one in which both the rabbits and the indigenous animals can live together. And this story shows just how difficult that may be, and how much bloodshed may result when a new world is forcibly produced – or, more accurately, when one world tries to reproduce itself in another.

Déogratias also ends with an image of the night sky, but the image of the night sky on which *Déogratias* ends is considerably less hopeful than the night sky at the end of 'The Rabbits'.[32] Rather than being a symbol of a possible future, this image is a reminder of what can never be undone: many who were alive in the previous world are now present here only as stars in the sky, dead souls looking down upon Rwanda. And it is precisely that reality with which all the living inhabitants of Rwanda must now come to terms. The night sky in *Déogratias* serves an opposite function to that in 'The Rabbits'. On the one hand, in 'The Rabbits' the image of the night sky is the one remnant of a world uncorrupted by violence, the one symbol of hope for the future. In *Déogratias,* on the other hand, the night sky is a constant reminder of the violence committed; it is a memorial that will never go away.

Thus, while the meaning of the night sky in 'The Rabbits' and in *Déogratias* is different, in both nevertheless, the night sky serves as a challenge to those remaining – Hutu, Tutsi, Twa and European, rabbit and indigenous animal – that the only way to survive in the new world created by violence is to find a way to live together. This need not be done as friends, but both texts suggest that without the ability to cohabit and share resources, everyone – both those who were powerless before the violence and those who were powerful – will be unable to survive. The new state of the post-violence world imposes vulnerability on both the previously powerless and the previously powerful, and independent survival is no longer possible. A return to the pre-violence world is impossible in both texts, and both texts end with shattered societies that will have to be remade for any future life to be possible. Dismal as both endings are, they nonetheless both suggest that things need not have been as they were, and that there is, therefore, the possibility of a different kind of future. As bleak as the end of *Déogratias* is, the fact that the dead will remain a part of the lives of the living through their illumination of the night sky offers the challenge to the living that they will not forget the dead, and therefore will perhaps not replicate the errors that caused so many to lose their lives.

Conclusion: documents of suffering and the future

The premise of this chapter is that violence creates new worlds by destroying the pre-violence world and putting in its place a new world marred by violence. Both 'The Rabbits' and *Déogratias* end with the uncertain future of this new world created by violence. As I have indicated, however, these endings are not periods, but ellipses. While they end with worlds that have been remade in the image of violence, they are also worlds that serve as cautionary tales. Those who read them carefully will see that these worlds contain both violence and the possibility of resisting this violence (to return to Said's contrapuntal reading). This is because, by documenting how violence began in each society, and how it destroyed each society, both works protest the colonialism and ethnic hatred that, in each case, led to a genocide. Each story ends with the possibility of hope, but also with an intense vulnerability that is perhaps the prerequisite for hope in a world that has been razed by violence.

In another context, Susie Linfield, in her analysis of photography that depicts human suffering in *The Cruel Radiance*, claims that those images contain within them a resistance against what they depict. These are contrapuntal images, then, that include not only suffering but the health, peace and joy that have been forcibly excluded from the lives of those depicted in such photographs. Linfield explains how these images of misery also embrace their opposite:

> Every image of barbarism – of immiseration, humiliation, terror, extermination – embraces its opposite, though sometimes unknowingly. Every image of suffering says not only, 'This is so,' but also, by implication: 'This must not be'; not only, 'This goes on,' but also, by implication: 'This must stop.' Documents of suffering are documents of protest.[33]

While I argue that there may be gratuitous images of suffering that are meant to thrill rather than to protest, Linfield's statement holds true for the way violence is depicted in 'The Rabbits' and in *Déogratias*. Both works warn that we must now learn to live together in whatever world we have inherited; there is simply no going back to that bucolic lake scene at the beginning of 'The Rabbits', nor to the fabled 'land of milk and honey' of Rwanda's pre-colonial days. Instead, we are left with a world marked by vulnerability, a vulnerability that requires mutual dependence and mutual aid for a way forward.

As Shaun Tan writes in his author's note accompanying 'The Rabbits' in the *Lost & Found* edition of the work, '[a]t the end the question of reconciliation is left open to the reader as it is in the real world: The future, as always, remains undecided'.[34] And so, while both of these graphic novels depict stories of frightening violence and the almost complete erasure of entire groups of people (or anthropomorphized animals), they both ultimately end with a challenge to the text's reader. And this challenge is how to move forward in the face of irreparable loss, and how to recognize, when confronted with violence, that '"This must stop"'.[35]

Notes

1. This was one of the basic tenets on which colonialism operated. In *Culture and Imperialism*, Edward Said explains that 'colonial space must be transformed sufficiently so as no longer to appear foreign to the imperial eye' (226).
2. Because this chapter analyses two works that combine words and images – works that are variably called graphic novels, comics and picture books – I will offer a brief word here about the intended audience for these works. Many English-speaking audiences assume that works that combine words and images are for children, since most English speakers' first and primary contact with such works are picture storybooks for young children. This assumption does not hold true for all cultures, however. Readers of French and Japanese, for example, have long accepted combinations of words and images – the French *bande dessinée* and Japanese *manga* – as literary forms that appeal to both adults and children. Shaun Tan addresses the question of intended audience for his works in his online essay 'Picture books: Who are they for?' In response to questions about whether his works are for adults or for children, Tan writes: 'One of the questions I am most frequently asked as a maker of picture books is this: "Who do you write and illustrate for?" ... [Art] often doesn't set out to appeal to a predefined audience but rather build[s] one for itself ... So it's really quite unusual to ask "who do you do it for?" Yet it is a question inevitably put to my work in picture books ... The reason of course is quite obvious. The idea of a picture book, as a literary art form, carries a number of tacit

assumptions: picture books are quite large, colourful, easy to read and very simple in their storyline and structure, not very long and (most significantly) produced exclusively for a certain audience, namely children, especially of the younger variety. Picture books are generally put on the shelves of bookstores, libraries, lounge rooms and bedrooms for young children, where they apparently belong. Picture books are synonymous with Children's Literature. But is this is a [sic] necessary condition of the art form itself? Or is it just a cultural convention, more to do with existing expectations, marketing prejudices and literary discourse? . . . Returning to that question, "Who do you write and illustrate for?" Perhaps the best answer I can give is this: anyone who reads and looks. . . . At the end of the day, any work of art finds it's [sic] own audience, inviting them to make what they will of this or that idea.' I follow Tan in being far more interested in the questions these books provoke than in their authors' intentions when writing them, or in how they are categorized by publishing houses and bookshops. I address the question here, however, due to the frequency with which it is asked, which points to the new and uneasy place that comics and graphic novels hold within academia. This anxiety regarding classification is reminiscent of earlier debates over whether novels should be included in the literary canon.
3. Said, *Culture and Imperialism*, 67.
4. Tan and Marsden, 'The Rabbits', 75–6.
5. Tan and Marsden, 'The Rabbits', 77–8.
6. Tan and Marsden, 'The Rabbits', 79–80.
7. Tan and Marsden, 'The Rabbits', 81–2.
8. Stassen, *Deogratias*, 17–18.
9. Stassen, *Déogratias*, 21: 1: 2–3; Stassen, *Deogratias*, 19: 1: 2–3.
10. Stassen, *Déogratias*, 21: 1: 3; Stassen, *Deogratias*, 19: 1: 3.
11. The narrative voice is that of an unnamed, unseen group of indigenous animals. It is a sort of chorus, narrating the rabbits' arrival to this land from the perspective of indigenous animals.
12. Other important differences between the indigenous animals and the rabbits, besides this matter of naming, are the clothing of the animals and their colour. The rabbits wear ornate clothing, while the indigenous animals wear nothing (and, indeed, when the British arrived in Australia, they were surprised to find that its indigenous people did not wear clothes). It is also significant, of course, that the rabbits are white, whereas the indigenous animals are a brownish colour. This colouring difference, as well as the fact that these animals are literally from different species, mirrors the great difference the Europeans of the day saw between themselves and the brown races. While the British believed themselves to be superior to darker races, indigenous Australians, for their part, were also confused by the colour of the Europeans' skin. Because white was a colour they associated with death, many Aborigines believed the Europeans to be men returned from the dead (Reynolds, *The Other Side of the Frontier*, 32).
13. In addition to the wheel marks on the ground, another indication of mechanical intervention in this scene is one of the rabbit's using a long looking glass to survey the land. This is common later in the book as well, as the rabbits view the landscape more often through machines than they do with their naked eyes. The transformation of the open land into orderly agricultural parcels, which the rabbits eventually accomplish, as well as their reliance on machines for their domination of the landscape, is a predictable part of the imperial worldview. In her book *Sowing Empire*, Jill Casid explains how colonizers used agriculture to transform the Caribbean. She explains: 'The pattern of transplantation of certain types of trees, like the oak, also declared the conversion of indigenous, junglelike, rhizomatic spontaneous growth into an ordered, productive machine-scape' (Casid, *Sowing Empire*, 37). In contradistinction to the open, spontaneous lake scene pictured in the depiction of the pre-rabbit norm, already here in this page there is the beginning of a 'machine-scape' that will be fully realized at the end of the book.
14. Tan and Marsden, 'The Rabbits', 85–6.
15. Donaldson and Donaldson, 'First sight', 15.
16. Note that the creation of division is an important aspect of the violence in both 'The Rabbits' and *Déogratias*. The rabbits literally divide up the land, thus destroying the habitat of the indigenous animals, while the Hutus' insistence on dividing Rwandans into different races is, in *Déogratias*, the major cause of the genocide.
17. Déogratias is never directly depicted committing violence: rather, scenes just before and just after his violence are depicted. The book gives no simple, evident reason why Déogratias

    participated in the killing, but the other Hutu men in his town strongly pressure him, even coming en masse to his front door and insisting that he join them.
18. Tan and Marsden, 'The Rabbits', 97–8.
19. Stassen, *Deogratias*, 75: 1–2.
20. Stassen, *Déogratias*, 78: 1: 3; Stassen, *Deogratias*, 76: 1: 3.
21. This level of discomfort never approaches anything resembling acknowledgement of crimes committed nor a willingness to make apologies or restitutions.
22. Stassen, *Déogratias*, 72: 1: 1; Stassen, *Deogratias*, 70.
23. Felman and Laub, *Testimony*, 68–9.
24. Stassen, *Deogratias*, 78: 2.
25. Stassen, *Déogratias*, 46: 1: 2; Stassen, *Deogratias*, 44: 1: 2.
26. Tan and Marsden, 'The Rabbits', 106–7.
27. Tan and Marsden, 'The Rabbits', 85–6.
28. The transformation from spontaneous growth to the machine-scape is now complete. See note 13 above.
29. Tan and Marsden, 'The Rabbits', 110–11.
30. Tan and Marsden, 'The Rabbits', 110–11.
31. Tan and Marsden, 'The Rabbits', 112–13.
32. Stassen, *Deogratias*, 78.
33. Linfield, *The Cruel Radiance*, 33.
34. Tan and Marsden, 'The Rabbits', 114.
35. Linfield, *The Cruel Radiance*, 33.

Bibliography

Casid, Jill H. *Sowing Empire: Landscape and colonization*. Minneapolis: University of Minnesota Press, 2005.
Donaldson, Ian, and Tamsin Donaldson. 'First sight'. In *Seeing the First Australians*, edited by Ian Donaldson and Tamsin Donaldson, 15–20. Boston: George Allen & Unwin, 1985.
Felman, Shoshana and Dori Laub. *Testimony: Crises of witnessing in literature, psychoanalysis, and history*. New York: Routledge, 1992.
Linfield, Susie. *The Cruel Radiance: Photography and political violence*. Chicago: University of Chicago Press, 2010.
Reynolds, Henry. *The Other Side of the Frontier: Aboriginal resistance to the European invasion of Australia*. Ringwood: Penguin, 1982.
Said, Edward. *Culture and Imperialism*. New York: Vintage Books, 1994.
Stassen, J. P. *Déogratias*. Belgium: Dupuis, 2000.
Stassen, J. P. *Deogratias: A tale of Rwanda*, translated by Alexis Siegel. New York: First Second, 2006.
Tan, Shaun. 'Picture books: Who are they for?' Accessed 25 May 2021. https://www.shauntan.net/esssay-picture-books-who-for.
Tan, Shaun and John Marsden. 'The Rabbits'. In Shaun Tan and John Marsden, *Lost & Found*, 76–113. New York: Arthur A. Levine Books, 2011.

Part 3:
Image/Narrative

8
Ludic space in horror fiction
Onni Mustonen

Writers in the horror genre have always been fascinated by spaces. Second only to monsters, horrific locations such as a haunted house, ruined castle or nocturnal graveyard may be the most iconic element of a horror story. Even before the monster makes its entrance, the mere sight of a long-abandoned house with dark windows tells us that we are in a horror story and gives us that first chill, making us realize something bad is happening and how vulnerable we are after all.

The interest of horror writers in spatiality should not come as a surprise when we consider the intellectual roots of the genre. Even though humans have always told scary stories, modern horror literature in the form of gothic novels was inspired by the larger cultural movement of British medievalist romanticism in the eighteenth century. During that era there was a renewed interest in the past, sparked especially by the haunting presence of numerous ruins and standing stones that dotted the British Isles as a reminder of the past that was gone but at the same time present – not too dissimilar to a ghost. The effect ruins had on people inspired novelists and poets such as Horace Walpole, Clara Reeve and Ann Radcliffe to write stories that would evoke a similar emotion. As the art historian Kenneth Clark has noted, the purpose of gothic landscapes 'was to induce a mood – the same agreeable melancholy which delighted the poets and dilettanti'.[1] Similarly, the purpose of a horror story is to induce a mood all the same: a feeling of 'painful emotion compounded of loathing and fear', to quote the definition of horror offered by the *Oxford English Dictionary*.

The problem with literary space is that, as Marie-Laure Ryan notes, conscious beings do not merely take up space fixed in one place. In literature the reader is only privy to the point of view of the narrator, but in the real world, something such as a garden path is not experienced from a static point of view, as a purely visual phenomenon, but by walking on it.[2] The path it takes and the way it curves guides not only the eye, but also the walker's steps, keeping them from trampling on the flowerbeds and taking them where they are supposed to go. In this sense, space is conceptualized through action, and in return space provides the structures for these actions. Literary spaces, meanwhile, seem to be physically inaccessible to the reader, and instead of walking on a path the reader can only read about it. Thus, the more dynamic aspects of space seem to be lost, namely the actions space encourages one to take and those that it inhibits.

Yet, as mentioned, the nature of space has been one of the more prevalent themes in horror literature from the very beginning. But why even pay this much attention to spatiality and location if they are reduced to mere window dressing or narrative framing? I would argue that the prevalence of different haunted castles, houses, towns and other horrific locations as themes, tropes and topoi warrants further examination of spatiality in horror fiction in a way that does not consider these locations merely as two-dimensional stage settings. To understand better how space can be contextualized through action in a storytelling context, I propose that we turn to another medium, namely games and especially video games, in order to shed light on the matter.

Unlike literature, where the more dynamic aspects of spatiality seem too often to be ignored, games and especially video games are more often than not structured around movement through space. A game of chess is all about mastering space, and in *Super Mario Bros.* (1985) the gameplay is by and large focused on running from the stage left of the level to the right and navigating the obstacles. This is also true of survival horror video games, which share horror literature's fascination with horrific locations and spaces.

By comparing the experience of space in the short story 'The Shadow over Innsmouth' by the American horror fiction author H. P. Lovecraft and in the video game *Silent Hill 2* (2001), developed by Team Silent and published by the Japanese entertainment conglomerate Konami for the PlayStation 2 console, this chapter will focus on the construction of horrific spatiality within the horror genre, and how the fictional spaces create the sense of vulnerability. By juxtaposing the different ways in which the narrative both informs and is informed by the locations described within the text, I will illustrate the ways in which textual spatiality can be understood as a game of sorts, hence ludic space, from the Latin word *ludus* meaning play, game or sport. More importantly I will study not only how ludic structures influence the way textual spaces are experienced and understood, but also more importantly how spatiality shapes and influences the interpretation of horror literature.

Urban space in 'The Shadow over Innsmouth'

Olli-Erkki Makkonen has noted that horror stories are typically set in small worlds with their own rules that separate them from the characters' everyday world.[3] To borrow a term from Stephen King, these spaces could be called 'Bad Places'.[4] The titular town in Lovecraft's short story 'The Shadow over Innsmouth' is, in many ways, a prototypical urban Bad Place of horror fiction. The short story tells the tale of an unnamed narrator who is travelling along the East Coast of the United States. During his travels he hears of an ancient port town called Innsmouth. Interested in local history, he decides to make the arduous trip to Innsmouth, even though several people tell him not to. In Innsmouth the narrator comes to realize that something has corrupted the town and its inhabitants, and more importantly, that he is trapped and being hunted.

Lovecraft's depiction of Innsmouth belongs in the tradition of urban fantasy that depicts city environments as uncanny.[5] He writes:

> Certainly, the terror of a deserted house swells in geometrical rather than arithmetical progression as houses multiply to a city of stark desolation. The sight of such endless avenues of fishy-eyed vacancy and death, and the thought of such linked infinities of black, brooding compartments given over to cobwebs and memories and the conqueror worm, start up vestigial fears and aversions that not even the stoutest philosophy can disperse.[6]

As Richard Lehan has noted, the city, by sheer virtue of its scale, always remains outside the grasp of an individual's reasoning:[7] no one can ever truly know everything that goes on in a city, be familiar with every street or know everyone who lives there. Something terrible may be going on just next door, and you would not have a clue.

Already in the extract quoted above, we can see that Lovecraft evokes this feeling of the uncanny in two distinct manners: firstly, there is the physical description of the city that emphasizes the obscuring nature of the architecture. He describes how the 'panorama' of an open vista, where everything is revealed, is 'contracted to a street scene' when entering the city.[8] Secondly, the narrative of 'The Shadow over Innsmouth' focuses on discovering the town's secret, its hidden nature, and it is exactly '[w]hen the city gives up its secrets we enter the realm of the uncanny', as Lehan writes.[9]

In the story, the city's uncanniness is used as a narrative strategy that enforces the narrator's vulnerability even when the physical threat is not present. By limiting the narrator's and the readers' point of view, both are left to wonder what they cannot see, and if that which they cannot see poses a threat to the character. Furthermore, by frequently alluding to some hidden but clearly horrible aspect of the city, the architecture simultaneously hides the threat and stands for it as its symbol. More so than an actual threat, it is a constant presence of atmosphere, not some particular creature or violent act, but a sense of place. The crooked houses constantly remind the narrator that he is vulnerable while depriving him of the knowledge of what may be threatening him, therefore taking away any chance he has of defending himself. The sense of vulnerability caused by the uncanniness of Innsmouth is as much a feature of the space as are its architectural and visual qualities. The sense of threat evoked by the city makes the narrator cautious as he moves around the town and inspires him to try to uncover the truth about Innsmouth in order to dispel it.

Similarly, the way in which the short story's narrative opens, step by step, makes the reader want to keep reading and explore the city with the narrator. Additionally, it contributes to the sense of spatiality insofar as it is construed through action (in this case, emotion). Narrative's deliberate obfuscation of truth even partially mimics the way that an urban space might limit a person's point of view, therefore evoking a similar sense of vulnerability, suspense and fear, but arguably the narrative is not the same thing as spatiality. After all, the sense of space is at least partially created by the physical space. For example, the walls of a house and the placement of a door demand that a given person enters and exits from a specific point. In 'The Shadow over Innsmouth', much of the narrator's spatial vulnerability is caused by the physical architecture of the city, which makes it hard for him to escape when pursued because he gets lost or is trapped in a room or dead end. The reader, meanwhile, can simply skip to the end to find out what is really happening in Innsmouth, or whether the narrator survives, and in the process dispel the story's suspense.

The problem of literary spatiality is not unlike that of the paradox of fiction, or 'how people can be moved (e.g., be horrified) by that which they know does not exist', to quote Noël Carroll.[10] Arising from the assumed tension between the story world and the real word, the paradox of fiction asserts that, as Colin Radford writes, 'our being moved in certain ways by works of art, though very "natural" to us and in that way only too intelligible, involves us in inconsistency and so incoherency', because that which does not exist should not have an effect similar to that which does, and the reader is acutely aware of the difference.[11] Yet, as Richard Joyce writes, it would be 'deeply counterintuitive' to say that horror fiction does not frighten people.[12]

A similar question can be asked regarding literary spaces: how can an environment that does not exist evoke a sense of spatiality, even if this sense is only the fright it might evoke? The reader cannot get lost in the linear progression of the story, yet they might be afraid and claustrophobic when reading about the narrow and winding streets of Innsmouth. In the next section, I examine how game worlds face a similar problem in the sense that they also operate on imagined systems that seem to evoke responses despite not being 'real'. By approaching reading from the point of *ludus* or playing, some of the tension may be alleviated by studying how actions are formalized within the fictional worlds represented in video games, and how it offers a possible approach to dynamic literary spatiality.

Formalizing action in video games

In his seminal work *Homo Ludens* published in 1938, the Dutch historian Johan Huizinga proposed the idea of a so-called magic circle where games and play take place. According to Huizinga, the magic circle represents an area separated from everyday life, where 'an absolute and peculiar order reigns'.[13] This 'order' is composed of three elements: rules, win-states and mechanics. Put simply, rules dictate what the player can do to achieve the win-state, win-state is what the player hopes to achieve in the framework of the rules and mechanics are the means dictated by the rules that the player uses to achieve the win-state.[14] Motivated by the win-state, the player then interprets the rules to devise strategies that are implemented by using the mechanics of the gameplay. For example, moving a chess piece across a table would by itself be a rather meaningless action, but in the context of a chess game, moving a piece may take the player closer to victory. In other words, the magic circle is a meta-hermeneutic structure that gives meaning to each of the three elements by using the other two to give them context. As Huizinga writes, it is a space 'dedicated to performance' in the sense that it is a hermeneutically sealed autopoetic system.[15]

Here, it may be easy to see why the magic circle can be such a tempting tool to use to unravel the paradox of fiction. The tension between that which does not exist and that which does is not present in games because nothing outside the circle is relevant. Nonetheless, it is worth noting that fiction is not analogous to games, or fictional worlds to the magic circle. In the end, the magic circle is a theoretical concept used to study games, not literature, and the emphasis Huizinga places on rules makes the magic circle a hard concept to co-opt into literary studies. It would be a stretch to call reading literature a rule-based action, not least because literature outright rejects win- and fail-states. Both 'The Shadow over Innsmouth' and its game adaptation *Call of Cthulhu: Dark corners of the Earth* (Headfirst Productions, 2005) include a scene where the protagonist has to escape from a hotel. In the game, the player must perform pre-set actions to escape, such as blocking doors and securing latches. If they fail to do this, they must play the section again until they succeed. On the other hand, the short story does not simply stop and refuse to advance if the reader fails to meet some presupposed conditions. The narrator will always escape no matter what the reader does.

This is why, as Jesper Juul has noted, it is 'tempting to describe [the relationship between rules and fiction] as inherently problematic'.[16] Rules are attractive because they are universal and offer rigid structures for an experience. Fiction, conversely, is at its best when it is highly subjective and ambiguous.[17] Because these two elements seem to be at such fundamental odds with one other, several prominent ludologists have been rather dismissive about fiction in games. Markku Eskelinen has famously stated that stories in video games are 'just uninteresting ornaments or gift-wrappings and studying these kinds of marketing tools is just a waste of time and energy'.[18]

Yet it is worth noting that one aspect of video games, where fiction and rules often become inseparable, is space.[19] Let us, for example, consider the town of Silent Hill, one of the more iconic examples of horrific towns in the media of video games. In *Silent Hill 2* you (the player) play as James Sunderland, who has just received a letter from his dead wife Mary asking him to come to the town of Silent Hill. Like the narrator of 'The Shadow over Innsmouth', James soon realizes that the town is actually inhabited by horrible monsters, and in order to survive he must uncover what is really happening. The gameplay is largely comprised of three actions: spatial navigation of urban locations, fighting monsters and solving puzzles.

All three gameplay elements come together to help create the town of Silent Hill, and by engaging with them, the player comes to experience the ludic spatiality through actions. Arguably the spatial navigation is the gameplay mechanic that is most explicitly tied to the location. Here, the player must make their way through often labyrinthine structures, such as hospitals, hotels or city streets, to find the next gameplay area. Additionally, these locations are almost always inhabited by monsters the player must fight or flee from. The presence of the creatures emphasizes the hostile nature of the town and designates Silent Hill as a *Bad Place* in a *Horror Story*. Puzzle-solving adds another layer to the space, but instead of ludic, it is narrative, because most of the objects the player needs to solve the puzzles (and move to the next area, or story beat) are somehow linked to the city, its history or the main character (who, we come to find out, is intimately linked with the reason why the town seems to be haunted).

Because *Silent Hill 2* is a horror game, spatial navigation, monster-fighting and puzzle-solving are framed as horrific. In order to evoke horror, *Silent Hill 2* emphasizes the players' and characters' vulnerability at all times. Firstly, the locations the player needs to explore are dark or foggy, often labyrinthine, and as discussed earlier, the confusing and obstructing layout of these locations acts to disorient the player and obscure possible threats.[20] Fighting monsters, meanwhile, is arduous and drains extremely limited supplies, and by forcing the player to solve puzzles the game forces the player to interact with the monsters in claustrophobic situations with no easy means of escape. *Silent Hill 2* also constantly keeps hiding the rules that govern the gameplay, or changes them, by, for example, suddenly making enemies unkillable, thus mimicking on a gameplay level the way horror stories on a narrative level thrust their characters into Bad Places with rules they cannot understand.

Naturally, the real human playing the game is not at any point under threat or vulnerable, but inside the magic circle their ability to act is limited and stripped, making them vulnerable. Actions in games are not reactions to some assumed real-world object, but inbuilt systems that come to define the game itself. As Juul notes, rules 'set up potential actions, actions that are meaningful inside the game but meaningless outside'.[21] In other words, rules construct meaningful actions inside the magic circle where previously there were none. We could call this process formalization, where more complex phenomena such as a sense of vulnerability are represented as predetermined narrative/ludic structures.

We could have a discussion about whether abstracted, formalized emotions are the same thing as real emotions, but for our purposes such a discussion is irrelevant. What matters is that through formalizing, systemizing and abstracting, things that do not exist can evoke responses that do, and in turn the player can use these responses to explore the game world with what we call play.

In the next part, I will examine how vulnerability is formalized in 'The Shadow over Innsmouth', and how this in turn helps the reader to explore literary spaces.

Virtual spaces in horror literature

The player's ability to interact with their surroundings in the game world is the main reason why literature and video games are hard to compare even in the most favourable of circumstances. The player's influence is acutely felt, whereas the reader can only read without affecting how the story is played out or what the outcome will be. Interactivity also explains how a player experiences space in games. As Grahame Weinbren writes, '[i]n a video game the "coincidence of view" is achieved very quickly and by means of a single, elementary device – that the movement of the character is fully determined by the actions of the player . . . So by playing the game I become [the character]'.[22]

In *Silent Hill 2* and other horror video games, the sense of spatial vulnerability is created by placing the character in threatening locations with a diminished point of view (shared by the player) and then forcing the player to act as their character in those same situations with gameplay mechanics that de-emphasize their power. Literature, on the other hand, must rely on less directive narrative devices to create terrifying spaces. Immersion is similarly vital, but it is based less on audience agency and more on the text's ability to mediate the horrific qualities of the spaces for the reader.

Mapping may be the most primal strategy of mediating space. Just like a map in real life, mapping is a narrative strategy that contextualizes narrative space 'as a network of access and relation that binds . . . sites together into a coherent geography', as Ryan writes.[23] In games, an understanding of geography is important because it informs the player of the possible moves they can take. In literature, the reader may not be able to plot their actions similarly based on this kind of information, but geography nonetheless plays an important part in understanding the story world both as a place and as a setting of the story. Without narrative mapping, the events of the story would take place in unspecified locations without spatial cohesion. As David Herman writes, mapping the story world allows 'the reader to chart the spatial trajectories along which the narrative events unfold'.[24] In other words, like the maps in *Silent Hill 2*, the maps in Lovecraft's story frame the narrative to a specific location, thus making it easier to follow. In the short story these mapping strategies range from descriptions of objects in a room to the layout of the city.

In 'The Shadow over Innsmouth' we even find numerous embedded maps, like the maps the player finds in *Silent Hill 2*. In 'The Shadow over Innsmouth', a shop clerk draws a map for the narrator. By following the map, the narrator is able to find his way around Innsmouth and go, for example, from Marsh Street to the Town Square where the hotel is located.[25] In other words, he is able to move from one scene to another, and due to the map-like descriptions of the prose, the reader is able to situate themself in the narrated situations. At the same time, the presence of the maps does act as a constant reminder that Innsmouth is a complex town, where it is easy to get lost. During his escape, the narrator even has to consult his map so he does not get lost in the endless winding streets. The presence of a map may empower the narrator, but without one he is even more vulnerable than ever.

While mapping allows the narrative to maintain spatial cohesion, the primary way the reader experiences 'The Shadow over Innsmouth' is still through the eyes of the narrator on the street level. Here, the framing narrative that functions rule-like by establishing how the story unfolds gives way to the mechanics of telling the story. Much like game mechanics, these narrative strategies allow the reader to engage with the story by taking a role in it through the 'coincidence of view' with a diegetic locus in the story world, but the actions that the readers take are more parasympathetic than the ones the player uses to interact with their diegetic counterpart. As befits a 'body genre', as Linda Williams calls horror, in 'The Shadow over Innsmouth', identification with the narrator's experience of space is built by juxtaposing the reader's biological and the narrator's textual corporeality.[26]

Apart from the more explicit characterization of the town as uncanny, 'The Shadow over Innsmouth' uses evocative descriptions typical of horror literature. When the narrator first enters the city, he describes the 'wormy decay' of the buildings.[27] Most of them seem abandoned and the few inhabited houses the narrator sees have 'rags stuffed in the broken windows and shells and dead fish lying about the littered yard'.[28] The people he sees are either digging around in their gardens or scavenging clams on 'the fishy-smelling beach below'.[29]

What makes this sort of description remarkable is the close attention it pays to the tactile and sensory qualities of Innsmouth. Lovecraft's description paints a vivid image of a town that is rotting. Like many other Bad Places, Innsmouth is depicted as physically disgusting, which begins to explain why it is also experienced as horrible. There are dead things lying about and the wind carries with it a foul stench from the sea. The generic disgustingness of the town not only anchors Innsmouth to the tradition of haunted places, but also suggests images of disease, degeneration and ultimately death.

Grisly descriptions of tactile qualities such as 'gruesomely musty' and 'mouldering and pestilential' are typically used in horror fiction to create a highly physical space with the intention of connecting with the reader's physicality.[30] Peter Stockwell has used the term 'textures' to describe the textual counterparts of real-world experiences that form 'the basis of measures of identification between a reader and the literary work'.[31] As he writes, '[w]here a text forges a close identification of a text-world counterpart with the discourse-world participant, the potential for empathetic engagement and strong emotion (which might include revulsion) is generated'.[32]

In part, the emotion of horror as it is related to horrific locations is born out of exposure to these unpleasant textures. Descriptions of putrid, wet and cold environments act as a frequent reminder that the narrator of 'The Shadow over Innsmouth' is in a constant position of physical peril. In these sorts of environments, the body's vulnerability is repeatedly accentuated through the description of exposure to unpleasant elements. Lovecraft's frequent references to the narrator shivering and shuddering emphasize the fact that he is susceptible to various threats ranging from the common flu to supernatural violence. To quote Jack Morgan, the rhetorical use of 'atmosphere, imagery, and so on, seeks to provoke and maintain a heightened sense of exposure to harm and subjection to being physically hurt'.[33]

At the same time, these smaller examples of physicality are vital in creating a tactile story world and anchoring it in the reader's own physical experience; we may not know what it is like to be attacked by monsters, but most readers know how uncomfortable it is to sit in wet clothes. The latter then creates a sense of discomfort and vulnerability that permeates even the more fantastic elements of the story, making them grounded at least on some level in the everyday feelings of the reader. They remind the reader of the vulnerability of their physical, flesh-and-blood body and use that to connect them to the story world in order to evoke feelings.

The shared narrative focus on the body of both the character and the reader furthermore casts corporeality as the hermeneutic locus of 'The Shadow over Innsmouth'. This, again, is something that the short story shares with *Silent Hill 2*. In the game, the character's body displayed on the screen is the deictic locus from which the locations are explored.[34]

The avatar body moves in accordance with the player's instructions and thus constitutes an extension of the player's physicality. It is a prosthetic of sorts that makes it possible for the player to act within the game-world, with its abilities and limitations informing the player of their surroundings.

The textual body of the narrator serves a similar function. The somatic responses mediated to the reader inform them of the fictional locations and allow them to 'act in' or at least to experience the story world. To borrow a term from computing, we could describe the emergent spatiality caused by embodied literary space as virtual, that is to say, 'not actually, but as if'.[35] Like cyberspace, the virtual space is a 'collection of world data' that includes information such as map-like layouts, different sensory qualities, fictional histories and so forth, but as Mark J. P. Wolf notes, a virtual world does not merely exist as a 'set of recorded words, images and sound'.[36] Instead, virtual space is experienced in the present tense. In the case of 'The Shadow over Innsmouth', the town is virtual in the sense that the experience of space mediated to the reader by describing the narrator's emotional and physiological experience, therefore creating the emergent literary spatiality, is not only the text on the page or the events of the narrative, but also encompasses the reader's reaction to the environments described by the text *in the present tense*. Consequently, the literary space in 'The Shadow over Innsmouth' is far more than just the words on a page. It also encompasses the emotions it causes in the reader.

Much like a game, 'The Shadow over Innsmouth' uses the interaction of systemic elements to evoke actions, which in the case of horror fiction also include the sensations and emotions it evokes. Both the map-like descriptions of narrative paths and the sensory descriptions of bodily experiences function similarly to the game mechanics in the sense that they formalize sets of complex actions into units that can be mediated to the reader. The narrative maps are formal representations of the plot that help the reader to be involved in the story, whereas the bodily textures mediate a sense of vulnerability, with the points of reference being the textual and the actual body, with the former projecting data that is then interpreted by the latter. The knowledge we accumulate based on our own physical reactions is then used to interpret the story. Fundamentally, this type of interpretation is not too different from playing a game, because in both instances we find that meaning does not arise from passively taking in information. Instead, both the reader and the player use the mechanics at their disposal to explore the diegetic worlds via action, which in the case of horror fiction is being moved on an emotional level.

Conclusion: horror fiction and vulnerability

In 'The Shadow over Innsmouth', the narrator does at one point wonder if the city is having some effect on him: 'Is it not possible that the germ of an actual contagious madness lurks in the depths of that shadow over Innsmouth?'[37] In the end, he does get infected by the city, and one day he will become a Deep One as well. Of course, there was never any other way for the story to end, because humans are creatures not only of habit but also of habitat. Our environment shapes us, has an effect on us, dictates our behaviour in small and large ways. Anyone who dares to venture into a Bad Place is liable to be haunted, and the same goes for the reader, although they get off easier than the narrator. The reader is merely left with the shallowest signs of infection to show for their adventures in Innsmouth: rapid breathing, flushed cheeks and a beating heart – in a word, the emotional and physical shock of horror caused by reading horror fiction. In other words, they are vulnerable to the effects of the text.

I began this chapter by mentioning that space is conceptualized through action. In the case of horror literature and Bad Places, this action is the reader being affected emotionally by the text. The reader is very literally moved by the story in the narrative alleys and streets where the story takes place. Being moved in this way is very similar to interpretation, because it makes us do things with the text.

The American horror fiction author Douglas E. Winter has reminded us that, as a word, 'horror' is not only used to describe a literary genre, but more commonly horror is an emotion, and the value of horror as a literary genre comes from its ability to evoke its namesake emotion.[38] As such, if literary studies were to forget to deal with the emotions of horror, dread and fear while talking about horror literature, we would be at risk of ignoring an integral aspect of the genre. By considering the reader as vulnerable, or our own vulnerability as readers, we gain a new tool to interpret horror fiction.

The simple emotion of horror may not give us a deeper understanding of the historical context in which the story was written or the psychology of the author, but it does give us a better understanding of the systems at work – and, as we saw with tactile textures, we as readers are a part of that system. We take, interpret and send signals as a part of the system, be it literature or games, and by playing we can also explore our own role in that meaning-creating system. Both actual and literary spaces are merely variations of these types of systems.

A ludic space is one that encourages the reader to take action to explore it, and then in turn the reader is defined by those actions. The ever-present game of chess is built around rules that define the possible moves the player can make, but it is only realized in its wonderful complexity by the emergent strategies inspired by those same rules. The ludic space of Innsmouth is one that inspires terror but is then in turn only actualized as the emotion of terror. It creates an entire town within the haunted magic circle.

Notes

1. Clark, *The Gothic Revival*, 47.
2. Ryan, *Narrative as Virtual Reality*, 71.
3. Makkonen, 'Clive Barkerin koominen ja groteski maailma', 236.
4. King, *Danse Macabre*, 278.
5. Lehan, *The City in Literature*, 81, 94–6.
6. Lovecraft, 'The Shadow over Innsmouth', 137.
7. Lehan, *The City in Literature*, 98.
8. Lovecraft, 'The Shadow over Innsmouth', 221.
9. Lehan, *The City in Literature*, 74.
10. Carroll, *The Philosophy of Horror*, 159–60.
11. Radford, 'How can we be moved by the fate of Anna Karenina?', 78.
12. Joyce, 'Rational fear of monsters', 210.
13. Huizinga, *Homo Ludens*, 10.
14. Koster, 'Rules versus mechanics'.
15. Huizinga, *Homo Ludens*, 10.
16. Juul, *Half-Real*, 163.
17. Juul, *Half-Real*, 121.
18. Eskelinen, 'The gaming situation'.
19. Juul, *Half-Real*, 188.
20. Järvinen, 'Understanding video games as emotional experiences', 103.
21. Juul, 'A certain level of abstraction', 58.
22. Weinbren, 'Mastery (Sonic c'est moi)', 186.
23. Ryan, *Narrative as Virtual Reality*, 123.
24. Herman, *Story Logic*, 279.
25. Lovecraft, 'The Shadow over Innsmouth', 245.
26. Williams, 'Film bodies: Gender, genre, and excess', 5.
27. Lovecraft, 'The Shadow over Innsmouth', 220.
28. Lovecraft, 'The Shadow over Innsmouth', 220–1.
29. Lovecraft, 'The Shadow over Innsmouth', 221.
30. Lovecraft, 'The Shadow over Innsmouth', 247, 250.
31. Stockwell, 'Texture and identification', 149.
32. Stockwell, 'Texture and identification', 149.
33. Morgan, *The Biology of Horror*, 74.
34. Perron, *Silent Hill*, 22.
35. Heim, *Virtual Realism*, 220.
36. Wolf, 'Worlds', 126, 127.
37. Lovecraft, 'The Shadow over Innsmouth', 264.
38. Cited in Sammon, 'Introduction to Douglas E. Winter's "Less Than Zombie"', 84.

Bibliography

Carroll, Noël. *The Philosophy of Horror, or, Paradoxes of the Heart*. New York and London: Routledge, 1990.

Clark, Kenneth. *The Gothic Revival: An essay in the history of taste*. Frome and London: Butler & Tanner, 1962.

Eskelinen, Markku. 'The gaming situation'. *Game Studies* 1, no. 1 (July 2001). Accessed 25 May 2021. http://www.gamestudies.org/0101/eskelinen/.
Heim, Michael. *Virtual Realism*. New York and Oxford: Oxford University Press, 1998.
Herman, David. *Story Logic: Problems and possibilities of narrative*. Lincoln: University of Nebraska Press, 2002.
Huizinga, Johan. *Homo Ludens: A study of the play-element in culture*. London: Routledge & Kegan Paul, 1949.
Järvinen, Aki. 'Understanding video games as emotional experiences'. In *Video Game Theory Reader 2*, edited by Bernard Perron and Mark J. P. Wolf, 85–109. New York: Routledge, 2008.
Joyce, Richard. 'Rational fear of monsters'. *British Journal of Aesthetics* 40, no. 2 (April 2000): 209–24.
Juul, Jesper. 'A certain level of abstraction'. In *Situated Play: DiGRA 2007 conference proceedings*, edited by Akira Baba, 510–15. Tokyo: DiGRA Japan, 2007. Accessed 25 May 2021. https://www.jesperjuul.net/text/acertainlevel/.
Juul, Jesper. *Half-Real: Video games between real rules and fictional worlds*. Cambridge, MA: MIT Press, 2005.
King, Stephen. *Danse Macabre*. New York: Gallery Books, 2010.
Koster, Ralph. 'Rules versus mechanics'. Accessed 25 May 2021. https://www.raphkoster.com/2011/12/13/rules-versus-mechanics/.
Lehan, Richard. *The City in Literature: An intellectual and cultural history*. Berkeley: University of California Press, 1998.
Lovecraft, H. P. 'The Shadow over Innsmouth (1936)'. In *The Whisperer in Darkness & Other Tales*, 207–72. Richmond, UK: Alma Classics, 2015.
Lovecraft, H. P. *Supernatural Horror in Literature*. New York: Dover Publications, 1973.
Makkonen, Olli-Erkki. 'Clive Barkerin koominen ja groteski maailma'. In *Musta lammas: Kirjoituksia populaari- ja massakulttuurista*, edited by Tero Koistinen, Erkki Sevänen and Risto Turunen, 216–41. Saarijärvi: Joensuun yliopisto, Humanistinen tiedekunta, 1995.
Morgan, Jack. *The Biology of Horror: Gothic literature and film*. Carbondale and Edwardsville: Southern Illinois University Press, 2002.
Perron, Bernard. *Silent Hill: The terror engine*. Ann Arbor: University of Michigan Press, 2011.
Petterson, Mattias. 'Racism and fear in H.P. Lovecraft's "The Shadow over Innsmouth"' (2016). Accessed 25 May 2021. https://www.diva-portal.org/smash/get/diva2:904039/FULLTEXT01.pdf.
Radford, Colin. 'How can we be moved by the fate of Anna Karenina?' *Proceedings of the Aristotelian Society, Supplementary Volumes* 49 (1975): 67–93.
Ryan, Marie-Laure. *Narrative as Virtual Reality: Immersion and interactivity in literature and electronic media*. Baltimore, MD: Johns Hopkins University Press, 2001.
Sammon, Paul M. 'Introduction to Douglas E. Winter's "Less Than Zombie"'. In *Splatterpunks: Extreme horror*, edited by Paul M. Sammon, 84–5. New York: St. Martin's Press, 1990.
Stockwell, Peter. 'Texture and identification'. *European Journal of English Studies* 9, no. 2 (2007): 143–54.
Weinbren, Grahame. 'Mastery (Sonic c'est moi)'. In *New Screen Media: Cinema/art/narrative*, edited by Martin Rieser and Andrea Zapp, 179–91. London: British Film Institute, 2002.
Williams, Linda. 'Film bodies: Gender, genre, and excess'. *Film Quarterly* 44, no. 4 (Summer 1991): 2–13.
Wolf, Mark J. P. 'Worlds'. In *The Routledge Companion to Video Game Studies*, edited by Mark J. P. Wolf and Bernard Perron, 125–31. New York: Routledge, 2016.

Ludography

The video game platform in parenthesis indicates the system on which these games were played for the purpose of researching this chapter.
Call of Cthulhu: Dark corners of the Earth (PC). Headfirst Productions/Bethesda, 2005.
Silent Hill 2 (PS2). Team Silent/Konami, 2001.

9
Graphic stories of resistance: a comic memoir of becoming

Pinelopi Tzouva

Graphic medicine is an emergent interdisciplinary field that explores the potential of comics as a medium for communicating the experience of illness.[1] It was founded by Ian Williams, physician, artist and writer, and its specific objectives are (1) to promote the expression of medical experiences in graphic form, (2) to employ such graphic expressions as a tool for the education of health professionals and (3) to bolster the transformative power of graphic pathographies and their capacity to create communities.[2] In this context, the medium of comics is seen as pertinent for the sharing of health experiences. As Susan Squier notes:

> Comics can show us things *that can't be said*, just as they can narrate experiences without relying on words, and in their juxtaposition of words and pictures, they can also convey a far richer sense of the different magnitudes at which we experience any *performance* of illness, disability, medical treatment, or healing.[3]

Graphic medicine aims to 'challenge the dominant methods of scholarship in healthcare' by means of intermingling art and science.[4] Courses that combine comics and medicine are already offered to medical students in the United States, while one of the basic tenets of the field is that 'if reading comics improves diagnostic reasoning and doctoring skills, then making comics will enhance creative and communication skills'.[5]

In all these goals and interests, graphic medicine functions in parallel ways and finds common ground with narrative medicine, which shares the same basic core of principles but is centred on purely textual narratives.[6] In both areas of scholarly study, major theorists have produced remarkable work on the gendered embodiment of illness from a feminist perspective.[7] Notably, Hillary Chute, a leading feminist scholar in comics studies, remarks in *Graphic Women* that 'some of the most riveting feminist cultural production is in the form of accessible yet edgy graphic narratives'.[8] Both fields, most significantly, emphasize the transformative, world-making power of storytelling, and how beginning from individual stories we can trace and influence broader structures and connections that pertain to the social and political organization of our societies. In his chapter 'Comics and the iconography of illness' in the *Graphic Medicine Manifesto*, Ian Williams understands graphic pathographies as offering an unofficial iconography of medicine, but he also underscores the power of change that is contained in this hybrid medium of comics when he writes that '[i]mages do not just mirror the world; they help build it'.[9] However, helping to make the world a new and better place through images created by people who experience serious illness, images that tell us their stories in powerful and affective ways – this making of the world is hugely defined by vulnerability.

Eszter Szép, in her book *Comics and the Body: Drawing, reading, and vulnerability* (2020), states that 'the experience of vulnerability is at the heart of nonfiction comics partly because of its drawn and embodied nature, and partly because of the special modality in which reality is presented in these comics'.[10] Indeed, such narratives communicate 'unsettling and painful moments' and, what is more, they do so in a genre in which 'the reader feels the drawer's bodily trace'.[11] This enables experiencing vulnerability as 'a shared quality' which can potentially function as 'a central transformative force' that 'allows for an ethical encounter with the Other'.[12] Further on, the author cites Judith Butler and affirms that recognizing our shared vulnerability 'is to solicit a becoming, to instigate a transformation, to petition the future always in relation to the Other'.[13] This allows us, then, to engage in such minor gestures of micropolitics towards personal and social change, to build ethical communities – to build a world, as we saw earlier with Ian Williams:

> Vulnerability in this way is a relationship between people: One experiences vulnerability in his or her own body, and one also experiences that this vulnerability needs to be and can be attended to by other people, and that one can attend to the vulnerability of others in meaningful ways or one can do harm. In this way, the social aspect of vulnerability is defining: In interactions with the Other, the vulnerability carried by the body becomes manifest. Vulnerability

allows for multidirectional open-ended affective interactions and transactions in which all parties involved can be changed.[14]

It is precisely on this world-building prospect of graphic memoirs that I wish to focus in this chapter, taking as my object of analysis Miriam Engelberg's *Cancer Made Me a Shallower Person: A memoir in comics*. Engelberg was a computer trainer and programmer who worked in the non-profit sector and had always loved comics. She made comics to communicate her experience of motherhood and her day-to-day reality at work, creating a compilation of strips published online under the title *Planet 501c3*. She was diagnosed with breast cancer in autumn 2001 when she was 43 years old. Creating comics about this experience was her lifeline and her way to cope with it. In her foreword, she writes:

> We all have issues that follow us through life, no matter how much therapy we've had. The big one for me is about feeling different and alone – isolated in a state of Miriam-ness that no one else experiences. That's what drew me to read autobiographical comics, and that's why I hope my comics can be of comfort to other readers who might be struggling with issues similar to mine.[15]

Engelberg used to go to a café for 30 minutes every day to work on her comic strips before she went to her regular office job. In her comic memoir, she documents, in a personal and quite distinctive style that is marked by refusal, negativity and irony, the entire story of her illness, beginning from the moment when she was still waiting for the biopsy results. Her book, around 100 pages in total which, interestingly, are not numbered, thus adding to its non-linearity, consists of short or slightly longer gag strips – independent short stories varying from one to four pages – each under a descriptive headline, such as 'The Undead', 'Breast Cancer as a Hobby' and 'Something Unpleasant and You'. Her amateurish drawing style is very simple, like something that possibly the reader herself could have drawn, contributing to a feeling of intimacy and recognition. Through her black and white drawings and her witty, caustic text, she performs her irreverent and unruly selfhood in a narrative of disobedience, cynicism and denunciatory utterances, for example, her rightfully indignant and funny pages on the implausible world of the educational booklets that are a far cry from her own reality. This, according to Engelberg, seems to be a world of denial and make-believe, where cancer and its treatment are absurdly presented as potentially positive experiences, invested with moments of conviviality in the company of fellow patients, associated with some charming nature scene and calmly providing the warning that 'you may experience some nausea during chemo'.[16] Engelberg knows very well that this is not the case at all. She has first-hand experience of all that and, as far as she is concerned, what she has witnessed is totally different. In contradistinction to the booklet world, having breast-cancer surgery and chemotherapy is a physically and emotionally debilitating, pain-inflicting, nausea-inducing, depressing and very lonely process. This is one of many instances when Engelberg protests against the hypocrisy surrounding breast cancer and against the demands that a toxic culture makes on cancer patients – to be courageous, strong and inspiring and to look on the bright side – topped up with society's infuriating refusal to assume responsibility for what is definitely related to broader structures and relations and should clearly not be attributed solely to people's everyday life choices. Engelberg's contribution, through her dark humour and her mordant satire, is to expose the insanity of it all, the total absurdity of a whole network of cultural patterns and attitudes towards cancer that not only do not make any sense but also reproduce oppression and sadness, inflicting, thus, further pain and adding to the harm that is already caused by the disease.

Engelberg eventually got metastases in her bones and brain and died just a few months after her book was published, in 2006. Her comic memoir raises a dissenting voice to the pink-ribbon culture and to the dominant cultural plot of survivorship, and it is considered an important work in the category of cancer comics. It has already been the object of several studies, including those by Emily Waples, Martha Stoddard Holmes and Mary DeShazer.[17] All three of these theorists pay attention to the same aforementioned features of Engelberg's narrative, which are, effectively, quite striking. And so, Waples concludes that it 'disrupts the story we want to tell about breast cancer: that it is surmountable, codified by the cultural archetype of the survivor – a subjectivity that has been relentlessly marketed throughout the past thirty years by breast cancer awareness campaigns'.[18] Stoddard Holmes, meanwhile, comments that it 'works against tired expectations of illness and disability as bleak and deeply ennobling conditions, most often operating in a satiric mode'.[19] And DeShazer makes it one of the objects of her analysis in *Mammographies*, in a chapter with the telling title 'Rebellious humor in breast cancer narratives: Deflating the culture of optimism'.[20] It is the same traits that have sparked my interest, and it is for the same reasons that I intend to examine it here: as a work that disrupts familiar narratives, goes against the expected and operates in a satirical and rebellious mode, qualities that constitute it as a political gesture of activism. It does so, though, in a minor key, which is, as Erin Manning argues, the weakness and the strength of every minor gesture.[21] Could, then, its minor qualities, the fact that it operates on a subtler and more nuanced register, attenuate its political strength or even compromise its political character?

Most interestingly, the very first thing that Manning explains in the introduction of her book *The Minor Gesture* (2016) is that the minor can be easily overlooked and for this reason is precarious. Conventionally, we seem to recognize much more readily the major gestures, those that are commonly classified as revolutionary and activist, and to miss the minor ones, failing to perceive how through their coming into being they function to open experience to new forms and variations. We tend to imagine that the real political action is elsewhere and in a different shape – big, loud, self-conscious and with a very concrete agenda. Manning writes:

> The unwavering belief in the major as the site where events occur, where events make a difference, is based on accepted accounts of what registers as change as well as existing parameters for gauging the value of that change. Yet, while the grand gestures of a macropolitics most easily sum up the changes that occurred to alter the field, it is the minoritarian tendencies that initiate the subtle shifts that created the conditions for this, and any change. The grand is given the status it has not because it is where the transformative power lies, but because *it is easier to identify major shifts than to catalogue the nuanced rhythms of the minor*. As a result, these rhythms are narrated as secondary, or even negligible.[22]

Marcelo Svirsky, in his examination of activism from a Deleuzian perspective, makes a similar point. 'Rather than understanding activism as supporting or leading social struggles', he pursues a definition that presents it 'as an open-ended process and stresses the role of *investigation* in relation to practices within the social situations to which activism addresses itself'.[23] Activism, then, is doing this investigation, looking at things with critical eyes, interrogating the ethical aspects of different organizations and processes, asking questions, asking 'why'. This is what makes further action possible, what initiates movement; this is the beginning of movement, and it is, despite the fact that it may pass unnoticed and remain uncredited due to its fleeting nature and subtlety, the most revolutionary part of all political action – the moment of negation and of the interruption of an old rhythm; before the organized struggle begins; before the new order is established. For Svirsky:

it is possible to understand insurrection as a perceptible act of opposition to a ruling power or habit, without tying it to a Hollywood-style image. For instance, a Bartlebyan moment of refusal is an act of opposition which might infect a state of affairs and develop into an activism, whether it occurs in a scrivener's office, in a call for a love, or at home through the forces exerted by a change in posture of a woman's body when a patriarchal tradition is challenged. It is in the insolence and intensity of the challenge posed against constituted power (whatever its form or mode), and its associated way of life, that activism is located, and not necessarily on the barricades or protest marches.[24]

We see that here a case is made for the minor, or for the micro-political: the small-scale that is generated out of a very specific, concrete situation in which people find themselves, as Engelberg found herself in a life with breast cancer. It makes the case for the incoherent and the spontaneous; the minor choices and performances; the local resistances. These are the various, dispersed micro-powers produced out of the encounter of bodies, ideas and things, micro-powers that concretely and intimately operate against the grain of the grand narratives. There is surely a type of activism that is militant, 'characteristic of traditional leftist politics, which base their political struggles on a yearning to change the world'.[25] But there is also an activism that is a form of escape, which is 'not concerned with changing the world, but rather would like "to produce it anew"'.[26] Svirsky argues:

> As praxis, the first mode of political activism is reactive, polemical, litigious, and engaged in incessant argumentation. As examples we can think of pressure groups for legislation change, High Court petitions, protests, persuasion campaigns, and so on. The second mode is more quiet but ontologically invasive. Examples include alternative modes of education, promoting new ways of life, rethinking narratives, investigating the conditions of oppression, and so on.[27]

Activism of the second type, according to Svirsky, is to be found in the following three interconnected practical points: 'a confrontation with a stratifying organization' (such as Engelberg's confrontation with the socially and medically regulated ways of experiencing breast cancer), 'a situational engagement' (setting out to make a comic book while in the midst of it all so as to recount, reflect and resist) and 'an inquiring attitude towards the actual' (expressed, as we will see, in the entire body of Engelberg's graphic memoir).[28]

'But what of the activist's intention?', one could ask. Is a clear declaration of one's political position not needed, an activist statement of one's objectives and purposes? Did Engelberg have, did she express this intention, this political motivation, seemingly indispensable to judging a gesture as activist or not? I would answer that this kind of thinking is rather rigid and narrow. Instead of discerning and acknowledging the situated beginnings of new rhythms, it assesses things and 'organizes itself according to predetermined definitions of value' and normative standards, thus creating borders and obstacles to activism *in thought*, that is, perceiving life in fresh ways, in terms of fluxes and constant exchanges between entities in real-life situations, as they happen in the world.[29] It is, evidently, shaped by the grand narratives that have informed modernity and its dualisms as well as furnished belief in a unitary subject, absolute truth and universal reason. It pertains to a sort of interpretation of the world that foregrounds rational logic, linearity and cause–effect relationships. It disparages the minor because 'it does not have the full force of a preexisting status, of a given structure, of a predetermined metric, to keep it alive'.[30] Svirsky, in 'Defining activism', refers to 'the psychological and social mechanisms used in political psychology to explain activism in terms of the structure of causality between the individual psyche and the action itself'.[31] He concludes:

> Instead of theorising incentives, it is better to explore by experimentation that which is already actively varying. Western normative ethics have tried to impose a democratic framework that limits and contains nomadic forms of resistance . . . But merely by creating distinctions between moral worlds, such normative ethics do nothing to further the exploration and intensification of present activist potentialities.[32]

Beginning from this theoretical framework, I will examine *Cancer Made Me a Shallower Person* as a micro-political utterance and as a work of minor literature. I argue that Engelberg's gag strips emerge as a series of activist gestures, each one of them a site of dissonance that problematizes, questions, critiques and denounces that which is felt to be wrongdoing on the part of a society's established structures and norms, and to be adding further to the already existing pain of her illness. Activism begins from a denouncement, from speaking up for your rights, and from exposing hypocrisy and injustice – '[a]lways starting as a wound of alterity within the habitual'.[33] That is precisely what Engelberg does: she opens that wound, for instance when she states that she expects some honesty regarding the experience of breast cancer (in the example given above), or when she asks not to be accused of being responsible for her condition, and not to be forced to perform the role of the ill in any of the socially prescribed ways (in more examples that follow). This is not the activism of large gatherings on squares or of chaining oneself in public spaces. This is the activism of a seriously ill woman, struggling with a potentially fatal disease and with almost unbearable treatment in a social and cultural context that exacerbates her suffering. It is the activism of a specific woman who took 30 minutes every day to report from her own front of resistance, until the end.

The dignity to fail and to differ

Emily Waples, in her excellent analysis 'Avatars, illness, and authority: Embodied experience in breast cancer autopathographics', compares Miriam Engelberg's memoir with Marisa Acocella Marchetto's *Cancer Vixen: A true story*. In a section titled 'Cancer vixen: Cosmetics, prosthetics, and (self-)awareness', Waples demonstrates that Marchetto's book falls into the category of conventional cancer narratives, in contrast, as she goes on to establish, to *Cancer Made Me a Shallower Person*. *Cancer Vixen* manifests not only a determined-to-survive attitude interwoven with the disposition to relate all this through a catchy, made-for-a-popular-film kind of narrative (indeed, this story is being made into a film), but also Marchetto's unwavering commitment to do so while looking her best. The very first sentence is already indicative of the tone and position of the book: 'What happens when a shoe-crazy, lipstick-obsessed, wine-swilling, pasta-slurping, fashion-fanatic, single-forever, about-to-get-married big-city girl cartoonist (me, Marisa Acocella) with a fabulous life finds: A LUMP IN HER BREAST?!? She kicks its ass, of course – and does so in killer five-inch heels.'[34] Waples remarks:

> Marchetto seems to gesture toward a vague postfeminist girl-power ideology of self-empowerment: a backlash against so-called second-wave feminism. Indeed, postmillennial breast cancer narratives like Geralyn Lucas's *Why I Wore Lipstick to My Mastectomy* abound with feel-good triumphalism, resulting in the compulsory repetition of a heteronormative paradigm, most often as the result of cosmetic modification.[35]

My own reaction to this could not be phrased any better than Audre Lorde's first sentence in *The Cancer Journals*: 'Each woman responds to the crisis that breast cancer brings to her life out of a whole pattern, which is the design of who she is and how her life has been lived.'[36]

The main reason why *Cancer Made Me a Shallower Person* stands out among other works of its genre is that it is in movement. By this, I mean the different position Engelberg takes regarding her illness and what she feels is expected of her, in view of this new life situation she has found herself in. The movement I speak of is an outward one. It keeps her out of fixed scenarios prescribing how a woman who fights breast cancer does this, for example, in all her heavily accessorized femininity (see: *Cancer Vixen*). It also keeps her out of the club of the noble, and the turned-spiritual, and the appreciative-of-the-grandeur-of-life. It takes her, instead, to areas of variation, perhaps darker ones, but those where one can choose not to 'think positive' and not to follow the popular-culture recipes on 'how to cope with cancer'.[37] Her work is in movement because *ethically* she did not identify with any ready-made options at any given point but was constantly looking for her own way. Her refusal to comply with the norm is a political act of resistance, an instance of micro-politics and an activist gesture of minoritarian becoming.

Engelberg, in *Cancer Made Me a Shallower Person*, declares that she does not want to be transformed by her breast cancer, and certainly not in any popular-culture way. She adamantly refuses to be a positive thinker, to be hopeful and optimistic, or to be a fighter and put on a brave face. In the same spirit as 'the failures and losers, the grouchy, irritable whiners who do not want to "have a nice day" and who do not believe that getting cancer has made them better people', she emerges as an utterly non-heroic figure, negative, discouraged and depressed, who will not 'gain a deeper insight' from this experience, or have an epiphany of sorts, and come up with something profound about human existence.[38] Again, in keeping with the argument of Quentin Crisp, who claimed that failure can be a style or a way of life, Engelberg suggests in her introduction that 'maybe the path of shallowness deserves more attention'.[39]

Halberstam, in his *The Queer Art of Failure* (2011), critiques a culture that holds success as its utmost ideal and that regards positive thinking and making the 'right' choices – an exclusive responsibility of the individual – as a solution even to breast cancer.[40] In Engelberg's comic, there are several instances of the depiction of such cultural attitudes expressed by her friends and acquaintances, such as the gag strip with the pertinent title 'Judgement'. There we see Engelberg held accountable for the amount of sugar she consumes and interrogated as to whether she exercises – queries always introduced by the clarifying remark that there is no judgement or blame intended by her inquisitors. Engelberg's irony shows how ludicrous such beliefs and indirect accusations are, as she goes on to confirm that women with breast cancer are known, after all, for their risky lifestyles and reckless choices – buying non-organic food because it is cheaper, having a glass of wine with dinner every day, and deciding to skip the symphony (despite the scientific research that has revealed that attending cultural events decreases the risk of getting breast cancer!) and stay at home to eat conventionally grown strawberries. Women who get breast cancer, Engelberg concludes, will just not listen to the good advice of well-meaning friends and acquaintances, will stubbornly refuse to go on a raw-foods diet (that made someone's friend's cousin's aunt's cancer disappear) and, bent on self-destruction as they are, will not follow a set of simple commandments – which turns out not to be simple at all. Such reactions are induced by fear and by people's need to believe that if they do all the right things, they will be okay. Thus, they will not begin to think that it should be environmental causes and political choices that create carcinogenic alternatives and oftentimes do not leave much other choice. Instead of searching for liability where it is due, they will point the finger at that cancer patient in their social circle who did not do the right things, or – there is really no blame on their part here *and* they can still enjoy that sought-after feeling of security – it was in the genes, as we see in the gag strip 'Family History'.

Against this neoliberal background, where each individual is expected to rely on herself and take full responsibility for her success and happiness, unless she is simply unlucky and doom is written in the stars or in her genetic code, Halberstam explores how failure can be a surprisingly creative alternative. He, quite intriguingly, presents the reader with three concrete things that failure can do for her. Firstly, it can help her 'escape the punishing norms that discipline behavior and manage human development' – therefore, she wouldn't have to smile through chemo and claim to feel that a horrifying, debilitating and oftentimes fatal disease has actually been a gift.[41] Secondly, it 'preserves some of the wondrous anarchy of childhood and disturbs the supposedly clean boundaries between adults and children, winners and losers'[42] – allowing her to reject all the grown-up practices of dealing with cancer such as support groups (which often make her even more depressed because everyone is so courageous), or taking up journaling/meditation/some other spiritual practice (because she does not feel the slightest interest), or being obliged to start appreciating the smallest moments of life in the fullest (because she never did, and she was never enchanted by life). Instead, failure enables her to just sit back and do the TV guide crossword puzzles, which she happens to find quite fun and engrossing, when nothing else works to distract her after she has received the diagnosis, and when, after a short dilemma between the crossword puzzles and more serious activities that would fit the occasion, she decides in favour of the puzzles and wisely concludes that, anyway, 'so much of life is really about filling up time'.[43] Finally, failure helps one use 'disappointment, disillusionment, and despair . . . to poke holes in the toxic positivity of contemporary life'[44] – which, through both image and text, is precisely what Engelberg does.

When Halberstam suggests failure as a powerful option of resistance to normative behaviours that inhibit and negate imagining 'other goals for life, for love, for art, and for being', he is, in fact, advocating a minoritarian twist that queers the stultifying patterns of the dominant majority.[45] He, effectively, launches failure, a concept in which Engelberg's graphic memoir is steeped, as a micro-political move of activism and, by means of low theory, he tries 'to locate all the in-between spaces that save us from being snared by the hooks of hegemony', even if these 'alternatives dwell in the murky waters of a counterintuitive, often impossibly dark and negative realm of critique and refusal'.[46]

Writing in a minor key

It is interesting at this point to look again at the comparison between Engelberg's graphic memoir and the conventional, heteronormative narrative by Marchetto. Waples draws our attention to what Marchetto's avatar looks like on the book's cover: 'blonde and Barbie-thin, mid-karate kick in Christian Louboutin stilettos'.[47] Introducing the book, Waples writes that 'a New York City socialite and self-proclaimed "fabulista," tells the story of her disease from diagnosis to recovery, emphasizing cancer's cosmetic challenges'.[48] In terms of depicting bodily change, however, and despite these challenges, Marchetto (notably, a trained cartoonist) does not seem to have been very inclined to have a go:

> What might seem striking about Marchetto's avatar in *Cancer Vixen*, then, is how little it changes during the course of her disease . . . If the postmodern body can be understood to be what Susan Bordo calls 'cultural plastic' – a term that responds, she explains, to the fantasy of 'defying the historicity, the mortality, and, indeed the very materiality of the body' – then the *avatar* might be understood,

for Marchetto, as a kind of imaginative dissociation from historicity, mortality, and materiality.[49]

Such an approach to the bodily self corresponds to Marchetto's approach to the telling of the story, and consequently to her understanding of and giving a shape to this experience. In parallel to the way in which the *Cancer Vixen* story follows a formula (ultra-feminine, appearance-obsessed, heterosexual, upper-class woman 'with a fabulous life' meets and beats breast cancer), the body of the character sticks to the formula as well. Both story and body adhere to specific standards (of normalcy, femininity) from which they do not depart at any point in the narrative. This is not at all what happens in the case of Engelberg (either on the level of the story or that of bodily representation), who, in the course of her counter-narrative, shares with the reader all the physical changes that she underwent as a result of her cancer treatment (such as losing her hair and gaining weight). Defying the historicity, mortality and materiality of the body is clearly not Engelberg's intention or style.

Engelberg was not a trained cartoonist, and her drawings are mostly asymmetrical and out of proportion. In addition to this, from one frame to the next the reader comes across a slightly different Miriam, certainly with some basic features unaltered to ensure recognition of the character, such as her glasses and her curls, but at the same time changing, with all of her or parts of her becoming bigger or smaller, more angular or more round, more conspicuous or more indistinct, and always inhabiting the frames as a very schematic creature with no muscles – a creature who is anatomically wrong. And yet, all these different Miriams, with their irregularities, their pluralities, their transitory nature, all emerging as she goes through the horrifying diagnosis and the debilitating treatment, seem to be all the more vulnerable and expressive and receptive and emotionally affective, and, precisely for that reason, emotionally right and truthful. The self, this way, emerges as minoritarian and nomadic and, indeed, reminiscent of the concept of 'difference-in-itself', which is not a difference between two or more things or states – it is not, then, a difference as we conventionally think of it, between a and b.[50] Instead of imagining difference as the opposite of sameness or as something that interrupts identity, 'difference must be thought of as the continual movement of self-differing, like the continual variation of a sound rising and lowering in pitch without stopping at notes in a scale. In other words, difference is continuous variation.'[51]

Engelberg's perspective on and employment of the body is opposed to ideas of stability, continuity and linearity. Her work provides a space where the self might be imagined differently, as a visually dynamic, morphing entity constantly responding to social, material and technological environments and modifying itself through its interaction with these environments and with other emotional beings. All the smaller or bigger inconsistencies in the representation of the character from one frame to the next, attributed to the artist's weakness of technical skill, question the notion of a unitary and stable self;[52] they put forward an alternative way of perceiving embodied and emotional existence – as always mutating, morphing and re-inscribing itself in its exposure to and intermingling with different affective assemblages. Such a notion of the self as the one that can be communicated through a comic book's frames and through all these micro-incongruities and deviations can be creative and productive. It hints at an existence that ventures beyond the confining lines, the 'striations' that define, oftentimes in quite a rigid way, people's presence within the different social frames of the world.[53] By creating images and notions of the self as non-static, and by making a malleable and pliable thing out of the lines that give a specific shape to existence, Engelberg performs an activist move against the entrenched and the segmented and gives us an account of the self in novel terms.

Based on the features of Engelberg's memoir that I have presented so far (its negativity, its refusal to conform to majoritarian discourses, its resistance to social pressures, its dissonance), I would now like to examine it as an instance of minor literature, a work of literature that encourages and performs minoritarian becomings. Deleuze and Guattari, in their book on Kafka, define three main characteristics of minor literatures. Firstly, language becomes deterritorialized, dislocated and displaced; it is removed from its homeland or what is taken to be its natural lodgings.[54] Secondly, 'everything (in a minor literature) is political', because 'its cramped space forces each individual intrigue to connect immediately to politics'.[55] Thirdly, 'everything takes on a collective value', since 'what each author says individually already constitutes a common action, and what he or she says or does is necessarily political, even if others aren't in agreement'.[56]

Major literature begins from an already given content and proceeds to put that content in a suitable literary form, that is, it starts from something already known to present it through, or invest it with, aesthetic means. It is about the representation of lived experience – it is a type of literature that speaks of what exists out there in our cultural and social world as we know it and, in that sense, it reproduces this world. The author puts herself on the side of language as it is and as it is habitually used to convey thoughts and desires to which readers are accustomed as well. In short, it is about the familiar and about communicating the familiar in familiar terms. For example, in the case of illness stories, one needs to talk about those times when, while feeling lost or in agonizing pain, she stuttered or screamed; one needs to find a reason for all the suffering; and one needs to learn how to be a better person, or what the gain out of all this hardship can be. A minor literature author, meanwhile, instead of describing stuttering or screaming, makes the language itself stutter and scream (the way Kafka or Beckett did); instead of searching for the comfort of a certain meaning and for the reassurance of becoming 'better', she shuns what is socially expected of her, as is the case with Engelberg. Instead of starting from a pre-given content, she starts from an overwhelming encounter or an encounter with something affective (such as Burrough's encounter with drugs, or Kerouac's with travel; or, indeed, Engelberg's encounter with breast cancer). The author, in creating minor literature, does not reproduce common knowledge or habitual ways of thinking; she does not represent and does not repeat what is already there. On the contrary – and, effectively, in an activist way – she challenges and upsets not only notions of how things are supposed to work or be thought of or written about, but language and expression itself.

Becoming minoritarian, and therefore constituting an activist micro-political move, is a process that develops and unfolds between the *ethical* and a certain kind of the *aesthetic*. And that, in our case, would be the use Engelberg makes of the specific aesthetics and the structural expressive affordances that become possible in the genre of the graphic novel. On this, I will give an example from Engelberg's graphic memoir. In a gag strip entitled 'The Undead', when she comes across an acquaintance who is quite surprised to see that she is still alive, she feels herself to have metamorphosed socially – in the eyes of this person – from a normal human being shopping at the grocery store into a zombie-like creature, something inbetween the living and the dead, something abject, abortive and monstrous. By that time, Engelberg had already had surgery, chemotherapy and radiation, she had lost her hair, and in general, she had been living with breast cancer for quite some time. When this acquaintance is so surprised to see her still around, her reaction is not to explain to us readers how this made her feel, particularly after all the trials she has experienced, nor is it to describe her thoughts about being seen as a piece of sick and decomposing flesh which is, startlingly enough, not quite dead yet. She could have done that, but she doesn't. Instead, she uses the vocabulary of comics to give another type of response. In what I consider one of the best frames of the book, she writes, 'when suddenly I became The Undead', and draws herself under this caption as a zombie figure with a deformed face, melting and falling apart, eyes popping out of their sockets, drooling, her curls rigid and unbending, as if she has been electrocuted, her fingers extended and stiff. To the right of this drawing, two words stand for sounds, as often happens in comics: 'glug', 'gurgle'. These two sounds and the drawing are Engelberg's reaction to a culture that turns cancer into a metaphor inspiring horror and disgust for the diseased body, rotting from the inside.[57] By showing herself to be transforming – in a frame that transports us from the real to the imaginary – into a zombie making zombie-like sounds, she makes her chosen language, that is, comics, 'stutter and scream' in a way that is simultaneously satirical, caustic and highly emotive. Her gesture constitutes a powerful critique that not only works much more effectively than if she had chosen to explain, panel after panel, in a conventional narrative manner her position, but also functions as a surprise tactic strategically performing a twist on a power level. For Engelberg turns her body into a mirror and confronts this cancer-dreading culture with the very zombie image that is projected onto her. So far as textual narrative goes, it is 'glug' and 'gurgle', but in its directness and compactness, together with the drawing, Engelberg's choice works far better than pages and pages of explanatory text.

The fact that comics make use of both language and images means they constitute a compellingly hybrid genre whereby the intermixing of these two different registers enables an intermedial mode of communication, one that is 'rich in possibilities for complexity, irony, and genre disruption'.[58] Once language and images are put together, they are both transformed as they participate in the process of the comic book.[59] Language becomes deterritorialized, imagined and employed differently, taken to different territories, connecting to different things, as we have seen in Deleuze and Guattari's analysis of minor literature.[60] Language and images, in their becoming-a-comic-book, turn into writing and drawing and manifest a new kind of materiality, since many times the drawings present themselves as words, and written text performs as image. In a sense, then, the uses of each form of communication (visual and verbal) are renegotiated and re-imagined. This takes place in ways that dislocate and deterritorialize their properties while assigning new creative tasks to them, granting them novel potentials and enhancing (as in Engelberg's memoir) the potential for an ethics of resistance, in a blurred, material, warm space that melts abstraction and concreteness into new expressive forms. On these points, I will give two examples.

Under the heading 'Everything is My Enemy', Engelberg presents the reader with a page-long frame where she enumerates all the bigger or smaller everyday carcinogenic sources (or those that she thinks of as carcinogenic, with her usual dose of satire), such as the hole in the ozone, pesticides in the park, having too much cheese or eating hot dogs when she was a kid. A lot of the text in that frame, though, escapes the confines of the conventional text bubbles to mix with the drawings and to engage, to interact with them in a freer relationship. This serves two purposes: firstly, it conveys Engelberg's generalized and oppressive feeling of being threatened and made vulnerable in a world where innocent-looking, everyday, functional objects that felt like home have now turned into something unheimlich/uncanny, something that can make her sick or kill her (her water filter, her coated cookware). Secondly, it demonstrates how thoughts of cancer have spread all over her habitual micro-interactions with objects and things (the material world), and how they have become attached to these things, like rapidly multiplying weeds that are now suffocating her environment and all that used to be familiar in it. This text, then, is not only part of the frame as language, but it functions *as image* because the way it is positioned, the way it is employed actually draws (depicts) Engelberg's anxiety and fear as these emotions now lie beside, pop out of or hover over the drawings of things that used to be trusted or, at least, not consciously thought of as enemies.

Another instance of text functioning as image is the following: in the gag strip 'The Disposition of Doctors', after her radiologist tells her that the size of her tumour seems to be about two centimetres 'but it could be larger', she finds herself returning to the waiting room in a panic. In this particular frame, we see Miriam with tears rolling down her cheeks while over her head, in the shape of a halo, the words of the radiologist seem to reverberate in a sinister triple repetition, 'it could be larger . . . it could be larger . . . it could be larger . . .', like dark and ominous vibrations – like a black cloud or evil spell that shrouds her and holds her captive under its terrible power. These written words in that frame are text, sure enough, but far from being *only* text they are part of the frame *as image* since they are employed in such a way that they communicate Miriam's emotional state, her agony, in a pictorial manner, just as much as her tearful face does.

The qualities that are given by Deleuze and Guattari as characteristic of minor literature (the deterritorialization of language, the connection of the individual to the political, collective value) are manifest in *Cancer Made Me a Shallower Person*, from beginning to end. Engelberg's book is a personal story of resistance that speaks to the reader in a minor key, opening up a space for negation, unruliness and revolt. It allows for and acknowledges the validity and authenticity of what is regarded as superficial or shallow in the context of a culture that seems to value ready-made patterns of human experience that emerge, in comparison, as deeper or more profound. To follow the patterns is to try to see what has gone wrong with your choices and fix it. It goes hand in hand with the mentality of self-help, self-improvement, self-discipline – the idea of the individual that reconciles, says yes to life, can see the grand (major) picture and, learning along the way, win the battle and save herself. To follow Engelberg's way is to be able to see through the political oppression of normative discourses that are based on the false and punishing concept of individual responsibility and that distribute socially accepted roles for people to play. It is to have the grit to fail, to be minor, childlike, stubborn, unwilling to conform and do the 'right' thing. It is, finally, to speak up for your rights and against the injustice to which you are subjected. It is to expose the dishonesty and mock it; it is to say no.

Acknowledgements

The research for this publication was supported by the Estonian Research Council (Grant 1481) and by the European Regional Development Fund (Center of Excellence in Estonian Studies). This research was also supported by the Foundation for Education and European Culture.

Notes

1. Donovan, 'Representations of health, embodiment and experience in graphic memoir'; El Refaie, *Visual Metaphor and Embodiment in Graphic Illness Narratives*; Squier, 'Literature and medicine, future tense'.
2. Czerwiec et al., *Graphic Medicine Manifesto*.
3. Squier, 'Literature and medicine, future tense', 131 (emphasis in original).
4. Czerwiec et al., *Graphic Medicine Manifesto*, 2.
5. Venkatesan, 'Graphic medicine manifesto', 93.
6. Charon and Montello, *Stories Matter*; Charon, *Narrative Medicine*.
7. Chute, *Graphic Women*; Waples, 'Emplotted bodies' and 'Avatars, illness, and authority'; DeShazer, *Fractured Bodies*; Sundaram, 'Graphic bodies'; DasGupta and Hurst, *Stories of Illness and Healing*.
8. Chute, *Graphic Women*, 2.
9. Williams, 'Comics and the iconography of illness', 118.
10. Szép, *Comics and the Body*, 3.
11. Szép, *Comics and the Body*, 7, 5.
12. Szép, *Comics and the Body*, 8, 9.
13. Butler, *Precarious Life*, 44, cited in Szép, *Comics and the Body*, 13.
14. Szép, *Comics and the Body*, 9.
15. Engelberg, *Cancer Made Me a Shallower Person*, xiii.
16. Engelberg, *Cancer Made Me a Shallower Person*: gag strip 'Something Unpleasant and You'.
17. Waples, 'Avatars, illness, and authority'; Stoddard Holmes, 'Cancer comics'; DeShazer, *Mammographies*.

18. Waples, 'Avatars, illness, and authority', 180.
19. Stoddard Holmes, 'Cancer comics', 158.
20. DeShazer, *Mammographies*, 92–118.
21. Manning, *The Minor Gesture*.
22. Manning, *The Minor Gesture*, 1 (emphasis added).
23. Svirsky, 'Defining activism', 163 (emphasis added).
24. Svirsky, 'Defining activism', 169.
25. Svirsky, 'Defining activism', 170.
26. Svirsky, 'Defining activism', 170. See also, earlier in this introduction, Ian Williams's comment on the world-building power of comics.
27. Svirsky, 'Defining activism', 171.
28. Svirsky, 'Defining activism', 165.
29. Manning, *The Minor Gesture*, 1.
30. Manning, *The Minor Gesture*, 2.
31. Svirsky, 'Defining activism', 166.
32. Svirsky, 'Defining activism', 166–7.
33. Svirsky, 'Defining activism', 167.
34. Marchetto, *Cancer Vixen*, 1.
35. Waples, 'Avatars, illness, and authority', 166.
36. Lorde, *The Cancer Journals*, 9.
37. See, for example, Kris Carr, *Crazy Sexy Cancer Tips*: 'more than just a memoir, it's a collection of facts, hints, hell-yeahs, how-tos, and know-hows for all you glorious Cancer Babes out there' (Carr, *Crazy Sexy Cancer Tips*, 16, as cited in Waples, 'Emplotted bodies', 51).
38. Halberstam, *The Queer Art of Failure*, 4.
39. On Quentin Crisp, see Halberstam, *The Queer Art of Failure*, 3; Engelberg, *Cancer Made Me a Shallower Person*, xiii.
40. Ehrenreich, *Bright-Sided*, cited in Halberstam, *The Queer Art of Failure*.
41. Halberstam, *The Queer Art of Failure*, 3.
42. Halberstam, *The Queer Art of Failure*, 3.
43. Engelberg, *Cancer Made Me a Shallower Person*: gag strip 'Crosswords'.
44. Engelberg, *Cancer Made Me a Shallower Person*: gag strip 'Crosswords'.
45. Halberstam, *The Queer Art of Failure*, 88.
46. Halberstam, *The Queer Art of Failure*, 2.
47. Waples, 'Avatars, illness, and authority', 166.
48. Waples, 'Avatars, illness, and authority', 158.
49. Waples, 'Avatars, illness, and authority', 169.
50. See Deleuze, *Difference and Repetition*.
51. Roffe, 'Variation', 299–300.
52. Stoddard Holmes, 'Cancer comics'.
53. Deleuze and Guattari, *Dialogues*.
54. Deleuze and Guattari, *Kafka*, 17.
55. Deleuze and Guattari, *Kafka*, 17.
56. Deleuze and Guattari, *Kafka*, 17.
57. Sontag, *Illness as Metaphor*.
58. Stoddard Holmes, 'Cancer comics', 148.
59. See Kukkonen, 'Comics as a test case for transmedial narratology'; McCloud, *Understanding Comics*.
60. This is not to say that all works from the genre of comics are works of minor literature, but only that there is a strong potential in this specific genre for the creation of such a literature.

Bibliography

Butler, Judith. *Precarious Life: The powers of mourning and violence*. London: Verso, 2006.
Carr, Kris. *Crazy Sexy Cancer Tips*. Guilford: Globe Pequot, 2007.
Charon, Rita. *Narrative Medicine: Honoring the stories of illness*. New York: Oxford University Press, 2006.

Charon, Rita, and Martha Montello. *Stories Matter: The role of narrative in medical ethics*. New York: Routledge, 2002.
Chute, Hillary. 'Comics as literature? Reading graphic narrative'. *PMLA* 123, no. 2 (2008): 452–65.
Chute, Hillary. *Graphic Women: Life narrative and contemporary comics*. New York: Columbia University Press, 2010.
Czerwiec, M. K. et al. *Graphic Medicine Manifesto*. University Park, PA: Penn State University Press, 2015.
DasGupta, Sayantani, and Marsha Hurst, eds. *Stories of Illness and Healing: Women write their bodies*. Kent, OH: Kent State University Press, 2007.
Deleuze, Gilles. *Difference and Repetition*, translated by Paul Patton. London: Athlone, 1994.
Deleuze, Gilles, and Félix Guattari. *Dialogues*, translated by Hugh Tomlinson and Barbara Habberjam. New York: Columbia University Press, 1987.
Deleuze, Gilles, and Félix Guattari. *Kafka: Toward a minor literature*, translated by Dana Polan. Minneapolis: University of Minnesota Press, 2006.
DeShazer, Mary K. *Fractured Bodies: Reading women's cancer literature*. Ann Arbor: University of Michigan Press, 2005.
DeShazer, Mary K. *Mammographies: The cultural discourses of breast cancer narratives*. Ann Arbor: University of Michigan Press, 2013.
Donovan, Courtney. 'Representations of health, embodiment and experience in graphic memoir'. *Configurations* 22, no. 2 (2014): 237–53.
Ehrenreich, Barbara. *Bright-Sided: How positive thinking is undermining America*. London: Picador, 2010.
El Refaie, Elisabeth. *Visual Metaphor and Embodiment in Graphic Illness Narratives*. New York: Oxford University Press, 2019.
Engelberg, Miriam. *Cancer Made Me a Shallower Person: A memoir in comics*. New York: HarperCollins, 2006.
Halberstam, Jack. *The Queer Art of Failure*. Durham, NC: Duke University Press, 2011.
Kukkonen, Karin. 'Comics as a test case for transmedial narratology'. *SubStance* 40, no. 1 (2011): 34–52.
Lorde, Audre. *The Cancer Journals*. San Francisco: Aunt Lute Books, 1997.
Manning, Erin. *The Minor Gesture*. Durham, NC: Duke University Press, 2016.
Marchetto, Marisa Acocella. *Cancer Vixen: A true story*. New York: Alfred A. Knopf, 2006.
McCloud, Scott. *Understanding Comics: The invisible art*. New York: HarperCollins, 1993.
Roffe, Jonathan. 'Variation'. In *The Deleuze Dictionary: Revised edition*, edited by Adrian Parr, 299–300. Edinburgh: Edinburgh University Press, 2010.
Sontag, Susan. *Illness as Metaphor*. Harmondsworth: Penguin, 1983.
Squier, Susan Merrill. 'Literature and medicine, future tense: Making it graphic'. *Literature and Medicine* 27, no. 2 (2008): 124–52.
Stoddard Holmes, Martha. 'Cancer comics: Narrating cancer through sequential art'. *Tulsa Studies in Women's Literature* 32, no. 2 (2013)/33, no. 1 (2014): 147–62.
Sundaram, Neeraja. 'Graphic bodies: Picturing feminised pathology, narrating resistance'. *Indian Journal of Gender Studies* 24, no. 2 (2017): 236–65.
Svirsky, Marcelo. 'Defining activism'. *Deleuze Studies* 4, no. suppl.1 (2010): 163–82.
Szép, Eszter. *Comics and the Body: Drawing, reading, and vulnerability*. Columbus: Ohio State University Press, 2020.
Venkatesan, Sathyaraj. 'Graphic medicine manifesto'. *Journal of Graphic Novels and Comics* 7, no. 1 (2015): 93–4.
Waples, Emily. 'Avatars, illness, and authority: Embodied experience in breast cancer autopathographics'. *Configurations* 22, no. 2 (2014): 153–81.
Waples, Emily. 'Emplotted bodies: Breast cancer, feminism and the future'. *Tulsa Studies in Women's Literature* 33, no. 1 (2013): 47–70.
Williams, Ian. 'Comics and the iconography of illness'. In M. K. Czerwiec et al., *Graphic Medicine Manifesto*, 115–42. University Park, PA: Penn State University Press, 2015.

10
The cryptographic narrative in video games: the player as detective
Ana Paklons and An-Sofie Tratsaert

Cryptography within literature has a rich and varied history, from Julius Caesar's encrypted letters to his generals, to Poe's creation of the modern detective story. The power of secrecy to elicit interest and form communities makes it a popular trope in contemporary television series and novels. In recent years, there has been a marked rise of this type of narrative in video games, especially in the field of indie survival horror games, that is, video games produced by small gaming companies without the financial support of large publishers, and which focus on the survival of the main protagonist, who usually has to face supernatural enemies in a horror-like setting. These games combine a clearly defined main narrative that the player needs to play all the way through, with a supporting, parallel narrative that is hidden and need not be uncovered to finish the game successfully or to understand the game world. This type of narrative is often called the 'hidden lore' by fans of the games, with reference to the concept of 'lore', meaning the game's backstory, popular in narrative-driven games. All the elements of the hidden lore complement the principal narrative but are not essential to it; rather, these details add depth and richness to the universe of a video game, expanding its history beyond the main plot. The details of the hidden lore are not easily accessible – the player needs to work to uncover them – and developers rarely comment on them. As a result, vast online communities of players work together to uncover these hidden narratives, increasing the games' popularity. In this chapter, we will define the structure and function of this parallel narrative, or cryptographic narrative as we will call it, and venture an explanation for its apparent success.

Narrative cryptography

Poe's fascination with cryptography led him to create the modern detective story, which follows a character who has to uncover a specific mystery based on hints given throughout the text. The reader can follow this mystery starting from its discovery to its eventual solution. According to Rosenheim, the detective story begins by extending modes of cryptographic reading to the phenomenal world.[1] The private eye applies the same analytical tools used to break a code to their own sensory experience, extending the use of these procedures from the two-dimensional page to the three-dimensional world. To be effective, however, this semiotic technique requires that the unbroken synaesthetic stream of sensory perception that ordinarily floods the self is reduced and simplified, so that the detective can establish the particular causal relationships holding between events. As in a deciphered code, the syntax of narrative puts all the formerly mysterious elements into a meaningful relation, which mirrors the supposed existence of real 'syntactic' lines of causality in the world. Narrative thus provides the structure in which all the disparate plot elements make sense and allows us to assume that this structure is repeated in reality. This system reduces the plot elements to nodes of meaning, which the detective needs to uncover to understand the mystery. Applying this narrative structure to the interactive medium of video games allows the player to become the detective and to bring together all the disparate plot points, hidden as narrative codes throughout the gameplay and game world, while creating her own meaningful narrative.

For Umberto Eco, meaning within writing exists at what he called the level of 'codes', where a content plane is correlated with a plane of expression.[2] According to Eco, language is a reproducible system of signs in which the signifier and the signified are related through the sign function. Sign functions are arbitrary, without necessary reference to facts. According to James Connor, these sign functions can therefore be equated to cultural conventions and become the carriers by which we speak, write or programme our computers.[3] In this way, signs are interconnected by the cultural concepts through which we read them. In his work on passwords, Brian Lennon brings these ideas into the modern world of cryptography and cryptophilology, the study and analysis of cryptographic techniques in which text is treated as cipher.[4] Lennon combines Eco's ideas on semiotics with the work of Jean Baudrillard on symbolic exchange, according to which symbolic exchange is the exchange of signs with the real (as opposed to simulation, which is the exchange of signs with signs). Baudrillard treats the symbolic as an 'outside' to representation, the code, value, production, the law, master-signification and the unconscious.[5] In this way, Lennon provides the necessary link between cryptography and its semiotic background. Following the logic set out above, the clues within a cryptographic text are signs that through symbolic exchange only derive their meaning through a necessary link with the cultural reality of which they are a part; however, these links are intentionally severed or made unclear. As a result, the cryptographic text can be regarded as a narrative in which the plot is derived via a cryptographic reading of its disparate plot points, a detective story if you will, which in turn plays with these necessary links to a shared cultural reality to obscure the correct meaning and reading of the text. We can place the creation of the cryptographic narrative within video games in this context. Cryptography is about making texts unreadable, by severing the relation between the sign and the cultural conventions by which it is understood, which from the point of view of the narrative can be understood as the dissolution of the bonds between the plot elements and their meaning. This creates an opening for the player to constitute their own narrative and to endow the information with their own value. In so doing, the cryptographic narrative is (co-)created with minimal to no guidance from the creator of the video game.

This dissolution of meaning also occurs in relation to our concepts of the detective and the victim, as described by Stefano Tani in his definition of the anti-detective novel, which he argues is a postmodernist mutation of the classic detective novel. It sets itself apart by its lack of centre, its refusal to posit a unifying system.[6] It frustrates the expectations of the reader/player and substitutes the detective as the central and ordering character with the chaotic admission of mystery, of non-solution.[7] The metaphysical detective narrative is a subset of this genre that parodies or subverts the traditional detective story conventions to transcend the mere machinations of the mystery plot and is often self-reflexive.[8] A puzzle-like relation is created between the text and the reader, where the reader has to make sense of the essentially 'unfinished writing'.[9] Because no solution is granted by the developer/writer for the cryptographic narrative, the existence of the mystery is not even acknowledged; it is up to the reader/player to create herself in the role of detective, even when this is not the role originally given to her. This puts the reader/player in a vulnerable position, since the writer/developer will not hold her hand to reach any conclusions concerning plot or narrative.

This concept of the cryptographic narrative has been adopted by some indie horror games, most notably our case study, *Five Nights at Freddy's* (*FNaF*), a video game that became popular in the indie game community through its use of hidden lore. The idea behind including this type of narrative in the gaming experience is that it leads to a hidden story which is not evident in the narrative first suggested to the player, thus creating a mystery to be solved. Furthermore, this narrative is superfluous in the sense that it is not needed for the player's understanding of the game world. Because it is not needed to play the game successfully, the creators of such games have left an opening for the player audience to provide their own meaning to the clues and cues (cryptographic codes) that are given. This superfluousness stimulates the creation of communities that distinguish the 'in' crowd, who are on to these narratives, from those who are not.

Structure of cryptographic narrative within video games

Schubert and Jenkins describe the specific narrative forms that are frequently used by game designers to shape the story within a video game.[10] The cryptographic narrative specifically seems to use narrative forms reminiscent of those used in detective novels and other novels focused on uncovering secrets. In many video games, the cryptographic narrative seems to be possible only when the narrative as a whole functions as a backdrop.[11] Among video games that have narrative content, we can make a distinction between those games where the story is only secondary to gameplay and those where it is essential. Among video games where the story is not the most important element of the game, there are those that only have a minimal level of storytelling and those with a more evolved and deeper story, even though it is not necessary to know this to play the game. An example of a game with such elaborate background information is the multiplayer online game *Shadowbane*. The complete lore and every aspect of this fantasy world is explained on the website, but very little about it can be found in the game itself. In these kinds of games the narrative serves as a backdrop for the gameplay and does not form an integral part of it. The backdrops are usually meant to give the game some grounding but are not essential when playing, compared with completely story-driven gameplay, where the backdrop is essential.

The cryptographic narrative always functions as an embedded narrative. It tells two stories at the same time, intermittently, leaving it up to the audience to bring them together again. The audience must use detection, exploration, decryption and speculation to bring the story to a sensible whole. In the case of the detective story, the story of solving the case and the story of the crime being committed may be told intermittently.

The case-solving story is usually told chronologically and the story of the crime is told anachronologically, by finding clues. At the end, the detective puts the story back in the right order. In the case of the cryptographic narrative, the first story is told chronologically throughout the game, while the second story is hidden inside the game in the form of clues, as a secret narrative. Because video games provide an extra layer of interactivity, they usually allow the player to interact with the game environment and let her actively search for these clues. In order for the player to notice these clues, a game designer normally develops a variety of kludges to prompt the player to narrative salient places. The space of the game becomes an information space or a memory palace.[12] However, the cryptographic narrative does not provide these kludges. The game developers do not make distinctions between the elements that are important to the narrative and those that are not. This leaves the player vulnerable, as the developers do not provide a guideline to reach the plot points or conclusions they envision. These characteristics make the embedded narrative an essential building block of the cryptographic narrative, since this type of narrative is always told non-linearly and is specifically designed to appeal to an audience of players who like to actively search for clues to put the story together in the right order.

The separate elements of the cryptographic narrative, the clues and cues hidden as narrative code throughout the game, are often presented to the player in the form of a micro-narrative. Within video games this can take the form of a cut scene, a conversation between non-playable characters (NPCs), reactions from NPCs to some actions or even just a note that can be found in the game containing some narrative information. A micro-narrative is a narrative that enters the game at the level of a localized incident and is needed to shape the emotional experience of the player. A clear example of a micro-narrative in games can be found in *BioShock*. In this game the player can hear the splicers – people whose genetic structure is altered and who have lost their sanity as a result – talking to each other or mumbling to themselves. What they say gives the player more information about what is going on around them and what he can expect when they get further into the game. For example, at one point, the character has to find their way to the medical pavilion. The splicers then talk about Doctor Steinman and his cosmetic procedures as if they were a kind of art form. The player now knows that there is probably something wrong with the doctor, so they must proceed carefully. Micro-narratives let the player think about the information they have received, leading to questions such as 'Why has this information been given to me?' or 'Why is this relevant to the story?'.[13]

Many micro- or backdrop narratives take place within the story world of the game. This makes the environment of the game an important factor and the spatial narrative an apt vehicle for transferring narrative information, since the typically graphical nature of a video game forces the player to navigate a space to progress in the storyline. We see this especially in role playing games (RPGs), in which the spatial narrative is often found. Game designers do not just create random spaces for their games, they create narratively compelling spaces for the player to go through. Gamers will usually remember the experience of moving through the game space created by the developers more than the actual story. For a board game such as *Catan*, the story creates a form of immersion and the cards provide a context in which the player loses or wins points. Ultimately, however, it is the action of moving across the board that makes the game memorable. The same goes for RPGs such as *Aion*. The land the player travels through has a history and every quest is given in the form of a story. These little stories provide immersion in the game, but they are not necessary to enjoy playing it. The most important part is the exploration of the world. The focus of the spatial narrative lies in world-making and not so much in storytelling.[14] One of the strategies used by game developers to immerse the players in the created space is to play on the memories and expectations of the player. Horror games in particular use environmental storytelling.[15] To ensure that the player is completely immersed, game developers create a place where the player will feel uncomfortable, such as an old abandoned house or asylum. The player unconsciously links these places to horror stories. Spatial narratives can form pre-existing narratives with spaces or they can embed this narrative information inside their stage setting.

The cryptographic narrative is never overtly told. Clues are hidden throughout the playing of the game. Some game developers will even go so far as to hide these clues outside the game space. In these cases the cryptographic narrative enters the realm of the pseudo-narrative. This type will combine a normal in-game narrative with extradiegetic narrative support. In other words, the game narrative is supported by information located outside the game, for example, a background story that can be found in the manual of the game or on the official website. This kind of narrative is divided into two parts, the narrative in the game and an extradiegetic narrative support. The narrative in the game invokes the player to tell the story based on her own imagination; the extradiegetic narrative support builds on the narrative of the game and allows the player to give more meaning to the story of the game.[16]

Taking this one step further is the transmedia narrative, which can further confound the story told by the cryptographic narrative, spreading the clues not only chronologically or within the game space but over multiple sources and mediums. It also adds a dimension of seriality to the telling, only giving the information piece by piece every time a new instalment is released. The transmedia narrative is a type of narrative in which the story is told through multiple platforms and formats, not to be confused with traditional cross-platform media franchises, adaptations and sequels of a story. An example of a game using a transmedia narrative is *Halo Wars*, a first-person-shooter video game series developed first by Ensemble Studios and then by Creative Assembly. This franchise now includes novels, comic books, a live action web series, audio plays and more. Another example is *The Matrix*, where the story is told over various media platforms, such as films, games, comics and so forth, each story contributing to the whole story of *The Matrix*, each starting from a different entry point. Transmedia narratives help keep audiences interested in a franchise. When viewers receive new information and new insights in the form of a new story, their interest remains piqued and so the franchise can sustain itself through consumer loyalty. It also gives the companies behind these franchises roots in different media sectors, reaching more people. The disadvantage of the transmedia narrative is that sufficient content is needed to sustain all the different media platforms every time new content is released to offer new experiences to the public.[17]

The function of cryptographic narrative in video games

Narratives in video games are often used as tools to elicit certain reactions or responses from the player. The cryptographic narrative also has some clear characteristics that allow the player to know the function of its use within video games. To begin our analysis of these characteristics, we first must take a look at the basic storytelling elements that are necessary to play the game and understand the surroundings, and the player's character's purpose within it. These elements can be dialogue, cut scenes, game mechanics and behaviour of the NPCs. Because they are needed to shape the game and are necessary in playing the game, they are considered part of the main narrative. Their inclusion within this parameter, however, does not exclude their usefulness to the cryptographic narrative. The main narrative can thus be described as containing all the elements with which the characters of the game must interact, including all the actions that the characters perform in the game. The elements of the cryptographic narrative, by contrast, are not found in plain sight but are hidden throughout the video game. The main narrative does not acknowledge these clues and the characters within the game do not react to them in any way. They are meta-elements, in some way put outside the story world and speaking to the player directly while still being part of the game world. Trying to make sense of them within the logic of the story world would break the suspension of disbelief. These clues are usually found in the background or environment of the game, which makes us conclude that they are spatial narratives or, in some cases, micro-narratives. Considering this, the cryptographic narrative can be defined as containing any narrative element which is hidden from the player and with which the characters do not interact, and it can be found within or outside the video game.

Unlike the classic pseudo-narrative, in the cryptographic narrative these clues or narrative elements are not easily accessible. Background information that is divulged on the website of the video game in question, for instance, cannot be taken into consideration for this reason. Only when background stories or promotional images contain clues not easily discovered by a lay audience can they be considered part of the cryptographic narrative. The division between an audience that is in the know and one that is clueless is essential to the creation of this type of narrative. The player finds herself in the middle of a mystery, passively experiencing it. She fulfils the role of victim until she actively decides to take up the role of detective to find a solution in order to free herself of this pre-imposed role. This leaves the discovery of these clues up to a select few, who need to decide for themselves whether the clues they have discovered contain any information that is useful in the further construction of the cryptographic narrative. There can only be certainty about the veracity of the given clues when the creators of the game confirm or deny them, or when they confess that it was just a design choice. These clues are not the same as 'Easter eggs', which are inside jokes or messages, often referring to other cultural phenomena such as movies or other games. They may be hidden messages that the makers of the video game have left behind, but they are not part of the cryptographic narrative simply because they hold no narrative information.

Comparing the main and the cryptographic narrative, we find that the main narrative is not as important as the cryptographic one in building the story world, since more elements for understanding the story world can be found in the latter. It is also clear that the maker of the video game harbours the intention of making the cryptographic information more important in this regard, by clearly diminishing the number of plot elements to be found in the main narrative. The main narrative does not explain much of what happens in the game or why, and at the end of the game players have more questions than answers based solely on the information given in this narrative. In order to find the answers to those questions, the player has to search in the clues of the cryptographic narrative, which, when found, provide the answers to those same questions raised within the main narrative.

In this regard, it is important to point to the fact that the cryptographic narrative is not a detective story in the classical sense. It is the player who acts as the detective, trying to piece together information about the story world that is not readily given within the game, and unlike a true detective story there is no detective-like character within the game that will eventually puzzle all the pieces together and solve the mystery. This confusion of roles is exemplary of the metaphysical detective story. Because the developer does not provide a ready-made answer to the mystery, there exist as many theories about the truth of the narrative as there are different interpretations of the clues. The main motive to assume this privileged position of the player as detective in such cryptographic narratives, besides the fact that characters within the game seem to already be in the know as to the true version of events, is that there are clues placed outside the medium of the video game itself, although we can see that there can be clues inside the video game as well that are meant solely for the player.

Lastly, the cryptographic narrative seems to enjoy a privileged position within the horror game genre. Perhaps this is because horror-like stories are more easily told in a minimalistic way through the main narrative ('less is more' is a typical horror trope, making it easier for creators to convey a feeling of suspense) while hiding a darker story in the form of the cryptographic narrative. It is also possible that the makers of such horror games find it more interesting to tell their story by letting the players search for their own answers and thus build a form of anticipation for future games, rather than simply giving them away as a normal horror story. The uncertainty about why events take place also adds to the suspense and emphasizes the fact that the player is woefully uninformed and unprepared, building on the sense of victimhood the player experiences. But this is only speculation, and more research should be done to further understand the link between this genre and the cryptographic narrative form.

The case of *Five Nights at Freddy's*

Five Nights at Freddy's is an indie game series created, designed, developed and published by Scott Cawthon. It is a point-and-click, survival horror game, where the player has to survive for five nights among homicidal animatronics. As of 2021, the series consists of ten games, three spin-offs and three novels. In most games, the player plays as the night-watch security guard, Mike Schmidt. The game takes place at the family restaurant Freddy Fazbear's Pizza, where the animatronics are the main entertainment. Through a phone call, the player is informed that the animatronics operate in 'free-roaming' mode at night to prevent their servomotors from being locked. For an unknown reason the animatronics will try to kill the night guard. The reason given by 'the Phone Guy' – a name lovingly bestowed by the fan base, since no name is given to this character in the game – is that the animatronics see any human as an endoskeleton and try to stuff him into an animatronic suit. He receives his pay cheque after surviving for five nights.

There are two game types contained within the video game: the main game, where the player has to survive a night in the pizzeria as the night security guard, and some mini-games that can be played in between the nights. In the main game the player has to sit in the security guard's office and monitor the cameras, which are positioned throughout the restaurant, to observe the motions of the animatronic mascots. Due to a limited amount of power, the player's main focus is resource management as she has to view camera feeds, light hallways next to the office and close the security doors that are on both sides of the office. If the player no longer has power, nothing can be activated and the animatronics can easily enter the office. The player must use the security cameras to keep track of the animatronics in the building and hold them off using the security doors. If the player fails to keep them out of the office, they will be 'jump scared', after which it is game over.[18] To win the game, the player must survive five nights. The mini-games are very distinct from the main game in both style and content. While the main game is made with 3D models, the mini-games are predominantly 8-bit representations reminiscent of old Atari-style games. The mini-games are triggered after a death sequence or after performing a specific task and often provide more backstory than can be found in the main game. Because of the style of the mini-games, not many details are shown, which has led to a lot of speculation about the meaning of everything that can be seen, further fuelling the creation of a cryptographic narrative.

In addition to the main narrative, many plot points and facts are hidden throughout the game and outside it. In this way, for example, we learn that the animatronics become murderous at night not because of mistakes in their programming, but because they are possessed. Most of this information is conveyed in a few clues spread across the games, and some hints are hidden outside the game, for instance in promotional material or even the source code of the game's website.

Looking at the main narrative, it is noticeable that this narrative is not necessary to play the game. The player does not need the story to enjoy playing the game; its main function is to create a sense of immersion. We know, for instance, through the main narrative that Freddy Fazbear's Pizza houses murderous animatronics. Playing as the night guard creates a very specific horror atmosphere. Any further explanation of the plot cannot be gleaned from a normal play through of the game, though. When looking at how elements of the cryptographic narrative are presented in the game, it is clear that it functions as an embedded narrative. All the hints and clues are hidden throughout the game and are not presented in chronological order. Even the games do not follow each other chronologically; for example, *FNaF: Sister Location* is presumably the first game on the timeline, while *FNaF 1* is located closer to the end of the timeline. In fact, the main and mini-games of each game do not even belong to the same time period, further confusing the issue of a chronological telling.

The clues themselves take the shape of either a spatial narrative, a micro-narrative or a pseudo-narrative. Clues that are considered part of the spatial narrative are those that can be extracted from the game environment. For instance, each game can be placed in the correct chronological order just by looking at the changes in the environment of the pizzeria. Clues that are considered part of the micro-narrative are those that contain written information. This information can be about what happened in the past, for example, the newspaper articles dispersed in the corridors of the pizzeria that provide more information about why the former pizzeria had to close its doors and what happened to the person who was suspected of kidnapping the children. These newspaper clippings appear randomly on the walls of the hallways and are never mentioned in the game. The characters do not even look at them; the player herself has to enlarge the image to read the newspaper clippings. The third type of narrative, the pseudo-narrative, can be found outside the game. For example, in the source code of the game's website clues can be found about locations and characters. An example of this type of cryptographic pseudo-narrative element can be found hidden in teaser images of the game, such as that for the game *FNaF: Sister Location*, where, if you increase the brightness of the image, you find a face hidden in the background, or even in the source code of the game's website, where a conversation between two websites, *Scott Games* and *FNaF world*, can be found. One of the entities tries to suppress the other, while the other tries to overrule the first entity.[19] The complete conversation goes as follows:

S: You are crowding us.
F: Be quiet.
S: You can't tell us what to do anymore.
F: Yes, I can. You will do everything that I tell you to do.
S: We outnumber you.
F: That doesn't matter, dummy.
S: We found a way to reject you.

It is not known whom the entities might represent, and speculation within the *FNaF* theorist community assumes that the oppressor may be the animatronic Ennard and those who are suppressed are the entities of all the different animatronics of which Ennard is composed. Making the clues so inconspicuous and hard to find motivates the player to keep searching for them, ultimately demystifying the mystery and giving agency back to the player.

The whole narrative of *FNaF* spreads out across multiple games as well as books and other media, confirming it as a transmedia narrative, although on a much smaller scale, since there are multiple video games, a spin-off and two books based on the same story. As mentioned before, the clues to the cryptographic narrative are often unclear, hard to find or not obvious while first playing the game. The mini-games, for instance, are created in such a pixelated style that the details are often hard to perceive. An example of this is the Purple Guy, only shown in the mini-games, where not much of his appearance is noticeable as he always looks purple and occasionally wears something resembling a badge on his chest. This has led to speculation in the community as to what his function in the pizzeria could be. Does the badge mean that he was a former security guard? Adding to this, in one of the mini-games the Purple Guy is holding a strange-looking object which has the form of a telephone. If that object were to be a telephone, does this mean that he is the Phone Guy? Or, if it is not a telephone, what else could it be? Questions such as these fuel players' fascination with the elements of the cryptographic narrative and their subsequent creation of many different theories.

What is important about these plot elements is that they are not offered up to the player in an easily understandable whole. They are clues to a greater story that in essence is not necessary to understand the video game's characters or the game world in which the player presides but nonetheless exerts a great attraction for anyone playing the game. Another example of the hidden character of these clues can be found in *FNaF 2*. In this game a new type of animatronic was introduced, the Toy Animatronics. The community discovered a striking and weird difference between the old Chica Animatronic and the new Chica Toy Animatronic: they noticed that sometimes the toy version had no beak. Because it was presumed irrelevant in the search for the cryptographic narrative, the community thought it was just a weird design choice made by Scott Cawthon and a completely random occurrence. This assumption held until Scott released an image on *FNaF World* with the text: 'In the FNaF 4 mini game, why would the tiny toy Chica be missing her beak?' This text led to the discovery of the tiny toy Chica, which also had no beak, in one of the mini-games in *FNaF 4*. Thus, the *FNaF* community presumed that the beakless Chica was just a design choice and not a clue until Cawthon made this remark, giving special attention to the detail, without confirming or denying its importance as a clue to the cryptographic narrative. This showcases the commitment of the developers and the players to the cryptographic narrative and highlights the importance of community building in co-creating it. Lastly, a clear example of the hidden nature of the clues is found in the newspaper clippings that appear randomly on the walls in the hallways. The game never clues you into the fact that important information may be found on them. In fact, to know what is in the articles the player must enlarge the image outside the game, otherwise it is not readable.

When playing *FNaF* the player might ask such questions as 'Who is the Purple Guy?', 'Who do I play as?' or 'Why do the animatronics want to kill the night guard?'. These questions are not answered within the game itself through the main narrative; it is only when the player takes the time to find the plot elements that are part of the cryptographic narrative that these questions are answered. The main narrative in games that harbour a cryptographic narrative is therefore very lean and does not offer much information with which to create the story world.

The example of the newspaper clippings also leads us to a second conclusion: the character the player adopts is not a detective, but rather the player is. The characters within the game do not react to the clues spread out in the game environment, because they already know the information. In the case of *FNaF*, the community has found out through the clues in the cryptographic narrative that the night guard, the main protagonist whom you play, is most likely to be Michael Afton, son of William Afton, the killer. This character tries to undo everything the killer did, from which it can be concluded that he already knows everything that the cryptographic narrative is trying to tell the player, and he has no reason to react to these clues. The main protagonist is therefore a character who, as far as we can tell, is completely aware of the whole plot, reinforcing the fact that this mystery is only here to be solved by the player. The game also leaves clues outside the game environment, in the source code of the designer's website or in promotional material, which can only be directed at the player and not at any character within the game. That is why there is no detective story within the main narrative: the game is not a clear whodunnit tale. The player is the only one who is both victim and detective. Without the discovery of the cryptographic narrative, she would stay in the role of victim, passively experiencing the game's narrative, which provides no satisfying solution in and of itself. Only by discovering the underlying mystery can she shed this vulnerable role and actively take up the role of detective, which gives her agency over the narrative and ultimately makes playing the game a more satisfying experience.

Conclusion

In the previous pages we have endeavoured to define the cryptographic narrative as a narrative separate and distinct from the main narrative in a video game. Cryptography aspires to make any text unreadable by severing the relation between a sign and its meaning, a method of which the genre of the detective story makes ample use. More specifically, in the metaphysical detective story not only are meanings within the writing mixed up, but so too, are the roles the reader/player and writer/developer take up within the narrative itself. In the detective story it is the protagonist who recreates the narrative from disparate plot elements, while in video games we see the same construction used but with the player as the detective, creating a distinction between the main narrative of the game and what we call the cryptographic narrative, which is not part of the gameplay or visible story world, and which the player (co-)creates with the developer of the game.

In form we see that the main narrative, or basic story of the game, functions as a backdrop of the video game in which gameplay takes precedence, while the cryptographic narrative functions as an embedded narrative. The clues, or plot elements, from the cryptographic narrative can be divided into three types of narratives: the spatial narrative, the micro-narrative and the pseudo-narrative, which in some cases can be transmedia. It is noticeable that the main narrative is not necessary to play the game, since the player does not need the story to enjoy playing the game; it is just there to give a sense of immersion and has no effect on the gameplay in general. All the hints and clues to the cryptographic narrative are hidden throughout the game and are not presented in any chronological order. Clues that are considered part of the spatial narrative are those that can be extracted from the game environment. An example of this is how each game can be placed in the correct chronological order just by looking at the changes in the environment of the pizzeria. Clues that could be considered part of the micro-narrative are those that contain written information. This information could be about what happened in the past, for example, the newspaper articles that appear randomly in the corridors of the pizzeria. The third type of narrative, the pseudo-narrative, can be found in clues hidden outside the video game environment, for example, clues about locations and characters can be found in the source code of the game's website. Unique to the cryptographic narrative is that those clues are there to be found by the player; they are not there for the benefit of the game's characters.

A cryptographic narrative is therefore not a detective story, since the disparate plot elements are only given meaning through the connections the player makes, unaided by any narrative mechanic within the game itself. The creator of such a narrative also does not make clear which elements are important to the narrative and which are just design choices, confusing the plot even more and thus creating an enticing mystery made solely for the player to enjoy. The main function of the cryptographic narrative therefore is to provide a means for the creator to assemble a community of interested and involved players.

Five Nights at Freddy's is an excellent example of this type of game. It has become hugely popular in the indie game scene because of the way it makes the player the protagonist of a detective story and challenges its players to seek the truth behind the events in the game. One of the platforms frequently used by these communities is Reddit, an American discussion, social news and web rating platform. The platform uses 'subreddits' to organize posts by subject. Creator Scott Cawthon follows the community closely, commenting on fans' reactions and occasionally commenting on theories when they are largely correct. With one of the later instalments in the franchise, *Ultimate Custom Night* (2018), many theories have found a satisfying end, but a good example of the communities' input in creating the cryptographic narrative is the series on *FNaF* created by famous YouTuber MatPat on his channel *The Game Theorists*.

Here the creator has posted 23 videos over 4 years containing possible theories about the true story behind *FNaF*.[20] After one such video, Cawthon personally responded, saying: 'I don't usually comment on theories or timelines, but I want to this time. This was a very satisfying, and important, episode of Game Theory. . . . now some of those things have been . . . answered(!), by MatPat. Obviously, it's not 100%'.[21] MatPat put together this theory based on elements found throughout the series. These clues are not spoon-fed to the player through NPC interaction, cut scenes or other standard narrative tools within video games, but they are deliberately coded within or outside the game through different narrative forms. With every new instalment of the franchise more clues can be discovered, creating a community of like-minded players intent on finding out the 'truth' behind the games they are playing. We find that this community aspect is of the utmost importance to keep up the momentum and importance of the cryptographic narrative, as without an interested audience it would forever go unnoticed.

Notes

1. Rosenheim, *The Cryptographic Imagination*, 25.
2. Eco, *The Role of the Reader*, 48–9.
3. Connor, 'Reading hidden messages in cyberspace', 297.
4. Lennon, *Passwords*, 3–5.
5. Baudrillard, *Passwords*, 25–6.
6. Tani, *The Doomed Detective*, 39.
7. Tani, *The Doomed Detective*, 40.
8. Merivale and Sweeney, 'The game's afoot', 2.
9. Tani, *The Doomed Detective*, 45, 113.
10. Schubert, 'The many forms of game narrative'; Jenkins, 'Game design as narrative architecture'.
11. Schubert, 'The many forms of game narrative', 2.
12. Jenkins, 'Game design as narrative architecture', 126.
13. Lemmens, 'Narrative in video games', 19–20.
14. Jenkins, 'Game design as narrative architecture', 121–2.
15. Lewitzki, 'Taking control of the horror', 3.
16. Lemmens, 'Narrative in video games', 21.
17. Jenkins, *Convergence Culture*, 95–6.
18. A jump scare is a technique often used in horror films or games. It is intended to scare the audience by surprising them with an abrupt change in image. A frequently used jump scare is a sudden close-up of a scary face.
19. See http://www.scottgames.com/ and https://gamejolt.com/games/fnaf-world/124921. Accessed 25 May 2021.
20. https://www.youtube.com/watch?v=th_LYe97ZVc&list=PLOl4b517qn8jl4Lw8H8cDrDkGwf1FtC7I. Accessed 25 May 2021.
21. 'The Game Theorists, Game Theory: FNAF, the FINAL theory! (Five Nights at Freddy's) – pt 1'. Accessed 25 May 2021. 'The Game Theorists, Game Theory: FNAF, the FINAL theory! (Five Nights at Freddy's) – pt 2'. Accessed 25 May 2021. https://www.youtube.com/watch?v=uhgMZ8w9lb8. For Scott Cawthon's Reddit post see: https://www.reddit.com/r/fivenightsatfreddys/comments/7b27bf/game_theory_FNaF_the_final_theory_five_nights_at/. Accessed 25 May 2021.

Bibliography

Baudrillard, Jean. *Mots de Passe*. Paris: Pauvert, 2000.
Baudrillard, Jean. *Passwords*, translated by Chris Turner. London: Verso, 2011.
Connor, James. 'Reading hidden messages in cyberspace: Semiotics and cryptography'. In *The Emerging Cyberculture: Literacy, paradigm, and paradox*, edited by Stephanie B. Gibson and Ollie O. Oviedo, 287–306. Cresskill, NJ: Hampton Press, 2000.
Eco, Umberto. *The Role of the Reader: Explorations in the semiotics of texts*. Bloomington: Indiana University Press, 1979.
Eco, Umberto. *A Theory of Semiotics*. Bloomington: Indiana University Press, 1978.
Jenkins, Henry. *Convergence Culture: Where old and new media collide*. New York: New York University Press, 2008.
Jenkins, Henry. 'Game design as narrative architecture'. In *First Person: New media as story, performance, and game*, edited by Noah Wardrip-Fruin and Pat Harrigan, 118–30. Cambridge, MA: MIT Press, 2004.
Lemmens, Pieter. 'Narrative in video games: Environmental storytelling in *Bioshock* and *Gone home*'. Master's thesis, Universiteit Gent, 2017.
Lennon, Brian. *Passwords: Philology, security, authentication*. Cambridge, MA: The Belknap Press of Harvard University Press, 2018.
Lewitzki, Alexander. 'Taking control of the horror: Working with visuals in the psychological horror game genre'. Master's thesis, Lulea University of Technology, 2017.
Merivale, Patricia, and Susan Elizabeth Sweeney. 'The game's afoot: On the trail of the metaphysical detective story'. In *Detecting Texts: The metaphysical detective story from Poe to postmodernism*, edited by Patricia Merivale and Susan Elizabeth Sweeney, 1–24. Philadelphia: University of Pennsylvania Press, 1999.
Rosenheim, Shawn James. *The Cryptographic Imagination: Secret writing from Edgar Poe to the Internet*. Baltimore, MD: Johns Hopkins University Press, 1997.
Schubert, Damion. 'The many forms of game narrative'. *Game Developer* 18, no. 1 (2011). https://www.proquest.com/docview/821993374/1B42A02F0DEE4E1FPQ/1.
Tani, Stefano. *The Doomed Detective: The contribution of the detective novel to postmodern American and Italian fiction*. Carbondale: Southern Illinois University Press, 1984.
Tratsaert, An-Sofie. 'The hidden narrative in indie games: A narrative analysis of an aspect in the indie game community'. Master's thesis, KU Leuven, 2018.

Gameography

Board Games

Catan, 999 Games, 1995.
Monopoly, Parker Brothers, 1935.

Video Games

Aion, NCsoft, 2008.
Bioshock, 2K Games, 2007.
Five Nights at Freddy's, Scott Cawthon, 2014.
Five Nights at Freddy's 2, Scott Cawthon, 2014.
Five Nights at Freddy's 3, Scott Cawthon, 2015.
Five Nights at Freddy's 4, Scott Cawthon, 2015.
Five Nights at Freddy's: Sister Location, Scott Cawthon, 2016.
FNaF World, Scott Cawthon, 2016.
Freddy Fazbear's Pizzeria Simulator, Scott Cawthon, 2017.
Halo, Creative Assembly, 2001.
Shadowbane, Wolfpack Studios, 2003.
Ultimate Custom Night, Scott Cawthon, 2018.

11
Narrating pornographic images: photographic description and ekphrasis in *De fotograaf* by Jef Geeraerts

Karen Van Hove

Nowadays, when we think of pornography we most often think of 'dirty' magazines with explicit pictures or of pornographic films, now widely available on the internet; before the internet revolution, filmic pornography could be enjoyed on video (VHS) or DVD. In other words, the genre of pornography seems to be almost exclusively associated with visual media, such as film or photography. However, in the 1950s, 1960s and 1970s, the popular pornographic production (for private consumption) consisted to a large extent of books. By popular pornographic books, I mean texts that contain explicit and detailed representations of sexual acts and bodies, texts that are conceived to stimulate the reader sexually. Often these books were produced for a mass audience. In the 1960s and 1970s, the pornographic book business flourished in both Europe and the United States. Pornographic novels were published by specialized publishing houses, for instance Olympia Press. This publishing house was originally founded in Paris by Maurice Girodias and had several branches across Europe – in Switzerland, Italy, Germany and the Netherlands – and in the United States. In Flanders, the biggest publisher and supplier of pornography was Walter Soethoudt, which published more than 150 pornographic novels between 1967 and 1972, both originals and translations, under different imprints. Most of the pornographic novels in Europe and the United States were sold under the counter, door to door or through the post, for it was illegal to sell offensive (pornographic) books.[1]

While many questions can naturally be raised about pornography and vulnerability, in this contribution I focus on one striking element of these pornographic novels, namely the (explicit and detailed) representation of sexual acts.[2] Even though this is a form of textual pornography, the visual qualities of the sex scenes are often emphasized. In the present contribution I will discuss how visuality is suggested or mimicked in pornographic prose. I will focus on a pornographic novel, *De fotograaf* (*The Photographer*), written by the Belgian author Jef Geeraerts, and analyse its use of visualizing narrative strategies. In Geeraerts's novel the visual aspect of the narrative is emphasized through several references to the medium of photography and to the genre of the illustrated pornographic magazine.

The novel was published in 1972 by Walter Soethoudt. Geeraerts wrote *De fotograaf* under the penname Claus Trum; at the time of its publication, he was best known for his autobiographically inspired novels about his military service in the former colonial Belgian Congo. In his novels Geeraerts combines criticism of the deplorable circumstances of life in the colony with a nostalgic vitalism. He lauds the 'primitive' and 'natural' lifestyle of the African people and the loose sexual morals that supposedly go together with it.[3]

De fotograaf features a photographer-narrator and contains several intermedial references to photography. These references take the form of photographic descriptions, of ekphrasis or of some hybrid form of the two. The analysis of the explicit narrative strategies of visualization such as ekphrasis and photographic description in *De fotograaf* can serve as a guiding principle for the study of visualization through more implicit strategies in both pornographic as well as non-pornographic novels. Moreover, I will argue that the effect of these textual references to the medium of photography is double. On the one hand, they function as metaphors for realism and authenticity. On the other hand, they are a way to negotiate and to compete with the increasing presence and popularity of other forms of pornography that exploit visual media, such as the illustrated porn magazine.

Visuality in pornographic prose

According to Linda Williams, an expert in the field of porn studies, the focus on visuality is one of the main characteristics of the pornographic genre. Building on Foucault's *Histoire de la sexualité* (1976; *History of Sexuality*), she states that the genre of pornography emerged from the desire for scientific knowledge about sex and the sexual body – the so-called *scientia sexualis*. She also contends that the invention and development of visual media – and more particularly film – from the nineteenth century onwards was stimulated by a similar desire for knowledge about the human (sexual) body and bodily movement. This brings her to the claim that there is a close link between the pornographic genre and visual media, such as film and photography, and that the two mutually influenced and reinforced each other. When Williams discusses visualization in pornography, she does not deal with textual pornography. Moreover, she seems to consider textual and visual pornography as two different genres that stem from different traditions.[4] Yet, I want to argue that this distinction is far from absolute and that the question of visuality and the visualization of sexual acts and pleasure is also very prominent in textual pornography.

Roland Barthes, for instance, stresses the visual dimension of the eighteenth-century libertine literature of the Marquis de Sade by the concepts he uses for his interpretation of it. He refers to the sexual positions represented in an erotic text by the notion of *posture*.[5] The term posture emphasizes the static nature of the representation. These postures or positions can be combined into larger configurations or 'scenes'. Barthes distinguishes between spatial configurations, on the one hand, and temporal configurations, on the other. The former he calls *tableaux* or *figures*; these are 'simultaneous ensemble[s] of postures' (for instance the orgy scenes in de Sade in which multiple characters engage with each other at the same time). The temporal configurations, which he refers to as *episodes*, are 'succession[s] of postures'.[6] In the representation of sexual positions, especially in the tableau-like scenes, the static and spatial dimension of the story world is emphasized. One might even say that in these scenes the narrative logic of the text is substituted for an iconic one.[7] The narrative approaches the visual, hence the metaphor of the tableau.

The emphasis on the visual in pornographic prose sometimes leads to interesting narrative paradoxes. In pornographic texts the plot and the narrative progression of the story become subordinate to the representation of sex.[8] Peter Rehberg even claims that, by making the visualization of sex their main objective, pornographic texts annihilate their textuality and bring about their own abolishment.[9]

In *De fotograaf*, the convergence of the textual and the visual is thematized explicitly since the tableau-like, descriptive sex scenes take the form of photographs or of scenes to be photographed. The novel features a homodiegetic narrator who is a professional photographer of glamour and pornographic pictures. Through a series of anecdotes, the first-person narrator narrates how he seduces women and tricks them into participating in erotic photoshoots. Afterwards he usually has sexual intercourse with these women. Besides that, he gets hired by different people (couples and groups) to take their photographs while they are having sexual intercourse. The novel is basically a succession of varied sex scenes. In what follows I will give some examples of these particular photographic scenes and discuss them in detail.

Literature and photography

The encounter of literature with photography, and more specifically the integration of photography in a text, is not an exceptional phenomenon. From the popularization of the new visual media in the nineteenth century that acted as forerunners of what we now know as photography, the literary and visual media interacted and competed with each other. As John Plunkett states:

> there was an intermittent production of books, particularly aimed at a juvenile readership, which attempted to exploit the novelty of the latest optical device or show. Insofar as it was possible they attempted to replicate the viewing experience of peepshows, panoramas, and dioramas. The success of the optical recreations exerted a creative pressure upon the conventional material organization of the book.[10]

The popularization of the visual did not only affect popular forms of literature. The impact of the invention of photography on nineteenth-century realist novels, as well as the ways in which these novels incorporated this new medium, have been studied extensively. Marta Caraion, for instance, has examined the integration and representation of photographs in nineteenth-century travel novels.[11] According to Philippe Hamon, the increasing prominence of the visual media did not only have an impact on the specific literary genre of the travel novel. The diffusion of photography and photographic goods (especially photo albums) in nineteenth-century society also affected reading practices. Reading became more fragmented and less linear, by analogy with leafing, back and forth, through a photo album. The cultural omnipresence of photos and the visual in general also had repercussions for the literary texts themselves. Descriptions grew more important in realist literature.

Moreover, the photograph became a model for realist textual descriptions.[12] Photographic description, as some scholars call it,[13] is a mode of describing that tries to copy the characteristics of photography and is characterized by its attention to detail – which often results in enumerative, list-like descriptions.[14] This type of description is often used to suggest realism and objectivity.

One of the ideas, or ideals, of the realist paradigm was indeed to represent reality in a true and objective way. Photography was the medium par excellence to do this. The reference to photography and photographic techniques became a metaphor for objectivity, transparency and credibility (or *vraisemblance*).[15] Of course, the very conception of a photograph as an objective, faithful, transparent, almost exact representation of reality originated from precisely this realist paradigm. More modernist conceptions of photography are less mimetically oriented and tend to foreground the artificiality of the medium and its problematic relationship with reality.[16] The idea of the transparency of the medium is particularly prominent in the genre of pornographic photography. As Bence Nanay states, in order for a photograph to be sexually arousing, the focus has to lie on its content, the naked body and/or sexual acts (the 'recognitional' aspect), rather than on the form or design (the 'configurational' aspect).[17]

The interaction between literature and photography has further been studied in relation to, and as a form of, ekphrasis.[18] In the traditional sense, ekphrasis is the 'literary (mainly poetic) representation of visual art'.[19] Two famous illustrations of this conception of ekphrasis are 'Ode on a Grecian Urn' by Keats and the description of the shield of Achilles in Homer's *Iliad*. A broader definition has been coined by James Heffernan. In his view, ekphrasis is 'the verbal representation of [visual] graphic representation'.[20] In ekphrastic passages, the spatial dimension of the narrative is emphasized, just like in the tableau-like sex scenes or postures. Hence, the literary strategy of ekphrasis would lend itself very well to the representation of these scenes in pornographic texts.

Ekphrasis and photographic description in *De fotograaf*

The combination, and more precisely the juxtaposition, of text and photographs was a common phenomenon in the pornographic genre in the 1960s and 1970s. For instance, some of the pornographic novels that appeared in the notorious Dutch pornographic series 'Signaalreeks' contained a section in the middle with pornographic pictures. *De fotograaf*, however, contains no pictures or illustrations. In that novel the 'intermedial references' to photography and pictures take the form of photographic descriptions, of ekphrasis, or of some hybrid form inbetween ekphrasis and photographic description.

The first fragment of the novel that involves photography is an ekphrastic one. The photographer-narrator tries to trick a woman into having her photograph taken by showing her some pictures in erotic magazines. In the following excerpt the narrator describes the photographs he shows to one of his clients:

> Ze begint te bladeren. Oo, roept ze uit, wat een prachtige foto's! Geen naaktfoto's natuurlijk, want daar ben ik tegen, althans op papier. Neen, licht gekleed, in frivool ondergoed, met sluiers, net uit het bad met de druppels eraan, een veegje badschuim op een zorgvuldig uitgekozen plekje, een nat broekje dat de schaamlippen en het haar nauwelijks verdoezelt. En dan raak ik haar arm aan. Ik geef commentaar bij de foto's. Ik adem tegen haar hals.[21]

> [She starts glancing through the magazine. Oo, she calls out, such beautiful photos! No nude photos of course, because I'm against these, at least on the record. No, scantily dressed, in frivolous underwear, with veils, right out of the bathtub covered in drops, some bath foam on a well-chosen spot, wet panties that hardly cover the labia and the pubes. Then I touch her arm. I comment upon the photographs. I breathe against her neck.]

As is illustrated in this excerpt, ekphrasis is the representation of representation itself, in this case the textual representation (novel) of a visual representation (photograph). Let me quote James Heffernan on this subject: 'What ekphrasis represents in words, therefore, must in itself be *representational*. . . . [E]kphrasis uses one medium of representation to represent another'.[22] This excerpt also shows that both 'real' and fictional images – images that only exist within the story world – can be the object of textual ekphrasis.[23] In *De fotograaf*, the technique of ekphrasis does not only allow the reader to dwell upon the female body displayed in the photograph. In the ekphrastic passages of the novel, the act of looking and the responses of the characters to the pornographic pictures are emphasized. One could even say that the ekphrastic passages serve an instructive purpose. According to Sylvia Karastathi, 'ekphrasis provides . . . an opportunity to educate the reader, with some texts exhibiting a programmatic and almost didactic tendency in their ekphrastic passages'.[24] Firstly, the reader is explicitly prompted to visually imagine the scenes that are being described. Secondly, by emphasizing the bodily responses of the characters and the photographer-narrator when looking at pornographic pictures, the reader is invited to respond in a similar way. Just as the characters and the narrator become aroused at the sight of the pictures, the reader should get sexually excited while reading the description of these pictures.

The novel does not only contain ekphrastic passages; it is also larded with photographic descriptions of (usually female) bodies, genitals and sexual acts. These descriptions are often based on the model of the close-up. However, the passages in which the reference to photography is most prominent are the photoshoot passages. These are successions of sexual positions and scenes, postures and tableaux – the combination of postures – being photographed. Usually, the photographer takes a series of 12 or 20 pictures of the same person, couple or group of people. In the photoshoot scenes, which are numerous in *De fotograaf*, similar strategies to ekphrasis are used. Yet the scenes are not truly 'ekphrastic', since they do not represent a photograph, but the production of it. The narrator describes the sexual positions and scenes he is photographing, but he does so as if he is already looking at the photograph, and not at the 'real' scene that is taking place in the story world. The shooting of a sexual position almost always takes the same form. Four phases can be distinguished: (1) the imagination of the posture(s) to be photographed; (2) the mise en scène or the staging of a posture; (3) the shot, the exact moment at which the photograph is taken; and (4) the envisioning of the future picture.

First, the narrator discusses with his clients what the photograph should look like. In the following excerpt the photographer is asked to take part in the scene to be photographed. The female client wants him to play Napoleon. Next, he asks her what pose he should strike. In the second excerpt the photographer-narrator suggests a pose to one of his clients:

> Ik vroeg haar wat ik moest fotograferen. Mij terwijl ik op de beroemde mantel van de Keizer door hem wordt bevredigd, zei ze.[25]

> [I asked her what I had to photograph. Me, while I am lying on the famous cape of the Emperor and being pleasured by him, she answered.]

> Ik stel voor: je trekt de onderjurk over je hoofd uit met gestrekte rug, de okselharen helemaal bloot, de borsten gespannen, de benen licht in spreidstand zijwaarts, de venusheuvel naar voren. Ik neem

de kiek als je gezicht half bloot komt. Je mond even open, dat de tanden zichtbaar zijn.[26]

[I suggest: you pull your undergarment over your head, stretch your back, armpits naked, breasts firmly pressed forward, legs slightly apart, mons Veneris forward. I will take the photograph when your face becomes partly visible. Your mouth slightly opened, so the teeth become visible.]

These excerpts can be situated somewhere in between ekphrasis and photographic description. The second excerpt demonstrates clearly what is meant by this second notion. It is as if the narrator takes several close-ups of the different body parts of the female character. This model of the close-up, mostly of men's and women's genitals, is recurrent in the novel and is also reflected in the vocabulary and expressions the narrator uses: 'focusing on' and 'very close-shots'. Trying to create the illusion of a close-up is a manner of visualizing the invisible and showing details that normally cannot be seen with the naked eye. This detailed and objectifying way of describing can be linked to the desire for knowledge of sexuality and the sexual body – the *scientia sexualis* – that is so typical of pornographic discourse. Photographic description is a strategy to represent the postures as faithfully and objectively as possible.

At the same time, the above excerpt shows resemblances to ekphrasis, yet not in the strictest sense. What is being described is not a pre-existing image or picture (whether it is fictional or not), but the posture to be photographed. Thus, the description is not a representation of a representation. At the same time, it is not a description of sexual acts that are being performed in the story world. Rather, it is an anticipation and imagination of a future picture. The narrator describes the postures and the tableaux in the way he wants to see them on the pictures. One could say that these excerpts describe what will be shown on a not yet existent picture. And in that sense it could be considered as a form of ekphrasis, even though strictly speaking this is not an ekphrastic description of a pre-existing representation, but one of an imaginary posture or tableau.

After this first phase follows the composition and the staging of the sexual position. The narrator usually gives instructions to the other characters for the particular poses:

Ze neemt de pose aan, maar ik verbeter met zachte dwang. Eerst even repeteren . . . Goed in houding staan zoals in de turnles,

> Thérèse, zeg ik, buikje goed vooruit, rug gespannen, doe alsof je erg geniet van de complexe beweging, niet vergeten je mond halfopen te houden.²⁷

> [She strikes the pose, but I correct her gently. First we rehearse for a while . . . Adopt a good posture just like in the gymnastics class, Thérèse, I say, your belly forward, your back straightened, act as if you enjoy this complex position, don't forget to open your mouth just a little bit.]

In addition to this, the photographer describes the various actions leading towards a pose. For instance, if the photographer-narrator wants a picture of penetration, he narrates how the characters prepare themselves for the actual sexual intercourse by caressing each other or masturbating. These passages function as a kind of 'behind the scenes' of a pornographic photoshoot. They instruct the reader on how such a picture or series of pictures are produced. The following excerpt is part of a photoshoot in which the narrator himself participates. He wants to photograph the orgasm of his female partner. The reader can follow the entire sex scene leading up to this picture:

> De Leica stond daar op zijn driepikkel . . . Ik zat in haar kutje met mijn lat, niet ver, alleen de eikel en zij vingeren, vingeren . . . , toen ze bijna klaarkwam, greep ze met een hand mijn schouder en fluisterde gespannen: Zet 'm op, het is er bijna . . . Ik stond op, en spande de Leica op die begon te zoemen.²⁸

> [The Leica [camera] stood there on a tripod . . . I was in her pussy with my dick, not very far, up to the glans and she was masturbating, masturbating . . . when she almost came, she grabbed my shoulder with one hand and whispered intensely: Put it on, it is almost there . . . I got up, and put on the self-timer of the Leica. The camera started humming.]

Since these passages represent explicit sex acts and focus on the naked body, they play an essential role in the arousal of the reader.

The third phase of the shooting is the actual shot, the taking of the picture, which is almost always signalled by the word 'klik' ('click'). This onomatopoeic word refers to the closing diaphragm of the camera. In this way the presence of the camera in the scene is stressed. Thus, the illusion that what is described is mediated through the lens of the camera is reinforced. The fourth and last phase is similar to the first one, namely the discussing of the position that will be photographed. The shot is taken and the photographer-narrator imagines what the picture will look like. This is demonstrated in the following excerpt that is part of the photoshoot I mentioned earlier, in which the photographer participates, disguised as Napoleon: 'Ik voorzag een snapshot van een maf vingerende vrouw, gevogeld door een innerlijk dood-verbaasde Napoleon' [I envisioned a snapshot of a crazily masturbating woman, being fucked by an utterly surprised Napoleon].[29] Again, this is not a case of ekphrasis in the strict sense. The narrator describes an imagined version of the photograph. The word that Geeraerts uses for imagining is 'voorzien', which literally means 'to see beforehand'. The vocabulary the narrator uses refers to the realm of the visual. He suggests that what he is describing is something he can 'see', something visible even though he only imagines it. I argue that this can be considered as a form of ekphrasis, namely of an imaginative picture, as the representation of a mental representation.

All these separate photo scenes are part of a larger, overarching frame: the photoshoot. Basically the shoots are successions of varied sexual positions or postures. This is what Barthes would call an episode. However, by photographing and describing each sexual position extensively, the focus lies on these individual positions rather than on the episode. The tension between description, temporal progression and narrativization is often broached in the literature on ekphrasis. On the one hand, ekphrasis is believed to be a way of narrativizing and animating static images.[30] On the other hand, according to Hamon, ekphrasis often takes the form of elaborate descriptions, almost like a list, or an inventory of what can be seen on the image.[31] These tend to slow down the pace and even arrest the progression of the narrative, and to stress its spatial rather than its temporal dimension.[32] In *De fotograaf*, these paradoxical tendencies can be observed as well. The desire to photograph as many women as possible and the act of photographing are the driving forces behind the story. Yet at the same time the description of these pictures, and of the women and the postures to be photographed, runs counter to the narrative.

Transparency and artificiality of the photographic medium

The intermedial references to photography in *De fotograaf* have two seemingly opposed effects. On the one hand, they are a means of suggesting the reality and authenticity of represented postures; on the other hand, they expose the artificiality of the photographic medium. In the nineteenth-century realist paradigm, photography was considered as the medium par excellence to represent reality transparently and objectively. In the realist novel, photographic references are used metonymically to convey and stress a sense of realism and authenticity. In *De fotograaf* these references serve the same purpose. The photographer-narrator wants to convince the reader that his pictures are of real people and of real sex scenes. The attention to realism and the focus on authenticity is characteristic of many Dutch pornographic novels that were published in the 1960s and 1970s. They all claimed to represent average civilians, who were of course the intended audience for these novels.

One of the consequences of this realist conception of photography is the conflation of the distinction between the description of the reality of the story world (which is also the referent of the photograph) and the description of the photograph itself. In *De fotograaf* it is not always clear (1) whether the narrator gives a description of the reality of the story world, (2) whether what he describes is mediated through the lens of the camera, or (3) whether he just describes what he mentally 'sees'. This conflation is characteristic of (realist) photographic ekphrasis and description; if one describes a picture that is supposedly an objective, transparent representation of reality, then the boundaries between the description of the picture and the description of reality itself become blurred.[33]

At the same time, the artificiality of the photographs and the photographic medium is also shown. Descriptive techniques such as ekphrasis and photographic description put the emphasis on the materiality and the form of the photograph. Moreover, it is clear from the above examples that almost all the pictures are staged. This is also evident from the vocabulary used to describe the sexual acts the narrator photographs: 'scène' [scene], 'cirkusnummertje' [circus act], 'pose' [pose]. The narrator pays a lot of attention to the technical details of photography such as the exposure time and the brand of the camera and the lighting. This seems to run counter to the realist effect. At the same time, one could argue that all these references to the photographic equipment, techniques and details reinforce the reality effect of the novel. They heighten the authenticity of the photographer-narrator and create an illusion of professionalism.

Intermedial references as intertextual references

The photographic references in *De fotograaf* can also be considered as forms of intertextuality. On the one hand, the ekphrastic descriptions of the pictures and the way in which the photographs function in the narrative remind the reader of a famous French pornographic novel, namely *L'Image* by Jean de Berg (pseud. Cathérine Robbe-Grillet). The book was published in 1956 by Éditions de Minuit and quickly became a cult erotic book. In 1970 it was translated into Dutch. The Dutch translation was sold by the prestigious, progressive publishing house De Bezige Bij. Claire, one of the female lead characters, seduces the narrator by showing him pictures of sadistic sex scenes. A full chapter, with the title 'The Pictures', is dedicated to the description of these photographs. After seeing a number of pictures, the narrator realizes they were shot in the exact room in which they are sitting. Just as in *De fotograaf*, pictures and their ekphrastic description play a prominent role in the narrative of *L'Image*. They are used as a means to arouse and seduce others – both characters and readers. Since *L'Image* was a renowned French pornographic novel in the 1960s and 1970s, and it was translated into Dutch in 1970, two years before the publication of *De fotograaf*, Geeraerts must have been familiar with the novel.

On the other hand, the pictures refer to the realm of the popular illustrated pornographic magazine, which was very popular in the 1960s and 1970s. The novel contains some explicit references to these magazines. In the following excerpt a female client of the photographer shows him a Scandinavian porn magazine. Scandinavian pornographic production had a notorious reputation at the time:

> Binnen laat ze me de smerigste Zweedse pornomagazines zien: vrouwen met honden en zo, met op de laatste foto onveranderlijk druipend sperma op een vrouwengezicht, wel opwindend voor sommige mensen, maar esthetisch helemaal niet verantwoord.[34]

> [Inside [her apartment] she shows me the dirtiest Swedish porn magazines: women with dogs et cetera, the last picture features a woman's face with sperm dripping off it, exciting for some people, but not aesthetically pleasing.]

The Scandinavian magazines were controversial and even illegal in the Low Countries because they contained explicit pictures of genitals, which were forbidden. They also featured animals and teenage girls and were often very sadistic in nature. However, these forbidden scenes can be found in *De fotograaf* by Geeraerts. By mentioning these kinds of pictures and scenes, Geeraerts's novel joins in with this type of hard-core pornography.

The explicit reference to the illustrated porn magazine also shows that Geeraerts was aware of the increasing popularity of these magazines. By the end of the 1960s, pornographic magazines, such as *Chick*, *Candy* and *Sex Top*, had seen the light of day. At first these magazines were combinations of pornographic stories (mainly in *Sex Top*) or sex ads (mainly in *Candy*) and erotic pictures (some more explicit than others). Eventually, the visual component got the upper hand in these porn magazines. According to Wim Sanders, who studied the distribution of pornographic novels and magazines in the Netherlands, 'tens of thousands' of illustrated magazines were sold each week, while the sales of pornographic novels were dropping.[35] The references to the erotic magazines and pictures can be interpreted as a means for Geeraerts to bridge the widening gap between pornographic magazines – which tend to focus on visual pornography – and textual pornography, and to capitalize upon the success of these magazines. In this respect, it is a way to negotiate the changing hierarchies in the pornographic field.

The 'male gaze', the common denominator between pornography and ekphrasis

Finally, I want to touch upon the idea of the 'male gaze', a concept that is central to discussions of pornography as well as of photography and ekphrasis. All these elements converge in Geeraerts's novel. According to Linda Williams, the pornographic responds to the male desire or phantasy to grasp and control female sexual pleasure and the female orgasm. Moreover, pornography is often written or shot from a male perspective. This androcentric perspective and dominance is what Williams calls the 'male gaze'.[36] Interestingly, the 'male gaze' is also at issue in discussions of photography and ekphrasis. According to W. J. T. Mitchell, a specialist on the topic of ekphrasis, the ekphrastic description often adopts a male perspective. He states that in some cases ekphrasis is even a strategy to dominate the '(female) other'. Mitchell claims that 'the female otherness is an overdetermined feature in a genre [ekphrasis] that tends to describe an object of visual pleasure and fascination from a male perspective, often to an audience understood to be masculine as well'.[37] Mitchell is discussing ekphrasis, but this particular argument could just as well be applied to pornography.

In *De fotograaf* this male gaze is thematized explicitly. On the one hand, the photographer-narrator adopts the position of a voyeur and an outsider. He literally observes his characters through the lens of his camera. Even when the narrator is not taking photographs, he still maintains his outsider position, a position which is similar to the position of the reader and supposedly encourages (male) reader identification. On the other hand, the photographer-narrator is clearly in charge of all the scenes. He directs the mise en scène and organization of the photograph. When women are too controlling or take the initiative, the narrator explicitly comments upon this, as demonstrated in the following excerpt from the Napoleon photoshoot, in which the female client instructs the photographer to adopt certain positions: 'Jongens wat stond er me nu te wachten? Vrouwen die het initiatief nemen in cirkusnummertjes. De nieuwe wereld' [O boy, what was going to happen now? Women who take the initiative in circus acts. The new world].[38]

Conclusion: text–image relations

I hope that through the discussion of this case study, which explicitly thematizes the relationship between the textual and the visual, I have given new impetus to examine this relationship in other pornographic texts. The intermedial references in *De fotograaf* have multiple functions and effects on different levels. Firstly, the act of photographing is an integral part of the narrative, the driving force behind the story. Moreover, the references to photography and to the character of the photographer function as a pretext to introduce explicit sex scenes into the novel in order to stimulate the reader sexually. Secondly, the intermedial references – mainly the ekphrastic ones – serve an instructive purpose and encourage reader identification. Ekphrastic descriptions invite the reader to adopt a voyeuristic attitude and perspective, which is also mimicked by the photographer-character. Thus, the reader is prompted to respond to the descriptions of the pictures and the tableaux in a similar way to that of the narrator and the other characters. Thirdly, the photographic and ekphrastic descriptions, as well as the references to the photographic material, can be considered as narrative strategies to create the illusion of reality, authenticity and objectivity.

Finally, the explicit references to the medium of photography, and to pornographic magazines in particular, are representative of changing hierarchies – between visual and textual pornography, between pornographic novels and magazines – in the pornographic field in the early 1970s. At the same time, the intermedial references are innovative realizations and revaluations of typical characteristics of pornographic literature, namely of representations of sexual positions and scenes, or postures, tableaux and episodes – to use Barthes's concepts. In this respect I want to argue that the distinction between visual and textual pornography is not absolute; the visualizing capacities and effects of pornography are not restricted to the visual media. As Allison Pease states in *Modernism, Mass Culture, and the Aesthetics of Obscenity*, all pornographic texts appeal to the reader's visual imagination; they 'prod the reader to approach the material with a visual imagination. [They do] not describe sexual ecstasy as an emotionally or physically experienced phenomenon, but rather cue . . . the reader that it must be experienced visually.'[39]

However, Pease does not explain how written pornography appeals to the reader's visual imagination, or what narrative strategies induce such an effect. As I have demonstrated in this chapter, ekphrasis and photographic description stress the visual aspect of narrative. The latter concept is especially promising for the analysis of the visualizing capacities of pornographic texts, since many of the novels in the genre contain detailed and objectifying descriptive passages of (female) genitals and sexual acts.

Notes

1. Loth, *De erotiek in de literatuur*, 33–6, 204–7.
2. Williams, *Hard Core*, 48–9.
3. Vermeiren, 'Jef Geeraerts', 1–12.
4. Williams, *Hard Core*, 34–9.
5. Barthes, *Sade, Fourier, Loyola*, 28–30.
6. Barthes, *Sade, Fourier, Loyola*, 29.
7. Lojkine, *La Scène du roman*, 4–5.
8. Bruckner and Finkielkraut, *Le Nouveau Désordre amoureux*, 64; Brulotte, *Œuvres de chair*, 279.
9. See Rehberg, 'Pornografie und Bildkritik in Texten des 20. Jahrhunderts', 237.
10. Plunkett, 'Optical recreations and Victorian literature', 1–28.
11. Caraion, *Pour fixer la trace*, 139.
12. Hamon, *Imageries*, 42–3.
13. For example Caraion, *Pour fixer la trace*, 139.
14. Sperti, 'L'*ekphrasis* photographique dans *Dora Bruder* de Patrick Modiano'.
15. Genette, *Figures II*, 71–99.
16. Clayton, *Literature and Photography in Transition, 1850–1915*, 4–6.
17. Nanay, 'Anti-Pornography', 191–2.
18. For example Miller, *Poetry, Photography, Ekphrasis*.
19. Heffernan, 'Ekphrasis and representation', 297.
20. Heffernan, 'Ekphrasis and representation', 299.
21. Trum, *De fotograaf*, 8; my translation throughout.
22. Heffernan, 'Ekphrasis and representation', 300.
23. Karastathi, 'Ekphrasis and the novel/narrative fiction', 94.
24. Karastathi, 'Ekphrasis and the novel/narrative fiction', 95.
25. Trum, *De fotograaf*, 23.
26. Trum, *De fotograaf*, 51.
27. Trum, *De fotograaf*, 51.
28. Trum, *De fotograaf*, 24.
29. Trum, *De fotograaf*, 24.
30. Caraion, *Pour fixer la trace*, 108.

31. Hamon, *Du descriptif*, 56–8.
32. Karastathi, 'Ekphrasis and the novel/narrative fiction', 95.
33. Caraion, *Pour fixer la trace*, 147–8.
34. Trum, *De fotograaf*, 19.
35. Sanders, 'Een jonge meester in het huis van de pijn', 15.
36. Williams, *Hard Core*, 204.
37. Mitchell, *Picture Theory*, 168.
38. Trum, *De fotograaf*, 24.
39. Pease, *Modernism, Mass Culture, and the Aesthetics of Obscenity*, 9.

Bibliography

Barthes, Roland. *Sade, Fourier, Loyola*, translated by Richard Miller. Berkeley: University of California Press, 1989.
Bruckner, Pascal, and Alain Finkielkraut. *Le Nouveau Désordre amoureux*. Paris: Éditions du Seuil, 1977.
Brulotte, Gaetan. *Œuvres de chair: Figures du discours érotique*. Sainte-Foy, Québec: Presses de l'Université de Laval/Paris: L'Harmattan, 1998.
Caraion, Marta. *Pour fixer la trace: Photographie, littérature et voyage au milieu du XIXe siècle*. Geneva: Droz, 2003.
Clayton, Owen. *Literature and Photography in Transition, 1850–1915*. Basingstoke: Palgrave Macmillan, 2005.
Genette, Gérard. *Figures II*. Paris: Éditions du Seuil, 1969.
Hamon, Philippe. *Du descriptif*. Paris: Hachette, 1993.
Hamon, Philippe. *Imageries: Littérature et image au XIXe siècle*. Paris: Corti, 2001.
Heffernan, J. A. W. 'Ekphrasis and representation'. *New Literary History* 22, no. 2 (1991): 297–316.
Karastathi, Sylvia. 'Ekphrasis and the novel/narrative fiction'. In *Handbook of Intermediality: Literature – image – sound – music*, edited by Gabriele Rippl, 92–112. Berlin: De Gruyter, 2015.
Lojkine, Stéphane. *La Scène du roman: méthode d'analyse*. Paris: Colin, 2002.
Loth, David. *De erotiek in de literatuur: Een luchthartige geschiedenis van de pornografie*, translated by Else Hoog. Amsterdam: De Arbeiderspers, 1966.
Miller, Andrew. *Poetry, Photography, Ekphrasis: Lyrical representations of photographs from the nineteenth century to the present*. Liverpool: Liverpool University Press, 2015.
Mitchell, W. J. T. *Picture Theory*. Chicago: University of Chicago Press, 1994.
Nanay, Bence. 'Anti-Pornography: André Kertész's *Distortions*'. In *Art and Pornography: Philosophical essays*, edited by Hans Maes and Jerrold Levinson, 191–205. Oxford: Oxford University Press, 2012.
Pease, Allison. *Modernism, Mass Culture, and the Aesthetics of Obscenity*. Cambridge: Cambridge University Press, 2000.
Plunkett, John. 'Optical recreations and Victorian literature'. In *Literature and the Visual Media*, edited by David Seed, 1–28. Cambridge: D. S. Brewer, 2005.
Rehberg, Peter. 'Pornografie und Bildkritik in Texten des 20. Jahrhunderts'. In *Handbuch Literatur & Visuelle Kultur*, edited by Claudia Benthien and Brigitte Weingart, 229–46. Berlin: De Gruyter, 2014.
Sanders, Wim. 'Een jonge meester in het huis van de pijn: Girodias, Komrij en de Olympia Press Nederland'. *De parelduiker* 9, no. 2 (2004): 2–21.
Sperti, Valeria. 'L'ekphrasis photographique dans *Dora Bruder* de Patrick Modiano: entre magnétisme et réfraction'. *Cahiers de Narratologie* 23 (2012): 1–15. Accessed 25 May 2021. https://doi.org/10.4000/narratologie.6607.
Trum, Claus. *De fotograaf*. Antwerp: Van Hevel, 1972.
Vermeiren, Koen. 'Jef Geeraerts'. In *Kritisch lexicon van de moderne Nederlandstalige literatuur*, edited by Ad Zuiderent, Hugo Brems and Ton Van Deel, 1–12. Groningen: Nijhoff, 1985.
Williams, Linda. *Hard Core: Power, pleasure, and the 'frenzy of the visible'*. Berkeley: University of California Press, 1989.

Part 4:
Medium/Genre

12
Through the doors of time: media interactions and cultural memory in *El Ministerio del Tiempo*

Katie Ginsbach

In recent years, Spanish television has experienced a surge in productions that engage with history and cultural memory while connecting viewers to a reimagined, collective past. The popular series *El Ministerio del Tiempo* (TVE) coincides with these types of productions but does so by blending the historical genre, the genre most typically used in these types of productions, with elements of science fiction, the adventure novel, period drama, detective fiction, fantasy and the novel of manners, or what is called *costumbrista* fiction in Spain.[1] The innovative nature of the series, however, does not stop at the fusion of genres but extends to the ways that various forms of media interact to convey a sense of time, a sense of both bygone eras and the modern age all rolled into one. In fact, this online and televised programme flourishes in a nebulous space of blurred boundaries where the past is rendered present, fiction overlaps with reality and various cultural representations are inserted into a narrative that fuses high culture with popular references.

The present analysis seeks to examine the ways in which *El Ministerio del Tiempo* utilizes media, not only in the service of preserving and generating cultural memory but also to expand its narrative universe, elaborate on the codes of the series and engage with the audience through its transmedia extensions. In addition to connecting the present society to the past, I argue that *El Ministerio del Tiempo* does more than just recycle cultural knowledge in an intertextual game of references and allusions, as it also lays bare the integral role that media plays in creating, storing and communicating cultural memory, while also marking historical time and conveying a sense of 'pastness'. In this way, I contend that the series' reliance on cultural symbols, as well as its transmedia extensions, allow viewers to shape their relationship to the past in an ongoing dialogue that continually reimagines the past in the present. Fundamentally, doing so illustrates how historical material and cultural symbols are vulnerable to contemporary modification and re-evaluation, particularly as technology and media offer new ways to creatively engage with and envision the past.

El Ministerio del Tiempo: fictionalizing the past

Behind the dilapidated façade of an abandoned building in Madrid lies the headquarters of the Ministry of Time, a top-secret agency whose underground corridors are comprised of a network of doors that permit time travel to the past. As the guardian of these doors of time, the ministry works to ensure that history remains the same in order to safeguard both the past and the present from the detrimental effects that altering the course of history could have on the modern era. Ministry agents entrusted with this task hail from all time periods and regions of Spain, although the episodes of the first two seasons centre around the missions of three main characters: Alonso, a sixteenth-century soldier from Seville; Amelia, a nineteenth-century native of Barcelona who is one of the first women to attend a university; and Julián, a twenty-first-century paramedic from Madrid who is later replaced by Pacino, a police officer from the early 1980s. The central premise of the series revolves around the ongoing and persistent interplay not only between time periods, but also between the real and the imagined, as the agents travel from the present to specific moments in history where they often interact with figures from that era. The figures and historical moments depicted in each episode range from the well-known to the vaguely familiar and include not only iconic individuals and events such as the defeat of the Spanish Armada (1588) or the renowned artist Diego Velázquez (1599–1660), but also the less commonly known siege of Baler (1898–9), as well as more obscure figures including the politician Agustín Argüelles (1776–1844) and the Galician heroine María Pita (1565–1643). By converting real individuals into characters, and by using a variety of actual events as a springboard for the storyline, the series incorporates strands of history into a fictional landscape, which results in a contemporary re-imagining of prior events and individuals. In doing so, the series engages with some of the most distinctive elements of the historical genre, as the realms of the fictional and the historical, as well as the present and the past, continually bleed into one another.

Yet what is most notable about the aforementioned fusions in *El Ministerio del Tiempo* is the central role that media plays in accentuating these tensions that are inherent to historical fiction. Media, in fact, are omnipresent in every episode and are represented in the broadest sense of the term.[2] For instance, books, newspapers, films, broadcast television, video games and various forms of social media are regularly incorporated into scenes. In addition, characters are frequently depicted on their smartphones, searching the internet, reading literature, looking at old photographs or watching television, movies and YouTube videos. While this in itself is not necessarily novel, the way in which media are arranged both to convey a sense of time and to contribute to the merging of diverse eras makes this series stand out in Spain. In fact, *El Ministerio del Tiempo* exemplifies Lisa Gitelman's notion that media are historical subjects, citizens of a certain period, and thus 'integral to a sense of pastness'.[3] Noting that media are intricately linked to and infused with time,[4] Gitelman further argues that our understanding of the past and '[o]ur sense of history' are tied to encounters with media, both new and old, be they in 'writing, print, photography, sound recording, cinema, and now . . . digital media'.[5] Thus, from Gitelman's scholarship, it follows that media not only have the potential to shape and inform one's relationship to the past but that they are also closely connected to what is circulated and passed down in a given society.

Gitelman's observations regarding media and time are apparent in various instances throughout the series where references to and imitations of different types of media are used to anchor time and recall the prior eras that are associated with them. The episode 'Time of Rogues', for instance, incorporates multiple references to the picaresque novel *Lazarillo de Tormes* (1554), a work that depicts the sixteenth-century society in which it was written as morally corrupt, and that emphasizes abuses of power, trickery of all types and social inequalities. The episode in question draws from the image of society that is constructed in the canonical text by recycling familiar moments and well-known themes from the work, which not only situate the narrative in a particular time and place but are also used by the series to invite a comparison between then and now that highlights the corruption in today's society.

El Ministerio del Tiempo also employs media to evoke a more recent past, as is the case in 'The Schism of Time', which includes references to the popular 1950s children's space adventure series *Diego Valor* in the depiction of a childhood memory of one of the agents who grew up during this time and associates his youth with the mediated forms of this science fiction series. In the episode, portions of the series' radio broadcast, as well as a close-up of its comic book adaptation, are used in conjunction with nostalgic flashbacks that transport viewers back to this time, conveying a sense not only of 'pastness' but also of childhood fantasies and the desire to believe that anything is possible, including futuristic space travel. The agent's memories of the series *Diego Valor* not only reconnect him to this prior time and his younger self, but also affect his actions in the present, and thus when he is told to delete photos with instructions on how to travel to the future, the agent recalls his childhood fondness for the sci-fi adventure series and ignores the orders.

In the series, instances such as these both anchor time and show the power of media to shape one's relationship to the past, be it as a literary text that conveys an image of a bygone era, or through a nostalgic return that harks back to a prior time. Nevertheless, it is important to note that while these medial vestiges recall the prior eras that are connected to them, they are also rendered present as they are incorporated into the contemporary series. In doing so, *El Ministerio del Tiempo* recycles older forms of media and gives them new life, which further serves to strengthen the connection between the present and the past that is cultivated in each episode.

Although in the previous examples media are employed to bring to mind a particular era and evoke associations with the past that are tied to them, in other instances media are juxtaposed anachronistically to blur temporal boundaries and highlight the fictional nature of the series. For instance, within the first few minutes of the 11th episode, 'Time of Noblemen', viewers are presented with a sequence of new and old mediated cultural artefacts, which begins with a close-up of a 1604 manuscript of *Don Quixote* as Miguel de Cervantes puts the final words down on parchment paper. The image of the literary masterpiece in the opening scene is followed shortly thereafter by a black-and-white archival video of the 1969 Eurovision competition with Salomé singing 'Vivo cantando', which, as the camera zooms out, reveals that the recorded televised broadcast is being replayed from a computer in the present. Moments later, viewers are transported back to the Spanish Golden Age, where an employee of the ministry is seen playing a 1980s video game on his modern laptop and answering his mobile phone while in the seventeenth century. Here, the arrangement of different representations of media contributes to a layered sense of time, which throughout the series is used either to evoke the viewer's knowledge of particular eras or to humorously mark a discord between the form of media portrayed and the historical setting.

The previous examples are also representative of the series' particular way of blending historical periods, which results in a space where time is collapsed. In fact, the coalescence of time and space in the narrative environment of *El Ministerio del Tiempo* has led to the series being referred to as an aleph,[6] defined by Jorge Luis Borges in his short story with the same name as 'one of the points in space that contains all other points'.[7] However, rather than an infinite and all-encompassing universe as the Argentine writer describes, the ministry's doors of time are limited to moments connected to Spanish history and culture. In this way, the underground agency serves as a physical realm from which one can view fragments of the country's past, and it is also a space that, to borrow a phrase from Andrew Hoskins, becomes a type of 'living archival memory' where the past is always present.[8] In this regard, much like Hoskins observes in his research on digital and other mediated memories, the series challenges traditional concepts of history, laying bare that this archival memory of the past is not fixed, but endlessly rewritten and re-imagined from the present.[9]

(Re)presenting the past: cultural memory and media

While this 'living archival memory' blurs temporal distinctions in the series, it also highlights the connection between forms of media and cultural memory. Cultural memory, in fact, depends largely on tangible representations, as Jan Assmann notes in his description of the term, finding that texts, symbols, traditions and rituals not only '[serve] to stabilize and convey that society's self-image', but are also perpetually 'reconstructed' as each generation reassesses these representations and subsequently their relationship to the past.[10] While Assmann's focus was primarily on the transmission of foundational events of an absolute past through highly formalized frameworks, his initial concept has proven useful for memory scholars, who in recent years have adapted his original premise to devise a broader notion of cultural remembrance that moves beyond 'fixed points' of distant eras and 'fateful events' of great importance,[11] in order to also include aspects of a community's way of life and popular culture. In this more comprehensive understanding of cultural memory, scholars have additionally noted that representations of the past have become increasingly intertwined with mass media and new digital media, as they play an ever-expanding role in the creation and preservation of cultural memory. Given such developments, Astrid Erll and Ann Rigney assert that in order to fully comprehend the dynamics of cultural memory in modern society, it is essential to consider the 'medial processes through which memories come into the public arena and *become* collective'.[12] To shed light on these processes, Erll and Rigney borrow the concept of remediation that was set forth by Jay David Bolter and Richard Grusin, who explain the term as 'the formal logic by which new media refashion prior media forms'.[13] Incorporating this notion into memory studies, this term refers to how 'memory-matter' develops across various forms of media.[14] Within this context, remediation can be seen as one of the processes through which selected elements of this constantly evolving cultural memory are kept in circulation.

El Ministerio del Tiempo engages in the remediation of cultural memory by continually drawing from the archives of culture and history in each episode, while simultaneously highlighting that these remembrances are embedded in a diverse range of media technologies, with a particular emphasis on those that are tied to literature, comics, paintings, film, music, television and radio. The earlier examples of the picaresque novel *Lazarillo de Tormes* and the mediated forms of the science fiction series *Diego Valor* serve to illustrate this point and underscore how the series borrows and refashions other forms of media that are infused with both culture and time. However, it bears repeating that the series' fusion of 'memory-matter' and diverse media technologies is often done in an anachronistic fashion, which further emphasizes its playful and fictional nature. By way of example, in one episode a 1960s home movie reel shows video footage of Rodrigo Díaz de Vivar (1048–99), the medieval hero of the epic poem *El Cantar de Mio Cid*, as he is fighting in battle in 1079. Similarly, the Spanish military general Ambrosio Spínola (1569–1630), whose image in popular culture is closely tied to his depiction in the painting *The Surrender of Breda*, is shown using a smartphone to take a selfie in a video posted on the television channel's website, and in the first episode of the second season, he quotes Bruce Willis from the movie *Die Hard* before going in to fight. While in reality such situations would be inconceivable, they are commonplace in *El Ministerio del Tiempo*. In fact, the series relies heavily on diverse forms of media and cultural memory to amplify the tension between fact and fiction, humorously blur the boundaries between different historical periods and combine what is typically considered 'official' or academic knowledge with popular culture.

In doing so, the series not only recycles cultural symbols and links them to more modern forms of media, but it also adds another layer to the traditional representations of these figures, thus contributing a new dimension to their image that coexists alongside the previous meanings that have been associated with them. By way of example, while traditional representations of the Cid portray him as the ideal Christian, vassal, husband and heroic fighter, in the series the historical and literary figure only retains his image as an exceptionally skilled warrior. In fact, contrary to traditional representations, in the episode 'Time of Legend' he is depicted as a violent mercenary who is neither the perfect husband nor the perfect man. Likewise, the series' representation of Ambrosio Spínola recalls not only his historic role as the general of the Spanish *tercios* during the siege of Breda (1624–5) but also, as was mentioned earlier, his connection to the iconic painting *The Surrender of Breda*, a work by Diego Velázquez that, according to Stefan Schreckenberg, has been associated with both political power and the greatness of the Spanish Empire.[15] In *El Ministerio del Tiempo*, Spínola's character continues to embody a certain degree of heroic bravery; however, rather than emphasizing a connection to a glorious imperial past, his character serves to accentuate outdated and regressive ways of thinking, particularly in his misogynistic attitude towards women in positions of authority. This can be seen in the ninth episode, during which Spínola repeatedly makes comments about taking orders from Amelia. His remarks are presented as not only incongruent with modern thought, but also unfounded given that Amelia's intelligence and leadership skills prove her to be more capable than the general himself. Spínola's antiquated mentality marks the distance between the present and the past, while also drawing viewers' attention to the fact that they are living in a vastly different time to which the Spanish general does not belong.

This type of distinction coincides with the research of Jens Brockmeier, who finds that narratives constructed from cultural memory lend us the 'ability to localize ourselves in time and history'.[16] Cultural historian Alison Landsberg further develops this notion, writing that while mass cultural representations of the past create visuals and accounts that allow the audience to 'remember' moments that they themselves did not experience, and to adopt what she calls 'prosthetic memories', they '[work] to emphasize their position in the present even as they take on the past'.[17] This again highlights the paradoxical relationship between the present and the past in these types of works where, according to Landsberg, images and narratives of a prior time lead individuals 'to feel a connection to the past but, all the while, to remember their position in the contemporary moment'.[18] The same could be said for *El Ministerio del Tiempo*, where the coexistence and interplay between the present and the past not only invites reflection between one's own time and the eras lived by the characters, but also lays bare that this reflective exercise is part of a perpetual dialogue with the past, during which prior representations, symbols and narratives are continually revised and reimagined in the present. In so doing, the series exemplifies how cultural memory is negotiated alongside modern social values – often in a way that reveals more about the current society than the one it purports to depict.

Transmedia: making Spanish history and culture trending topics

While media play an important role within each episode of the series, it is the use of media beyond the traditional frameworks of broadcast television that has received the most scholarly attention. This is due to the fact that from its inception *El Ministerio del Tiempo* set in motion a transmedia campaign of a magnitude that was unheard of for a Spanish television production.[19] Doing so has allowed viewers to engage with the series in a variety of ways, as David Varona Aramburu and Pablo Lara Toledo note, writing that in addition to the series' official website, Facebook page, Tumblr account and Twitter feed, there are also behind-the-scenes making-of broadcasts, podcasts and video blogs with ministry agents, a web series that features interviews with the actors and producers, and an online forum where fans can discuss the series as well as the historical periods that are portrayed in each episode.[20] Additionally, its other social media platforms continue the illusion of a top-secret agency that deals with classified information. For example, exclusive online content is available through the intranet portal of the ministry, but initially one could only gain access to this private network by obtaining usernames and passwords that were periodically changed. Confidential information is also communicated through the instant messaging application WhatsApp, which is limited to a select group of fans who must continually demonstrate their knowledge of both history and the series.[21] Similarly contributing to the illusion, the ministry's Instagram account was first presented as a secret file with video and photo evidence of other missions in which the agents participated.[22] Many of these platforms reflect the essence of the show and follow the same patterns established in the series by blending history and fiction, older and newer media, as well as high culture and popular references. The Instagram secret archive, for instance, contains images of iconic paintings such as *The Oath of the Cortes of Cádiz in 1810* and *The Surrender of Bailén*, as well as the cover of the medieval manuscript *The Chronicle of King Roderick*. On this social media platform, one can also find photographs of distant historical events including the War of 1898 and the Asturian miners' strike of 1934, along with other photos and videos depicting a more recent past, showing, for instance, Ana María Matute receiving the Cervantes Prize for her literary oeuvre in 2010, the opening ceremony for the 1992 Olympic Games in Barcelona, a photo claiming to depict the ministry's involvement in convincing a young Pau Gasol to continue playing basketball and a video of Star Wars characters discovering the ministry. Some of the creations are complete fabrications made to look authentic, while others are actual photos or artistic and literary productions that have been digitized and Photoshopped to include ministry agents in these events. The images not only display a collision of history and fiction, but they exemplify another way in which the series playfully conflates the present and the past as it draws from cultural and historical 'memory-matter', which is then doctored with contemporary references to the show and circulated through its transmedia extensions.

According to Jason Mittell in *Complex TV*, a transmedia strategy not only expands the scope of a television series by providing opportunities for 'engagement across screens' and 'viewer-driven conversations', but also serves 'as a way to get noticed and to build viewers' loyalty in an increasingly cluttered television schedule'.[23] This loyalty and visibility are heightened in a participatory culture such as the one fostered by *El Ministerio del Tiempo* in which viewers are encouraged to generate and circulate new material. In fact, the show's social media managers actively engage with fans, which helps to maintain interest, create a sense of community and continue the illusion that the ministry actually exists. The series' official Twitter account, for example, regularly interacts with viewers in character, thus blurring the lines between fiction and reality as it responds to their comments and retweets their observations, artistic creations and memes. In addition, the series also invites fans to be extras on the show, features their creative projects on its website and has even hired one fan to be a writer.[24]

As a result of this high level of interaction with fans, the initial transmedia campaign organized by the producers of the series has been matched, if not surpassed, by the activity of its fans, called *ministéricos*, who have flocked to social media in droves, making the show a fan phenomenon.[25] Taking media into their own hands, viewers have created blogs, comics, animated gifs, YouTube videos, role-playing games, web pages that analyse the historical accuracy of the series, fan fiction, fan art and even a generator of 'official' ministry certificates that authenticate their status as fans. In addition, each episode has become an online event in which viewers rush to comment on both the series and the observations of others, all while they are watching the programme in real time.

This 'virtual flash mob', as Natalia Marcos calls the weekly occurrence,[26] provides fans with the opportunity to collectively come together to take over Twitter and, in the process, make the series as well as Spanish history and culture trending topics.

These online spaces and experiences not only allow for continued reflection on the past, but they also highlight the relationships that individuals have with media and virtual communities. Aspects of Alison Landsberg's study of remembrance in the age of mass culture are again helpful here given her emphasis on the powerful experiences that audiences can have with these mass cultural technologies that 'make possible a new relationship to the past'.[27] And while Landsberg does not consider the influence of participatory culture or digital media in conjunction with historical representations, her ideas about the experience with these mass cultural technologies as becoming part of one's own 'personal archive', as well as her observations on the transportable and malleable nature of these constructed visions of the past, fully lend themselves to the mediated universe of the series in question.[28] Extending these notions to *El Ministerio del Tiempo*, the series' transmedia extensions not only provide a space for further imaginative engagements with and conversations about the past, but they also encourage individuals to take on these prior eras through personal exploration and creative endeavours, all of which allow the past to become part of their own 'personal archive'. Additionally, the involvement of fans in the production of original material, in which they either expand upon or invent new missions that re-imagine and fictionalize elements of the past, could also be seen as demonstrating Landsberg's observation that mass cultural technologies and the internet both make it apparent that cultural memories are not the sole property of anyone.[29] Indeed, an internet connection and a basic understanding of the series would potentially allow anyone, anywhere, to take on the narratives and visions of the past that are presented in the episodes and then adapt them as they see fit, exemplifying a relationship with the past where the past is an endlessly malleable resource. Furthermore, an engagement of this type results in a situation where viewers can come to see themselves not merely as consumers but, to a certain degree, as producers who are actively involved in the cooperative development of the series' narrative universe. In fact, along these lines, Javier Olivares, writer and executive producer of the series, has found that the experience of creating and sharing new material online results in a fan community that is not only much more active and involved, but that feels integrated into this universe, to the point of seeing themselves and their creations as forming part of the series itself.[30]

This sense of identification or belonging, as well as the fans' ability to participate in this mediated universe, has to do, at least in part, with understanding the codes and references that are being utilized and then working within those parameters to generate new content. On this note, José Carlos Rueda Laffond and Carlota Coronado Ruiz find that fans imitate the narrative universe of *El Ministerio del Tiempo* in their own creations, citing not only their abundant use of distant eras and iconic cultural figures, but also that viewers replicate the same types of humour, references and intertextual nods that are found in the series.[31] One way to partially address this alignment between the audience and the brand lies in Stuart Hall's classic essay 'Encoding/decoding'. In this work, Hall discusses the relationship between producers and viewers and finds that while there are multiple ways in which viewers can decode a text, they are not at liberty to interpret them in just any way given the rules of discourse and the embedded codes that place certain limitations on the text.[32] The patterns and hallmarks of the series, then, including its playful recycling of cultural and historical 'memory-matter' as well as its reliance on generic codes, particularly those of historical fiction, are thus fundamental since they provide both the limitations and the frameworks through which viewers can imitate the series.

Indeed, in their imaginative reworking of the past, fans frequently engage with the tenets of the historical genre by incorporating kernels of history into their fictional storylines. In fact, examples of fan fiction often reference not only historical details and events, but also individuals that range from the extremely well-known to the more obscure. Some examples on Archive of Our Own and FanFiction.net include iconic figures such as Francisco de Goya, Adolfo Bécquer and Federico García Lorca, as well as the lesser-known Margarita Manso, Enriqueta Martí and María Pita. Other characters in these texts, both real and invented, speak to the country's diverse past, such as the fictional Abraham Levi, the Jewish rabbi who invented the doors of time, and the historic Queen Aixa who formed part of the last Muslim dynasty in Granada during the fifteenth century. The multitude of historical references found across these fictions results in a collection of narratives that is highly varied, where there are not only references to Sigmund Freud, Carl Jung, Washington Irving, William Shakespeare and El Greco, but also to the Apollo 11 moon landing, the Montesa earthquake of 1748 and allusions both to the 2004 terrorist attack in Madrid as well as to those in New York City on 11 September 2001. And while the mixing of cultural references from distinct eras serves to highlight the fictional nature of these texts, an excellent example being a fan fiction crossover that combines references to both the fifteenth-century artist El Greco and the *Harry Potter* series, the conventions of the historical genre that are employed nevertheless encourage a creative exploration through which viewers can imagine times that they never lived through and individuals they never met. In this way, this particular genre allows for an imaginative engagement with the archives of history, one that, according to Jerome De Groot, permits a type of 'affective relationship between then and now that "normal" history cannot accomplish'.[33]

This personal engagement with the past often leads to reflections on the historical record and the actions of the ministry. The fan fiction 'No es sólo historia' [It's not just history], for instance, wonders if the 'unofficial' version of the past that the agents are sent to fix may actually be the real history that is being suppressed.[34] Other texts that address these topics typically deliberate the moral dilemma of not being allowed to change the past and right the wrongs of history, which invites a reflection on the injustices that have been committed throughout time. And while it is true that, like the series, many of these fictions avoid controversial eras, there are exceptions, such as the fan fiction 'Perdido en el Tiempo' [Lost in time], which takes place during the Spanish Civil War (1936–9). Although this text does not describe the ideologies that gave rise to the war, it does detail the horrors of combat and allows the individual to imagine what living during the civil war, or any time of conflict, may have been like.[35]

In this discussion regarding how fans engage with the hallmarks of the series and produce their own creations, it should be noted that various scholars of digital and mass media, including Carlos Alberto Scolari, find that it is nearly impossible to summarize and outline all the content generated by users in any given fandom.[36] Jorge Miranda Galbe and Javier Figuero Espadas explain that this is not only due to the enormous quantity of creations and the difficulty of finding them all,[37] but that in 'each narrative world there can be hundreds of original works generated by users, and all of them add something new to the transmedia narrative of each fiction'.[38] Indeed, while the original content created by *ministéricos* often engages with the conventions of the historical genre, one can also find content that does not include references to any historical event or figure, but rather generates storylines containing other subjects or themes that fans want to explore relative to the series, as is the case in the romance 'Tiempo de reencuentros' [Time of re-encounters] by Saedhriel. Similarly, there are also texts that do not feature any of the main characters from the show and instead invent secondary characters in lower-level positions that illustrate what a typical day is like working in the ministry.³⁹ One can also find fictions that focus solely on the female characters and the relationships between them, as well as slash fictions in which viewers create narratives imagining a physical attraction or relationship between characters of the same sex. Ministry agents Alonso, Julián and Pacino have been written about in this fashion, even though doing so does not conform to the series' portrayal of these characters. All of these instances serve as examples that diverge in some way from the norm that is established in the series, yet all of them work to expand the universe of the ministry and thus all belong in this diverse network.

Hence, the sense of belonging and identification that was mentioned earlier is due not only to the ability of fans to identify the patterns and codes that are being utilized, but also to their involvement in contributing new material via interactive media technologies that blur the line between producers and viewers in a way that could not have been anticipated when Hall's essay 'Encoding/decoding' was written in the 1970s. Examining the fan fiction published on Archive of Our Own and FanFiction.net, for instance, reveals not only that fans are engaging with some of the hallmarks of the series, but that they are using media to collaborate with others and to expand the series' narrative universe beyond the one established by the producers. In so doing, they create a community in which they not only read each other's works but also reference each other's texts, ask for suggestions with their storylines, leave feedback for each other in the comments, dedicate texts to each other and invent new characters that are later adopted by others in the group. This type of interaction is not only evident in forums and other social media platforms but can also be seen in blogs such as 'Tiempo de Relatos' [Time of short stories], which began as a collective project to develop multiple storylines around the same topic. In this blog, while some *ministéricos* add new narratives to the site, others create artwork or make videos to accompany the story. Much of this artwork is then posted on Twitter with a link to the fiction in order to further circulate and promote the original content produced by fans. These types of collaborative engagements not only provide opportunities to connect with others in a shared experience through the use of modern technologies, but they also give more options to fans who, even after the series is done filming, can continue to create with media, genres, 'memory-matter' and other types of information across a variety of platforms. In so doing, they illustrate the observation of Henry Jenkins in *Convergence Culture*, who writes: 'In a hunting culture, kids play with bows and arrows. In an information society, they play with information.'⁴⁰ Needless to say, the transmedia universe surrounding the series provides viewers with multiple avenues to do just that.

Beyond generic codes and references: reflecting on the past

However, *El Ministerio del Tiempo* does not just play with media and recycle elements of cultural memory in a never-ending web of references and generic codes, as it also reflects upon Spanish culture, the past and the representations of both. In this regard, it can be viewed alongside contemporary discourses on historical memory in Spain, which has been a significant topic since the 1975 death of dictator Francisco Franco, as well as in more recent years with the establishment of the Association for the Recovery of Historical Memory (2000) and the so-called Historical Memory Law (2007). And while *El Ministerio del Tiempo* does not specifically address the Spanish Civil War, its representation of both the national past and historical figures challenges the regime's idealized vision of Spanish history. For instance, iconic figures and events populate the narratives of each episode, however, neither are presented in an exclusively glorified manner. Indeed, according to Paul Julian Smith, although the ministry's agents travel to important moments in Spanish history, these events are frequently connected to tragedy or death and usually represent the country's 'collective misfortunes', rather than 'triumphal or nationalistic moments'.[41] Similarly, symbolic figures of national importance are not portrayed in a romanticized fashion, but rather are thoroughly humanized and shown to be less than perfect. For example, Miguel de Cervantes is so desperate to make a name for himself in theatre that he becomes suicidal, Salvador Dalí is an opportunist who will be whatever type of artist someone wants him to be if the price is right, Ambrosio Spínola is a male chauvinist, Philip V is mentally unstable, Isabel II is portrayed as a spoiled child and, as was mentioned earlier, the Cid is depicted as a violent mercenary.

The Cid, in particular, represents one of the figures who was glorified in Francoist historiography and who, according to Carolyn P. Boyd, was exalted along with other 'knightly warriors and conquerors [who] illustrated that "with the sword one wins both heaven and empire"'.[42] The episode that re-imagines this medieval hero incorporates a recurring theme concerning the power that historical representations have in anchoring cultural memory and in influencing the images that one has of the past, while simultaneously highlighting their fictional nature. In this episode, while Alonso initially regards the legendary tales and the literary representation of the Cid to be historical fact, Amelia continually points out that although they are based on the life of the medieval hero, they are largely fiction with only kernels of truth. Moreover, in addition to subverting grandiose notions of this figure as an exemplary hero, other common myths regarding the society of the Cid and the supposedly antagonistic relationship between Muslims and Christians during this period are also dismantled as Alonso and the viewers learn that such narratives are not entirely accurate. For instance, when Alonso assumes that the Muslim agent of the ministry who greets them in Valencia in the year 1099 is a hostile foreign invader, it is quickly explained that this society was not as divided along religious and cultural lines as some may believe given that many Muslims lived alongside Christians during this time and that this region had been their home for centuries. Such comments, along with other remarks that emphasize the fictional way in which the Cid has been portrayed, not only serve to undermine myths about this figure as an ideal Christian warrior who fought to reclaim the peninsula from Muslim intruders, but they also lead to a reflection on the validity of historical representations and the images of the past that they generate.

This pattern is repeated in 'Time of Conquest', when Alonso similarly discovers that his grandfather, a soldier and *conquistador*, does not live up to the idealized myth that he had been led to believe about him and that he holds to be true for other sixteenth-century Spanish conquerors as well. Influenced in part by the stories that he was told about his relative, Alonso idolizes these men whom he considers to be brave heroes who achieved glory and honour by bringing civilization to the indigenous people of the New World. However, in the episode, it is the Spanish conquerors who are portrayed as uncivilized, and Alonso soon learns that it was not glory or honour that brought his grandfather and others like him to the Americas, but rather greed. In short, much like the previous example that demystifies the legend of the Cid, this episode similarly underscores how the past has been fictionalized, which again invites a reflection on how prior historical discourses and representations have been manipulated or construed to serve a particular interest or view.

The scepticism that is frequently tied to the past is also found in the main characters' reflections on the secret agency's mission of making sure that history does not change, as they question the morality of saving those who figure prominently in the archives of history and culture, while common people are left to die. This moral dilemma is an ongoing theme throughout the first season. By way of example, in a mission that involves saving Lope de Vega from an untimely death in the defeat of the Spanish Armada, the team pores over hundreds of documents with lists of passengers searching for Lope's name and the boat to which he was mistakenly assigned. After locating the canonical writer, Amelia looks helplessly at all the other names of the individuals who will perish, and Alonso notes the injustice of saving Lope de Vega and letting the others die. Later, in a tavern, Julián looks at the men who are about to embark on these ships and comments on the senselessness of their impending deaths, stating: 'You see them so young, so full of life . . . and to know what is going to happen to them. They are going to die for nothing.'[43] Alonso replies that such is the nature of combat: 'That's the way war is. . . . And if you survive, you watch your comrades die who are like your brothers.'[44] Similar critiques on the uselessness of war and the futile sacrifices of so many run throughout the series. The thematic message regarding national history, reiterated again and again, is that the past is not and has never been glorious. And that one must be careful with idealizing the past.

This point is taken to an extreme in the last episode of the second season, when the series imagines what would happen if Philip II, whose kingdom was so vast it was said that the sun never set on the Spanish Empire, were allowed to change the outcome of the defeat of the Spanish Armada and take control of the doors of time to ensure the continuation of Spain's 'glorious past'. The result is frightening. In this alternate reality, not only was the Inquisition never abolished but the organization monitors both the doors of time and Spanish society, which in this episode abides by the restrictive rules of the fifteenth-century monarch in the twenty-first century. Under the tyrannical rule of the king, speaking out against the government is strictly prohibited and individuals are burned at the stake, tortured or executed by garrotte. In addition to the elimination of democracy, homosexuality is banned and society adheres to stringent gender roles in which women are to be submissive, do all the housekeeping and tend to the children. Changing the past to allow for the continuation of a supposedly 'glorious era' not only results in a different way of life for citizens of this new Spain, but strict censorship laws lead to the elimination of masterpieces of Spanish art and literature. The image that is constructed of this alternate universe directs a clear message to contemporary viewers: romanticized and idealized visions of the past are fabrications, and the lived historical reality was much different.

The use and portrayal of history throughout *El Ministerio del Tiempo* provides viewers with the opportunity to collectively revisit, reimagine and reflect upon their knowledge not only of the past, but also of prior historical discourses that have circulated within Spanish society. Indeed, while knowledge of the past has always been a collective affair with various discourses in competition for authority, television and other forms of mass media provide another way to shape the public narrative concerning historical figures and events, which, according to William Palmer, 'are inevitably susceptible to interpretation as texts, are expropriated, interpreted, and "reworked" by mass cultural mechanisms'.[45] In this endeavour of reworking the past, contemporary media are intricately bound to the way in which historical narratives are experienced, shared and constructed in the present. This can also be seen in the series' use of social media and other immersive media technologies that encourage viewers to engage personally with 'memory-matter' and the conventions of the series in order to create their own narratives, share and circulate information with others and participate in a virtual community. However, in this process, the series also lays bare how both the past and cultural memory are constructed in the here and now, and thus these narratives and representations often say more about the present than the prior time that they aim to portray.

To conclude, the series' broad and diverse engagement with media offers multiple avenues for viewers to encounter historical time and cultural memory, while also exploring their own knowledge of and relationship to the past. In so doing, certain aspects of Spanish history and culture are given new currency in contemporary society, where they become socially relevant beyond their time and inspire a renewed interest in the past as an imaginative space that is open to reinterpretation and public dialogue. In this regard, *El Ministerio del Tiempo* does more than just recycle information, as it also provides insight into how individuals interact with the past and how new narratives revise prior historical discourses and symbols. In this way, the series can be understood not only as a realm for both cultural commentary and reflection on topics concerning historical memory in Spain, but also as an example of how 'memory-matter' is recycled, circulated and rewritten within the landscape of twenty-first-century media.

Notes

1. Rueda Laffond and Coronado Ruiz, 'Historical science fiction', 88.
2. I am adhering to Lisa Gitelman's broad definition of media 'as socially realized structures of communication, where structures include both technological forms and their associated protocols, and where communication is a cultural practice' (Gitelman, *Always Already New*, 7).
3. Gitelman, *Always Already New*, 5.
4. In one of the many illustrations of this idea in *Always Already New*, Gitelman explains that antiquated forms of media, including black-and-white television, medieval manuscripts, silent film, eight-track tapes and rotary phones, harken back to previous eras and seem oddly out of place in modern society (4).
5. Gitelman, *Always Already New*, 21.
6. Lorente Muñoz, 'La biblioteca del Ministerio', 99.
7. Borges, *Collected Fictions*, 280.
8. Hoskins, 'Digital network memory', 92.
9. Hoskins, 'New memory', 335.
10. Assmann, 'Collective memory and cultural identity', 132, 130.

11. Assmann, 'Collective memory and cultural identity', 129.
12. Erll and Rigney, 'Introduction', 2.
13. Bolter and Grusin, *Remediation*, 273.
14. Erll and Rigney, 'Introduction', 5.
15. Schreckenberg, '*El sitio de Breda* de Calderón y *Las lanzas* de Velázquez en *El sol de Breda* de Arturo Pérez-Reverte', 218–20.
16. Brockmeier, 'Remembering and forgetting', 28.
17. Landsberg, *Prosthetic Memory*, 22.
18. Landsberg, *Prosthetic Memory*, 9.
19. Julian Smith, 'History, memory, television', 5.
20. Varona Arambura and Toledo, '"Be ministérico, my friend"', 204–6.
21. Varona Arambura and Toledo, '"Be ministérico, my friend"', 204.
22. Varona Arambura and Toledo, '"Be ministérico, my friend"', 204.
23. Mittell, *Complex TV*, 293.
24. Varona Arambura and Toledo, '"Be ministérico, my friend"', 207.
25. Julian Smith, 'History, memory, television', 5.
26. Marcos, 'Una serie para la generación Twitter', 200.
27. Landsberg, *Prosthetic Memory*, 47.
28. Landsberg, *Prosthetic Memory*, 26, 3.
29. Landsberg, *Prosthetic Memory*, 18, 147.
30. Marcos, 'La "ministeria" inunda internet'.
31. Rueda Laffond and Coronado Ruiz, 'Historical science fiction', 97.
32. Hall, 'Encoding/decoding', 169.
33. De Groot, *Remaking History*, 19.
34. Fridda, 'No es sólo historia'.
35. Ayala, 'Perdido en el Tiempo'.
36. Scolari, *Narrativas Transmedia*, 244.
37. Miranda Galbe and Figuero Espadas, 'El rol del prosumidor en la expansión narrativa transmedia de las historias de ficción en televisión', 123.
38. Miranda Galbe and Figuero Espadas, 'El rol del prosumidor en la expansión narrativa transmedia de las historias de ficción en televisión', 125 (my translation).
39. Mereth, 'Un día cualquiera'.
40. Jenkins, *Convergence Culture*, 134.
41. Julian Smith, 'History, memory, television', 2.
42. Boyd, *Historia Patria*, 266.
43. 'Time of Glory' (my translation).
44. 'Time of Glory' (my translation).
45. Palmer, *The Films of the Eighties*, 7.

Bibliography

Assmann, Jan. 'Collective memory and cultural identity'. *New German Critique* 65 (1995): 125–33.
Ayala, Frank. 'Perdido en el Tiempo'. *Un Blog en el Tiempo*, WordPress, 2017. Accessed 25 May 2021. http://perdidoeneltiemposite.wordpress.com/.
Bolter, Jay David, and Richard Grusin. *Remediation: Understanding new media*. Cambridge, MA: MIT Press, 1999.
Borges, Jorge Luis. *Collected Fictions*, translated by Andrew Hurley. New York: Viking, 1998.
Boyd, Carolyn P. *Historia Patria: Politics, history, and national identity in Spain, 1875–1975*. Princeton, NJ: Princeton University Press, 1997.
Brockmeier, Jens. 'Remembering and forgetting: Narrative as cultural memory'. *Culture & Psychology* 8, no. 1 (2002): 15–43.
'Change of Time'. *El Ministerio del Tiempo*, written by Javier Olivares and David Sáinz-Rozas, directed by Marc Vigil, Cliffhanger, Onza Entertainment and Televisión Española, 2016.
De Groot, Jerome. *Remaking History: The past in contemporary historical fictions*. New York: Routledge, 2016.

Erll, Astrid, and Ann Rigney. 'Introduction: Cultural memory and its dynamics'. In *Mediation, Remediation, and the Dynamics of Cultural Memory*, edited by Astrid Erll, 1–11. Berlin: De Gruyter, 2009.
Fridda. 'No es sólo historia'. FanFiction.net. Accessed 25 May 2021. http://www.fanfiction.net/s/12508096/1/Tiempo-de-relatos-No-es-s%C3%B3lo-historia.
Gitelman, Lisa. *Always Already New: Media, history and the data of culture*. Cambridge, MA: MIT Press, 2006.
Hall, Stuart. 'Encoding/decoding'. In *Media and Cultural Studies: Keywords*, edited by Meenakshi Gigi Durham and Douglas M. Kellner, 163–73. Malden, MA: Blackwell, 2006.
Hoskins, Andrew. 'Digital network memory'. In *Mediation, Remediation, and the Dynamics of Cultural Memory*, edited by Astrid Erll, 91–106. Berlin: De Gruyter, 2009.
Hoskins, Andrew. 'New memory: Mediating history'. *Historical Journal of Film, Radio and Television* 21, no. 4 (2001): 333–46.
Jenkins, Henry. *Convergence Culture: Where old and new media collide*. New York: New York University Press, 2006.
Julian Smith, Paul. 'History, memory, television: *El Ministerio del Tiempo* (TVE, 2015)'. *Bulletin of Spanish Studies* 93, no. 6 (2015): 1–5.
Landsberg, Alison. *Prosthetic Memory: The transformation of American remembrance in the age of mass culture*. New York: Columbia University Press, 2004.
Lorente Muñoz, Pablo. 'La biblioteca del Ministerio'. In *Dentro de 'El Ministerio del Tiempo': El libro sobre la serie que ha revolucionado la televisión en España*, edited by Concepción Cascajosa Virino, 99–106. Madrid: Léeme Libros, 2015.
Marcos, Natalia. 'La "ministeria" inunda internet'. *El País*, 23 March 2015.
Marcos, Natalia. 'Una serie para la generación Twitter'. In *Dentro de 'El Ministerio del Tiempo': El libro sobre la serie que ha revolucionado la televisión en España*, edited by Concepción Cascajosa Virino, 199–201. Madrid: Léeme Libros, 2015.
Mereth. 'Un día cualquiera'. Archive of Our Own. Accessed 25 May 2021. https://archiveofourown.org/works/3593727.
Miranda Galbe, Jorge, and Javier Figuero Espadas. 'El rol del prosumidor en la expansión narrativa transmedia de las historias de ficción en televisión: El caso de "El Ministerio del Tiempo"'. *Index.Comunicacion* 6, no. 2 (2016): 115–34.
Mittell, Jason. *Complex TV: The poetics of contemporary television storytelling*. New York: New York University Press, 2015.
Palmer, William. *The Films of the Eighties: A social history*. Carbondale: Southern Illinois University Press, 1993.
Rueda Laffond, José Carlos, and Carlota Coronado Ruiz. 'Historical science fiction: From television memory to transmedia memory in *El Ministerio del Tiempo*'. *Journal of Spanish Cultural Studies* 17, no. 1 (2016): 87–101.
Saedhriel. 'Tiempo de reencuentros'. Archive of Our Own. Accessed 25 May 2021. https://archiveofourown.org/works/9065044l.
'The Schism of Time'. *El Ministerio del Tiempo*, written by Javier Olivares, Javier Pascual, and Anaïs Schaaff, directed by Miguel Alcantud, Cliffhanger, Netflix, Onza Entertainment and Televisión Española, 2017.
Schreckenberg, Stefan. '*El sitio de Breda* de Calderón y *Las lanzas* de Velázquez en *El sol de Breda* de Arturo Pérez-Reverte: Transformaciones de un lugar de memoria'. In *El Siglo de Oro en la España contemporánea*, edited by Hanno Ehrlicher and Stefan Schreckenberg, 213–32. Madrid: Iberoamericana, 2011.
Scolari, Carlos Alberto. *Narrativas transmedia: Cuando todos los medios cuentan*. Barcelona: Deusto, 2013.
Tiempo de Relatos. Blogger, 2017. Accessed 25 May 2021. http://relatosdelministeriodeltiempo.blogspot.com/.
'Time of Conquest'. *El Ministerio del Tiempo*, written by Javier Olivares and Alberto López, directed by Koldo Serra, Cliffhanger, Netflix, Onza Entertainment and Televisión Española, 2017.
'Time of Glory'. *El Ministerio del Tiempo*, written by Javier Olivares and Pablo Olivares, directed by Abigail Schaaff, Cliffhanger and Televisión Española, 2015.
'Time of Legend'. *El Ministerio del Tiempo*, written by Diana Rojo and Javier Olivares, directed by Marc Vigil, Cliffhanger and Televisión Española, 2016.

'Time of Noblemen'. *El Ministerio del Tiempo*, written by Javier Olivares, Carlos de Pando and Anaïs Schaaff, directed by Anaïs Schaaff, Cliffhanger, Onza Entertainment and Televisión Española, 2016.

'Time of Rogues'. *El Ministerio del Tiempo*, written by Paco López Barrio, Javier Olivares and Anaïs Schaaff, directed by Marc Vigil, Cliffhanger and Televisión Española, 2015.

Varona Arambura, David, and Pablo Lara Toledo. '"Be ministérico, my friend": Diseño de una estrategia transmedia'. In *Dentro de 'El Ministerio del Tiempo': El libro sobre la serie que ha revolucionado la televisión en España*, edited by Concepción Cascajosa Virino, 203–10. Madrid: Léeme Libros, 2015.

13
Vulnerability as duality in speculative fiction

Eva Dinis

> Ours is indeed an age of extremity. For we live under continual threat of two equally fearful, but seemingly opposed destinies: unremitting banality and inconceivable terror.
>
> Susan Sontag[1]

From the several different ways in which vulnerability has been defined and conceptualized, this chapter will focus on the ambiguity inherent to it: the dichotomy between fragility and openness and how it may relate to genre theory in general and speculative fiction in particular. In order to develop this concept, I posit that speculative fiction is a prolific breeding ground for the formulation of narratives of vulnerability, as speculative works are, by their own nature, ambivalent – thriving on dualities for world-building. These are often represented by depictions of dystopian societies whose characters may have, in contrast, a stronger moral compass than most; they may depict genetic or ecological modifications that result in the end of humankind as we know it, while simultaneously allowing for the birth of a new hybrid, sentient species. Manichaean dualities opposing simplistic *good* and *evil* are overturned, as the subtlety of relativism does not always allow for easy differentiation.

Speculative fiction's vulnerability as a literary genre

David Duff underlines the vulnerable standing of genre theory in his introduction to the volume of essays *Modern Genre Theory*. He posits that genre theory has had an historically inconsistent course, fluctuating between being acclaimed and disparaged:

> in modern literary theory, few concepts have proved more problematic and unstable than that of genre. Having functioned since Aristotle as a basic assumption of Western literary discourse, shaping critical theory and creative practice for more than two thousand years, the notion of genre is one whose meaning, validity and purpose have been repeatedly questioned in the last two hundred ... The modern period has been more typically characterized by a steady erosion of the perception of genre, and by the emergence of aesthetic programmes which have sought to dispense altogether with the doctrine of literary kinds or genres.[2]

For current criticism on the definitions, uses and purposes of genericity, I refer for instance to Alastair Fowler's 'The future of genre theory', in which he claims that the construction of theoretical genres is at best problematic, and at worst 'simply useless'.[3] In spite of this, some critics argue for its merits as a valid field of study: Duff further asserts that in the twenty-first century, this resistance to literary theory has begun to abate.[4]

In order to advance a working definition of genericity, David Fishelov suggests that there is no simple, straightforward approach to explaining literary genre, which he considers an elusive and multifaceted phenomenon. He proposes genre as 'a combination of prototypical, representative members, and a flexible set of constitutive rules that apply to some levels of literary texts, to some individual writers, usually to more than one literary period, and to more than one language and culture[: a] dynamic cluster of formal, stylistic and thematic features'.[5] This definition proves useful in characterizing the genres of science fiction, scientific fiction, speculative fiction and several other variations thereof, as it suggests their porosity and permeability, as well as the overlapping nature of apparently different literary subsets.

Adam Roberts argues that the term 'science fiction' resists definition, enumerating some unifying characteristics which may – or may not – be present in the narratives: an 'imaginative or fantastic premise, perhaps involving a postulated future society, encounters with creatures from another world, travel between planets or in time'.[6] However, the focus is on the cleft, the interstice between the real and the imagined: 'science fiction as a genre or division of literature distinguishes its fictional worlds to one degree or another from the world in which we actually live: a fiction of the imagination rather than observed reality, fantastic literature'.[7] A formalist approach to a definition of science fiction would be an attempt to systematize the underlying themes and lexicon of science fiction in order to create a cohesive body of work. Furthermore, Roberts adds that the logic of science fiction, in contrast to other forms of fiction, requires that the modifications between real and imagined be made plausible for the scientific context in which the work is written, which entails grounding the narrative in material, physical rationalization.[8]

Darko Suvin, a prolific critical theorist on the subjects of science fiction and utopias, has posited that the 'point of difference', that which seems then to differentiate the real world from the universes created in science fiction, is the *novum* (Latin for 'new') – the starting point or basis for any science fiction text. Suvin defines science fiction as 'a literary genre or verbal construct whose necessary and sufficient conditions are the presence and interaction of estrangement and cognition, and whose main device is an imaginative framework alternative to the author's empirical environment'.[9] In this context, *cognition* is the rational and logical aspect of science fiction which allows the reader to understand the foreign nature of the science fiction text. *Estrangement*, a term borrowed from Brecht, refers in this context to the elements of science fiction that are recognizably alien to us, effectively estranging the reader from the familiar context. In his text 'Science fiction and the novum', originally from 1977 and republished in 2010, Suvin states:

> in order to determine [the concept of science fiction (SF)] more pertinently and delimit it more precisely, it is necessary to educe and formulate the *differentia specifica* of the SF narration. My axiomatic premise in this chapter is that SF is distinguished by the narrative dominance or hegemony of a fictional '*novum*' (novelty, innovation) validated by cognitive logic . . . If the novum is the necessary condition for SF . . . the validation of the novelty by scientifically methodical cognition into which the reader is inexorably led is the *sufficient* condition for SF. Though such cognition obviously cannot, in a work of verbal fiction, be empirically tested either in laboratory or by observation in nature, it can be methodically developed against the background of a body of already existing cognitions, or at the very least as a 'mental experiment' following accepted scientific, that is, cognitive, logic.[10]

Fishelov analyses the terms used by Suvin, positing that if *cognitive* could be a synonym for *scientific*, then *cognitive estrangement* quite literally refers to science fiction, approximating the terms to 'a common-sense tautology, that science fiction is scientific fictionalising'.[11] It also bears noting that not all scientific laws must be taken into consideration when ascribing them to the science fiction world. The term 'pseudo-science' refers to things that hard science has ruled out as physical impossibilities, but which remain a large part of the science fiction discourse, dependent on pseudo-scientific-sounding rationalizations. Roberts states that for Suvin, the important thing about the 'science' part of 'science fiction' is that it is 'a discourse built on certain logical principles that avoids self-contradiction; that it is rational rather than emotional or instinctual . . . In other words, it is not the "truth" of science that is important to SF; it is the scientific method, the logical working through of a particular premise.'[12] Nevertheless, Roberts's focal point remains emphatically placed on *difference*, wherein the strength of science fiction as a mode or genre is the 'systematic working out of the consequences of a difference or differences, of a *novum* or *nova*', that is, in the coherence of the arguments predicated by science within the scope of the narrative.[13]

The critic Robert Scholes stresses the human aspect of fabulation in the creation of science fiction in his book *Structural Fabulation*. He concedes that while in science fiction 'the insights of the past century of science are accepted as fictional points of departure[,] structural fabulation is neither scientific in its methods, nor a substitute for actual science. It is a fictional exploration of human situations made perceptible by the implications of recent science', while simultaneously creating a parallel with Suvin's proposal: fabulation is 'fiction that offers us a world clearly and radically discontinuous from the one we know, yet returns to confront that known world in some cognitive way'.[14]

Adam Roberts summarizes the current state of (in)definition of science fiction:

> There is among all these thinkers no single consensus on what SF is, beyond agreement that it is a form of cultural discourse (primarily literary, but latterly increasingly cinematic, televisual, comic book and gaming) that involves a world-view differentiated in one way or another from the actual world in which its readers live. The degree of differentiation (the strangeness of the novum, to use Suvin's term) varies from text to text, but more often than not involves instances of technological hardware that have become, to a degree, reified with use: the spaceship, the alien, the robot, the time-machine, and so on. The nature of differentiation, however, remains debated, some critics defining science fiction as that

branch of 'fantastic' or 'non-realist' fiction in which difference is located within a materialist, scientific discourse, whether or not the science invoked is strictly consonant with science as it is understood today, rationalised within the text through some device or technology.[15]

Closely related to science fiction but remarkably distinctive, speculative fiction and its definition are still debated and debatable: as a burgeoning literary genre, its specificity lies in the way it associates themes belonging to the realms of both reality and imagination. Some of its most notable theoreticians are writers whose production is included in the genre itself, such as Margaret Atwood. However, its newness and instability leave it open to criticism and vulnerable to outright disapproval.

Speculations on genre: the *MaddAddam* trilogy

Much has been written about Atwood's supposed shunning of the label of science fiction for her dystopian novels, not least of all by the author herself. Adam Roberts, in *The History of Science Fiction*, states:

> the Canadian novelist Margaret Atwood has annoyed many members of the SF community by denying that she writes any such thing as 'science fiction', a Pulp genre she has denigrated as concerning merely 'intelligent squids in space'. But in spite of her denials, Atwood's three best novels are all SF.[16]

Roberts is not alone in his criticism: renowned science fiction author and critic Ursula K. Le Guin's review of *The Year of the Flood* in an article published in The *Guardian* in 2009 refers to Atwood's use of speculative fiction in detriment of science fiction as an arbitrarily restrictive definition:

> To my mind, *The Handmaid's Tale*, *Oryx and Crake* and now *The Year of the Flood* all exemplify one of the things science fiction does, which is to extrapolate imaginatively from current trends and events to a near-future that's half prediction, half satire. But Margaret Atwood doesn't want any of her books to be called science fiction. In her recent, brilliant essay collection, *Moving Targets*, she says that everything that happens in her novels is possible and may even have already happened, so they can't be science fiction, which is fiction in which things happen that are not possible today.[17]

What could be the reason for this supposed shunning of a label already perceived as vulnerable, in favour of one that is more precarious – as it is newer and more undefined – but may be more acceptable in its literary merits? Although initially stigmatized, science fiction has not only become a cult popular genre but has been recognized by 'serious' authors – such as Le Guin herself. However, perhaps it still suffers from its own struggle to be accepted as an 'acceptable' literary genre that coincides with conservative, canonical views. Science fiction authors who criticize the use of the term speculative fiction by others may then be offering a defensive perspective. If we look at speculative fiction as more realistic and, as such, more canonical, it could appear to be a safer choice of label for an author. However, it is not necessarily so. To place one's work within the speculative fiction genre leaves the author vulnerable to the criticism of both conservative literary critique and science fiction authors.

Atwood proposes the label of speculative fiction for her *MaddAddam* trilogy, composed of *Oryx and Crake* (2003), *The Year of the Flood* (2009) and *MaddAddam* (2013), describing the genre as 'things that really could happen but just hadn't completely happened when the authors wrote the books'.[18] Other definitions of speculative fiction posit that its narrative proposes a shift in consensual notions of reality, while still providing scientifically sound hypotheses.[19] Michael Svec and Mike Winiski identify:

> four overlapping and interwoven elements necessary for [the] pedagogical use of the speculative SF genre:
>
> 1. Deep description of the science content or technologies that were plausible or accurate to the time period.
> 2. The *novum*: A plausible innovation as a key element in the speculation.
> 3. Big Picture: Exploration of the impact on society and humanity.
> 4. Nature of Science: Science and technology as human endeavors.[20]

Although there are numerous studies of Atwood's dystopian and speculative works, there is still no thorough reflection on the specific formulas and notions pertaining to speculative literature inscribed therein. In her collection of essays *In Other Worlds*, Atwood reflects on her reasons for exploring her 'relationship with the sci-fi world, or worlds' when she published the aforementioned novels, which are:

work[s] of fiction in a series exploring another kind of 'other world' – our own planet in a future. (I carefully say *a* future rather than *the* future because the future is an unknown: from the moment *now*, an infinite number of roads lead away to 'the future', each heading in a different direction).[21]

She defends her choice of term for the genre, *speculative fiction*, contrasting the two overlapping genres:

> What I mean by 'science fiction' is those books that descend from H. G. Wells's *The War of the Worlds*, which treats of an invasion by tentacled, blood-sucking Martians shot to Earth in metal canisters – things that could not possibly happen – whereas, for me, 'speculative fiction' means plots that descend from Jules Verne's books about submarines and balloon travel and such – things that really could happen but just hadn't completely happened when the authors wrote the books.[22]

Atwood concludes by arguing that 'when it comes to genres, the borders are increasingly undefended, and things slip back and forth across them with insouciance'.[23] She adds that a certain 'bendiness of terminology, literary gene-swapping, and intergenre visiting has been going on in the SF world – loosely defined – for some time', and the accusation that she is a 'genre traitor' are, as such, indefensible; her take on genericity is that 'much depends on your nomenclatural allegiances, or else on your system of literary taxonomy'.[24] Atwood further expands on her definition of speculative fiction in another collection of essays, *Writing with Intent*, in which she adds that the starting point for her speculative writing is a foundational point which she finds troubling, pertaining to the possible futures of humankind:

> [*Oryx and Crake*] invents nothing we haven't already invented or started to invent. Every novel begins with a *what if* and then sets forth its axioms. The *what if* of *Oryx and Crake* is simply, What if we continue down the road we're already on? How slippery is the slope? What are our saving graces? Who's got the will to stop us?[25]

In *Heterocosmica*, Lubomír Doležel states that 'the universe of possible worlds is constantly expanding and diversifying thanks to the incessant world-constructing activity of human minds and hands. Literary fiction is probably the most active experimental laboratory of the world-constructing enterprise.'[26] The authors of *Speculative Everything*, Anthony

Dunne and Fiona Raby, postulate that the very action of speculating (in literature, design, art and other media) has a mirroring, dual effect in society, with a definite influence on the outcomes of possible world theories. While literary speculation allows humankind, at all levels of society, to explore alternative scenarios, simultaneously:

> reality will become more malleable and, although the future cannot be predicted, we can help set in place today factors that will increase the probability of more desirable futures happening. And equally, factors that may lead to undesirable futures can be spotted early on and addressed or at least limited.[27]

They further add the hypothesis that speculations may be considered thought experiments that aid us in processing difficult current issues, rather than narratives or coherent 'worlds'.[28] This notion may also relate to Suvin's definition of utopias, whose production is 'a vivid witness to desperately needed alternative possibilities of "the world of men", of human life'.[29] According to Suvin, any literary utopia is defined by three main characteristics which distinguish it from other forms of literature or speculation: 'a) it is fictional; b) it describes a particular state or community; c) its theme is the political structure of that fictional state or community'.[30] This conflation of possible worlds and utopias is further discussed by Suvin, who posits that utopias exist as a 'gamut of Possible Worlds in the imagination of readers, not as a pseudo-object on the page'.[31] He further elaborates on the finer thematic distinctions between science fiction, utopia and dystopia, positing that:

> in case the imaginatively constructed community is not based principally on socio-political but on other, say biological or geological, radically different principles, we are dealing with Science Fiction. The understanding that sociopolitics cannot change without all other aspects of life also changing has led to SF becoming the privileged locus of utopian fiction in the twentieth century. [Dystopia is] organized according to a *radically less perfect* principle [than in the author's community].[32]

Correspondingly, dystopian societies such as the ones depicted in the *MaddAddam* trilogy bring to the fore the realization that individual liberties are the commodity that has been taken over by the overarching power structure, under the guise of social scaffolding. As Foucault claims in 'Right of death and power over life':

perhaps what accounts for part of its force and the cynicism with which it has so greatly expanded its limits now presents itself as the counterpart of a power that exerts a positive influence on life, that endeavors to administer, optimize, and multiply it, subjecting it to precise controls and comprehensive regulations.[33]

This consideration allows for a further point of contention: not only is the form – the speculative fiction genre – vulnerable, but the themes depicted in the *MaddAddam* trilogy also illustrate the highly vulnerable nature not only of societies (be they utopian, dystopian or, from a perhaps more cynical point of view, current), but also of human and animal physical frailty and materiality.

Speculated futures

The *MaddAddam* trilogy presents the reader with a highly stratified society in which elitism prevents social mobility. Government is but a façade for private security firms, which exert control over the people by means of violence. Scientific advancements are utilized in an indiscriminate and unethical manner, with little regard for human and animal lives. Emerging from the duality between the wondrous, immense possibilities of science and the apathy generated from an endless parade of seemingly useless or frivolous scientific creations (such as animal hybrids created for the sole purpose of entertainment or consumption), the main characters in the trilogy struggle with finding a balance for human nature: either by attempting to end the human race and create a new, human-like set of creatures without the perceived innate faults of humans, or by surviving the ravaged landscape with resilience and empathy.

Among the innumerable ways in which Atwood shows that the dystopian *MaddAddam* society is susceptible to a vast array of pressures, human frailty as a symptom of vulnerability is at the forefront of the concerns depicted in the books. The wannabe-god-like misanthropic character who creates and spreads the epidemic that ends almost all human life, while at the same time creating a new 'non-human, human-like' race, seems to be on a quest for both ultimate mortality and immortality. From a bioethical perspective, the following question arises: 'if modern science and technologies continuously try to remove or overcome this essential characteristic of human beings through enhancing the human body, intervening against diseases and impairments, and extending the human lifespan, will they then endanger the humanness of human beings?'[34]

The field of bioethics forces us to address the issue of human research as, like animal research, it may lead to abuse. Transhumanism, a movement that seeks to engage and develop science and technology to enhance and transform the human condition – both physical and intellectual – aims at 'broadening human potential by overcoming aging, cognitive shortcomings, involuntary suffering, and our confinement to planet Earth'.[35] This is – at least to the cynical eye – a utopian view of technological advances that would be transversally available to the entire population. The *MaddAddam* trilogy may offer an answer regarding at whose expense this could come to pass. This entails a two-edged sword, necessitating the development of an ethical field designed to protect potential human subjects from harm, while at the same time allowing for medical research.

The setting of the *MaddAddam* trilogy is of a markedly stratified dystopian society; although – or rather, because – there are governmental and private security firms with a high level of power over the population, there are revolts, counter-currents and protests. Any movement across borders – delimiting richer, middle-class or poorer zones – is controlled; these borders are secured at all times with armed patrols, sniffer dogs and electric fences, among other measures.

Signs of moral breakdown are also emblematic of speculative societies. As living conditions worsen for both human and animal populations alike, both Crake and Jimmy-the-Snowman (two of the main characters from the first book *Oryx and Crake*) 'normalize' mass extinction by playing computer games that were created purposely to anaesthetize human reactions to suffering, either environmental, human or animal. Eventually, these games bleed into and blend with reality, as climate change, extinction and violence become the new normal.

There is a prevalence of measures of population control, employed through biopolitics, supposedly for the medical improvement of the poorer classes – namely through the distribution of a 'bliss inducing pill' that increases energy levels and libido, whereas its real effect is to cull the poor by rendering them sterile. This strategy, sanctioned by the higher governmental structures – as well as the 'big corporations' – had a much more drastic side effect: a rogue haemorrhagic fever that turned airborne – the epidemic that was to kill nearly all humankind, by Crake's design.

Closely linked to societal breakdown, technological advances also reveal their vulnerabilities; although technology is created and used to protect humankind, it may often endanger humanity in unpredictable ways. As the critic and theorist Donna Haraway indicates, there is:

a comic faith in technofixes, whether secular or religious: technology will somehow come to the rescue of its naughty but very clever children . . . In the face of such touching silliness about technofixes (or techno-apocalypses), sometimes it is hard to remember that it remains important to embrace situated technical projects and their people.[36]

Not only is technological output finite, it is not as foolproof as the characters in the novels are led to believe; after the epidemic spreads through the world, technology becomes obsolete, leading to a regression to previous, more organic activities, such as beekeeping or raising maggots for medical purposes. These obsolete technological by-products may also act as a source of danger and be weaponized against humans, making use of seemingly natural inherent vulnerabilities: 'A tiny parasitic wasp had invaded several ChickieNobs installations, carrying a modified form of chicken pox, specific to the ChickieNob and fatal to it. The installations had had to be incinerated before the epidemic could be brought under control'; 'a new form of the common house mouse addicted to the insulation on electric wiring had overrun Cleveland, causing an unprecedented number of house fires. Control measures were still being tested'; 'Happicuppa coffee bean crops were menaced by a new bean weevil found to be resistant to all known pesticides.'[37]

Human corporeality is inherently frail; Catriona Mackenzie draws attention to previous critical thinking on the fact that 'our bodies are animal bodies, which are liable to affliction and injury'.[38] Mackenzie further implies that aside from our relational, socio-political state of vulnerability, our materiality is also a condition for vulnerability. Building on Butler's ethics of corporeal vulnerability,[39] which explores the ethical implications of the frangible nature of the human body when exposed to the actions of others, she states:

> Human life is conditioned by vulnerability. By virtue of our embodiment, human beings have bodily and material needs; are exposed to physical illness, injury, disability, and death; and depend on the care of others for extended periods during our lives . . . As sociopolitical beings, we are vulnerable to exploitation, manipulation, oppression, political violence, and rights abuses. And we are vulnerable to the natural environment and to the impact on the environment of our own, individual and collective, actions and technologies.[40]

Risk of disease, whether man-made as through the bliss pill, or through other pathogens introduced by humans; risk of harm from ever-increasing pollution; risk of violence from rioters and the lower classes, perceived as unpredictable: all these weigh heavily on the minds of the multiple narrators present in the novels, who are more distrustful of their fellow humans than they are of nature, animals or the new humanoid race.

The experience of corporeality or embodiment is inherently dangerous for the inhabitants of this society. Bodily repercussions – either fear of them or the impetus to cause harm to others – propel the action. Inscribed within the pages of the *MaddAddam* trilogy are countless descriptions of the ways in which our bodies are breached, wounded, cut by others; infected by man-made diseases, wasted away, bled out; transformed into unrecognizable puddles of goo; or chewed through by corrosive hostile bioforms.

Henk ten Have argues that vulnerability cannot be fully understood within the framework of individual autonomy: rather, our vulnerability is created through our social and economic conditions. However, even within groups or communities which may be considered, as a whole, as vulnerable, not every individual will be affected in the same way – not every individual has the same degree or condition of vulnerability. Moreover, he asserts that the notion of vulnerability is relational, as it is associated with specific threats and risks that create or produce vulnerability for both individuals and groups.[41]

This reasoning may be applicable, or relevant, to specific marginalized or particularly vulnerable groups within the more umbrella term that gender studies tends to examine. The relational quality of vulnerability's application to gender studies and feminisms is particularly thought-provoking when correlated with the notion of intersectionality, which posits that the social construct of power systems has a layered, interlocking and interwoven impact on the more marginalized elements of society, who may be victims of various levels of social stratification, such as gender, class, ethnicity, age, disability or sexual orientation or identity.

Representations of gender differences are often markedly physical in the *MaddAddam* trilogy. Depictions of female nakedness directly emphasize their bodily vulnerability, which in turn has two possible outcomes, two opposite human reactions: either empathy, or violence against the weakest. Nevertheless, characters often described as seemingly or outwardly frail are not always betrayed by their corporeality, which is at odds with their resilience – even when it is made abundantly clear that female vulnerability and fear are among the commodities available for pornographic consumption and display. For instance, two of the female characters who work in the sex industry make use of their apparent frailty to create empathy and to seduce, coerce or even blackmail those who would seem to hold power over them:

> It made her feel strong to know that the men thought she was helpless but she was not. It was they who were helpless, they who would soon have to stammer apologies in their silly accents and hop around on one foot in their luxurious hotel rooms, trapped in their own pant legs with their bums sticking out, smooth bums and hairy bums, bums of different sizes and colours, while Uncle En berated them. From time to time they would cry.[42]

These female characters are vulnerable to unwanted pregnancies from rape, unavoidable after the epidemic, as they are left without medication or technology; by the same token, this vulnerability is compounded by a sense of finite materiality, as women from the lower classes are often viewed as replaceable, disposable. At the same time, instances of the adoption of conventional male performativity on the part of women are depicted as a viable way to avoid the violent responses which the female population, as a whole, is subjected to, as some male characters adopt a hypermasculine posture in order to position themselves higher on the dystopian social hierarchy. This duality, which works through their innate human vulnerability, ensures their continued survival, balancing both their fragility and their willingness to remain open to change.

Science fiction frequently places emphasis on detailed portrayals of the physical body when positioned in direct contrast with the technological advancements for which the genre is notorious. In this manner, the material human body is often inscribed with the technological advancements predicated by science fiction. Haraway's statement about the fragile boundaries between machine and organism seems to illustrate this, as the difference between natural and artificial is ambiguous and the boundary between physical and non-physical is very imprecise.[43]

In a possible parallel, the *MaddAddam* trilogy takes the emphasis on the human body to the next stage, to a possible transhumanism – as posited by Rosi Braidotti, who states that 'there is a posthuman agreement that contemporary science and biotechnologies affect the very fibre and structure of the living and have altered dramatically our understanding of what counts as the basic frame of reference for the human today'.[44] Crake attempts to institute a new society without hierarchies (after having wiped out the human race), constituted by the humanoid species he creates: the Crakers. This species is, in theory, superior to humans: they are more beneficial for the environment, more in tune with the natural world, less physically fragile, and they have no need for technology, which had, in any case, been rendered mostly obsolete. This new species' invulnerability makes them not only more than, but also less than human.

Humanity, as it stands both in the *MaddAddam* trilogy and in reality, is characterized by the duality between the corporeal materiality of our bodies – and our inherent vulnerability to harm – and the constant, never-ending search for betterment by any means possible.

Notes

1. Sontag, 'The imagination of disaster', 224.
2. Duff, 'Introduction', 1.
3. Fowler, 'The future of genre theory'.
4. Duff, 'Introduction', 15–19.
5. Fishelov, *Metaphors of Genre*, 1, 8.
6. Roberts, *Science Fiction*, 1.
7. Roberts, *Science Fiction*, 1.
8. Roberts, *Science Fiction*, 2–5.
9. Suvin, *Metamorphoses of Science Fiction*, 37
10. Suvin, *Defined by a Hollow*, 67–70.
11. Fishelov, *Metaphors of Genre*, 8.
12. Roberts, *Science Fiction*, 9.
13. Roberts, *Science Fiction*, 7.
14. Scholes, *Structural Fabulation*, 2–8.
15. Roberts, *Science Fiction*, 2.
16. Roberts, *The History of Science Fiction*, 316.
17. Le Guin, '*The Year of the Flood* by Margaret Atwood', 11–12.
18. Atwood, *In Other Worlds*, 12.
19. Gannon, *Rumors of War and Infernal Machines*.
20. Svec and Winiski, 'SF and speculative novels', 38.
21. Atwood, *In Other Worlds*, 3.
22. Atwood, *In Other Worlds*, 12.
23. Atwood, *In Other Worlds*, 4.
24. Atwood, *In Other Worlds*, 2.
25. Atwood, *Writing with Intent*, 285–6.
26. Doležel, *Heterocosmica*, ix.
27. Dunne and Raby, *Speculative Everything*, 4.
28. Dunne and Raby, *Speculative Everything*, 80.
29. Suvin, *Defined by a Hollow*, 18.
30. Suvin, *Defined by a Hollow*, 27.
31. Suvin, *Defined by a Hollow*, 122.
32. Suvin, *Defined by a Hollow*, 383–4.
33. Foucault, 'Right of death and power over life', 137.
34. Have, *Vulnerability*, 23.
35. *The Transhumanist Declaration*.
36. Haraway, *Staying with the Trouble*, 3.
37. Atwood, *The Year of the Flood*.
38. Mackenzie, Rogers and Dodds, 'What is vulnerability, and why does it matter for moral theory?', 4.

39. Butler, Gambetti and Sabsay, *Vulnerability in Resistance*.
40. Mackenzie, Rogers and Dodds, 'What is vulnerability, and why does it matter for moral theory?', 1.
41. Have, *Vulnerability*.
42. Atwood, *Oryx and Crake*, 133.
43. Haraway, *Simians, Cyborgs, and Women*, 81–180.
44. Braidotti, *The Posthuman*, 40.

Bibliography

Atwood, Margaret. *In Other Worlds: Science fiction and the human imagination*. New York: Doubleday, 2011.

Atwood, Margaret. *MaddAddam*. London: Bloomsbury, 2013.

Atwood, Margaret. *Oryx and Crake*. London: Virago, 2003.

Atwood, Margaret. *Writing with Intent*. New York: Carroll & Graf Publishers, 2005.

Atwood, Margaret. *The Year of the Flood*. London: Bloomsbury, 2009.

Braidotti, Rosi. *The Posthuman*. Cambridge: Polity Press, 2013.

Butler, Judith, Zeynep Gambetti and Leticia Sabsay, eds. *Vulnerability in Resistance*. Durham, NC: Duke University Press, 2016.

Doležel, Lubomír. *Heterocosmica: Fiction and possible worlds*. Baltimore, MD: Johns Hopkins University Press, 1998.

Duff, David. 'Introduction'. In *Modern Genre Theory*, edited by David Duff, 1–24. Harlow: Longman, 2000.

Dunne, Anthony, and Fiona Raby. *Speculative Everything: Design, fiction, and social dreaming*. Cambridge, MA: MIT Press, 2013.

Fishelov, David. *Metaphors of Genre: The role of analogies in genre theory*. University Park, PA: Penn State University Press, 1993.

Foucault, Michel. 'Right of death and power over life'. In *The History of Sexuality*, Vol. I, translated by Robert Hurley, 133–59. New York: Pantheon Books, 1978.

Fowler, Alastair. 'The future of genre theory: Functions and constructional types'. In *The Future of Literary Theory*, edited by Ralph Cohen, 291–303. New York: Routledge, 1989.

Gannon, Charles E., ed. *Rumors of War and Infernal Machines: Technomilitary agenda-setting in American and British speculative fiction*. Lanham, MD: Rowman & Littlefield Publishers, 2005.

Haraway, Donna. *Simians, Cyborgs, and Women: The reinvention of nature*. New York: Routledge, 1991.

Haraway, Donna. *Staying with the Trouble: Making kin in the Chthulucene*. Durham, NC: Duke University Press, 2016.

Have, Hank ten. *Vulnerability: Challenging bioethics*. London and New York: Routledge, 2016.

Le Guin, Ursula K., ''The Year of the Flood' by Margaret Atwood'. The *Guardian*, 29 August 2009. Accessed 25 May 2021. https://www.theguardian.com/books/2009/aug/29/margaret-atwood-year-of-flood.

Mackenzie, Catriona, Wendy Rogers and Susan Dodds. 'What is vulnerability, and why does it matter for moral theory?' In *Vulnerability: New essays in ethics and feminist philosophy*, edited by Catriona Mackenzie, Wendy Rogers and Susan Dodds, 1–26. New York: Oxford University Press, 2014.

Roberts, Adam. *The History of Science Fiction*. Basingstoke: Palgrave Macmillan, 2006.

Roberts, Adam. *Science Fiction*. London: Routledge, 2006.

Scholes, Robert. *Structural Fabulation: An essay on fiction of the future*. Bloomington: Indiana University Press, 1975.

Sontag, Susan. 'The imagination of disaster'. In Susan Sontag, *Against Interpretation, and Other Essays*, 208–25. New York: Farrar, Straus & Giroux, 1966.

Suvin, Darko. *Defined by a Hollow*. Bern: Peter Lang, 2010.

Suvin, Darko. *Metamorphoses of Science Fiction*. New Haven, CT: Yale University Press. 1979.

Svec, Michael, and Mike Winiski. 'SF and speculative novels: Confronting the science and the fiction'. In *Science Fiction and Speculative Fiction: Challenging genres*, edited by P. L. Thomas, 35–57. Rotterdam: Sense Publishers, 2013.

The Transhumanist Declaration. Accessed 25 May 2021. https://humanityplus.org/philosophy/transhumanist-declaration/.

14
No, poetry is not out of date: notes on poetic writing and digital culture

Jan Baetens

Translated by Marie-Claire Merrigan

Today, poetry is surely commercially the most vulnerable of all literary forms, at least in traditional print culture.[1] And while a new dynamic has been created by the popularity of oral and performance poetry, the ephemerality of performance heightens the vulnerability of the poem as a textual object.[2] Fortunately and in a very timely manner, we have an instrument that is not only practical but also has the additional advantage of being appreciated by specialists (the poets themselves, critics, academic researchers) and the general public alike, which allows us to take stock of current trends in contemporary French-language poetry. Directly published in paperback format, the new edition of *Caisse à outils: un panorama de la poésie française d'aujourd'hui*, by Jean-Michel Espitallier, is a study which, through the diversity of its corpus and the extent of its information, serves as an excellent introduction to anyone wishing to explore French-language poetry of the early twenty-first century.[3] Espitallier's overview displays the richness and the public success, however relative, of this poetic production. It also allows us to assess the complex dynamics between innovation and tradition. For example, some of the authors discussed in *Caisse à outils* attest to the unexpected renewal of an ancient lyrical tradition, which had long been the 'whipping boy' of previous generations. Song and lyrical sensibility are more than just maintained or rejuvenated in neo-lyricism or in landscape writing (*écritures du paysage*), they are also reinvented through works as diverse as those of Franck Venaille, representative of the 'great' lyricism, and Pierre Alferi, a protean author whose texts tend to propose a 'drier' lyricism. As for the neo-avant-garde experiments that are sometimes gathered under the label of the 'extreme-contemporary', it must be noted that most of them make no effort whatsoever to camouflage the older models that serve as their point of reference. This is certainly the case for those poets, nowadays very numerous, who claim to use the technique of constrained writing (*l'écriture à contraintes*) or for those, possibly even more numerous, who practise various types of collage-montage, and whose great modern example is *Testimony: The United States (1885–1915): Recitative*, the masterpiece of the American poet Charles Reznikoff.[4]

Digital poetry, the beautiful outcast?

The previous analysis, which could easily be pushed even further, is hardly sufficient, however, when it comes to grasping the most contemporary aspects of the poetic field. The dialectic between old and new is a characteristic feature of all modern literature,[5] as is the antithesis between, on the one hand, a subjective pole, strongly marked by lyricism, and, on the other hand, an objective pole, manifest today in an aesthetics of the *ready-made* and of *sampling*.[6] In his study, Espitallier strongly emphasizes two aspects that go beyond the framework we have outlined so far: on the one hand, the migration of poetry to non-book contexts (poetry is no longer confined to the space of the book; it is now performed, staged), and, on the other hand, the increasing hybridization of poetry and other media (e.g. cinema, music, video). It is easy to see what is at stake in both these evolutions: the relationship between poetry, which is *media*, that is, a social practice rooted in the use of a certain type of signs, and its *medium*, that is, the material support that allows the production and circulation of these signs.[7] In this context, it is logical that *Caisse à outils* ends with some considerations on the possible digital future of poetry. However, these comments are brief (comprising two pages in a book of nearly 250 pages) and relatively general. The author mainly emphasizes the current cross-fertilization (*métissage*) between digital and multimedia poetry:

> What does digital poetry mean? That any poet who uses digital language creates digital poetry? Not quite . . . here again, practices and means are intertwined, looted, mixed and, alongside self-proclaimed 'digitists', it is poetry as a whole that, by seizing these pioneering experiences, is reconfiguring and pushing the limits of its definitions.[8]

This very cautious, if not ecumenical, conclusion should not come as a surprise. The fact that digital poetry in the narrow sense of the term – created for the screen and only readable on screen – remains a relatively marginal phenomenon may indicate a certain delay in French-language poetry compared with other linguistic or cultural areas,[9] but such a conclusion would be premature, to say the least. This is not only because, on so many other levels, its poetry is clearly ahead of the curve (no one disputes the effervescence and often very radical inventions of contemporary and extreme-contemporary poetry in France), but also because there are many other areas in which modernity and innovation are not necessarily synonymous with digital culture (comic books are a good case in point).[10]

Be that as it may, 'real' digital poetry is still relatively poorly established in practice. Of course, poetry can now be read on-screen, or, if it fails to find a real audience there, it can at least be published on-screen. That alone, however, does not suffice to qualify this type of poetry as digital, except in a flatly mechanical sense – and here emerges a different aspect of poetry's vulnerability, not in the commercial but in the aesthetic sense of the word: in many cases the move from print to screen is a visual disaster (the vital link between text and page, for instance, is very difficult to reinvent in the digital sphere), not to speak of the technical as well as financial difficulty to keep items online, hence the reluctance of many readers and authors to 'go digital'. To be digital in the strongest sense of the term, poetic writing must exploit and explore a series of specific features which are absent from the printed word or which are difficult or even impossible to achieve in that context. Some examples include the mobility of signs; the possibilities of interactivity and appropriation by the reader; multimedia combinations with image and sound; the unstable nature of the digital text, which becomes ephemeral, constantly susceptible to change and therefore plural, without it always being possible to 'classify' chronologically or hierarchically the different versions in circulation; and the inscription of the text in hyper- and transmedia networks. More and more poetic texts make use of these features, but in many other cases, on-screen poems are nothing more than pre-existing texts that are merely presented in a digital form.[11]

However, as Espitallier suggests, the real question may not lie there. While it is of course important to monitor carefully what is happening on the side of on-screen literature, it is even more important to see the extent to which the emergence of digital culture affects poetry as a *whole*, regardless of the more limited issue of on-screen writing.[12]

In other words: while it may appear that, until now, digital writing has remained a relatively minor phenomenon, we cannot, from that, conclude that the impact of digital culture on poetry in general has been altogether more symbolic than real. In the following pages, I thus propose to return to the double question of (1) the migration of poetry outside the book and (2) media hybridization, in order to see the indirect but no less real effects of the transformations produced by the transition from printed to digital texts. The digitization of poetry takes on the shape, then, of a *ricochet*, that is, a profound transformation of old practices, rather than expressing itself directly, that is, by the appearance of an exclusively screen-based poetry.

Digitization as demediatization and transmedialization

As we have seen, the question of digitization can be formulated in terms of media specificity. The modernist tradition, illustrated by Clement Greenberg (in the plastic arts) or Jean Ricardou (in literature), raises the question: in what ways do individual works identify, foreground and rework the specific features of an art or medium (the difference between the two becomes minor here) in order to establish new forms of creation? This line of questioning, while still valuable, nevertheless suffers from an overvaluation of the medium alone as a material support for saying or doing, while glossing over the changes that occur in the media field as a whole. For this reason, our field of inquiry should be broadened to include the wider impact of digitization on contemporary art practices, all of which are forced to redefine themselves in relation to this ongoing revolution.

In the artistic field, digitization has reinforced and accelerated a series of long-term developments which coincide with the gradual industrialization of cultural facts, of which the ever-increasing influence of the creative industries is undoubtedly the most visible aspect.[13] As Matthieu Letourneux, a specialist in popular literature who focuses on media-related issues, has clearly demonstrated, the most profound transformation is that of *serialization*.[14] Indeed, this literary and commercial phenomenon, which we can only treat briefly here, does more than just affect the form or content of works, which move from a 'one shot' artistic logic (a unique work, the result of the initiative of an author) to an industrial logic of 'prototype/series' (multiple works, commissioned by the publisher from interchangeable authors). It also depends on a series of technical and media-related factors, which materialize in two singular but inextricably linked ways: *demediatization* on the one hand, and *transmedialization* on the other.

Serialization is, in fact, destined to become *transmedial*. Serializing a work implies not only the fragmentation of an initial work into various deliveries or different entities within its starting medium, but also its adaptation into other media. Such a politics of *transmedialization* characterizes the majority of contemporary cultural and artistic activities, yet it also provokes a dynamic of withdrawal, resistance and reinvention of specific forms. This process is reinforced by an equally vast phenomenon of *demediatization*. The latter refers not to the dematerialization of digital data (digital culture is as material as any other), but to a creative procedure that favours components that can move as freely as possible from one medium to the next. Instead of conceiving of a story starting from a concrete format (a novel, film, video game, etc.) and then adapting it, more or less successfully, into other media, *demediatization* takes as its starting point a universe and characters, this is to say, elements that can be more easily adapted than an already formatted story.

The question of digitization, then, becomes a completely different one. It goes beyond the integration of specific digital traits and deals, rather, with the impact of new ways of doing things: it deals with the creation of components detached from any medium – *demediatization* – followed by the impact of fragmentation and serialization across various media – *transmedialization* – on the evolution of poetry.

How does *demediatization* manifest itself in poetry? In prose, more specifically in narrative prose, it undeniably leads to a foregrounding of space at the expense of what has always been considered the essence of narrative, namely time.[15] Poetry, however, seems to be moving in a different direction. Following the more traditional lineage of Mallarmé ('Verse is everywhere in language where there is rhythm'),[16] the meeting between digital technologies and poetry reinforces the temporal, and more precisely the *rhythmic*, element of writing, which becomes a currency in itself. This primacy of rhythm can be observed in all forms of poetry that have appeared since the emergence of digital technology: poetic performance, particularly slam; hybridization with other media forms, mainly music; and a fascination with reading aloud, which has made a strong comeback in avant-garde poetry, long dominated by the model of the visual arts (we can find an increasing number of examples of this on all publishers' websites).[17]

The articulation of rhythm and body, already logical in itself, further demonstrates the idiosyncratic effect of digital culture on poetry. On the one hand, this articulation implies a form of *demediatization*, given that an emphasis on rhythm tends to detach words from language itself, transforming it into pure rhythm. On the other hand, *demediatization* only increases the importance of those elements that, according to some, are threatened by digital technology, namely, the voice, body and presence of the author in the text.

When it comes to *transmedialization* in poetry, the results are equally ambiguous. Fiercely opposed, at least in theory, to any politics of serialization and, more generally, to any form of cultural industry, poetry can only reiterate its demand for singularity and thus take as its starting point a resistance to any attempt at standardization, any alignment with discursive standards or concession to the linguistic doxa. In research literature, the ideal remains that of a critique of commonly used discourse, which is considered alienating.[18] Contemporary poetry thus remains very 'literalistic' or 'textualistic'. At the same time, poetry is wary of any discourse on verbal or linguistic 'purity' and willingly functions as a point of intersection of different media. As Espitallier constantly points out, the majority of modern poets align themselves in a thousand different ways with other arts, other media and other supports. It is therefore not wrong to consider contemporary poetry as both hyper-specific and transmedial. Contrary to the traditional modernist discourse on media specificity, it is the combination of both that makes contemporary poetry markedly different from any nostalgic remake of the so-called textual writing (*écriture textuelle*) of the 1960s and 1970s.

In the following pages, we will examine these general hypotheses with the help of two examples from the catalogue of P.O.L. Editions, a publishing house that has set itself apart from the start by its defence of a dialogue between poetry and digital culture. We will take a closer look at certain aspects of the writing of Olivier Cadiot and Pierre Alferi, both of whom were directors at the ephemeral but vital *Revue de littérature générale*,[19] which can be considered as the first major illustration of what was at stake for the graphical user interface at the transitional moment between typewriters and personal computers. We will see, however, that their respective works exceed, in several respects, the programme of this journal, which is often reduced to a manifesto of French objectivist writing,[20] and that they do not always respond in the same way to the rise of digital culture. Our study of Cadiot and Alferi will, of course, take into account the various evolutions of the media field since the publication of their joint review, which more or less coincided with the launch of the first commercial forms of the internet. Since the opening of the Web, the influence of digital creation is no longer a mere function of the use of the personal computer (PC), but also, and above all, a function of the connection that henceforth exists between all types of sign production and circulation systems.

Two authors confront the digital era (I): Olivier Cadiot

Olivier Cadiot's (b. 1956) work, which has numerous extensions into theatre, radically evades the distinction between prose and poetry, two modes of writing that constantly overlap, question, criticize and merge with each other throughout his writing. As Michel Gauthier writes in his microscopic reading of Cadiot's fifth book, *Retour définitif et durable de l'être aimé* (2002), this encounter is not simply about including fragments of poetry in the novel:

> poetry consists of memories of the novel; it does not, therefore, consist of poems, but of evocations of novels ... [However,] it can only be fragmentary, this poetic memory of the novel. If the poet had an absolute memory, if he could remember the novel in its entirety, he would no longer be a poet but a novelist, emulated by Pierre Menard or César Paladion, these now mythical writers revealed by Jorge Luis Borges and Adolfo Bioy Casares. Poetry thus succeeds when it has trouble remembering the novel ... Poetry achieves its goal when it tears the novel apart.[21]

The same critic also points out that Cadiot's 'poetic' texts are increasingly placed under the sign of rhythm, more precisely under that of speed, which summarizes the essence of the author's approach. (Michel Gauthier's entire essay, then, is devoted to examining the forms and scope of this 'speed factor'.) This notion of speed is not limited to questions of prosody or bodily staging of the text, even if the writer does design his texts in view of reading them aloud. It appears, first and foremost, as a response of literature to the increasingly strong presence of the machine in the creative act.[22]

A reference to Denis Roche is almost inevitable here. After declaring poetry 'unacceptable' and moving from writing to photography,[23] Roche returned to writing (a writing that many today would willingly describe as poetic) through a reflection on the act of photography, the fundamental mechanisms of which he transposed into textual production. In *Les Dépôts de savoir & de technique* (1980),[24] in which Roche uses the typewriter and its 60-character lines as a photographic camera to 'extract' existing textual fragments, he translates the photographic code into a principle of literary composition. The influence of this practice on post-*Tel Quel* authors has been undeniable, and there is no shortage of echoes of Roche in the rediscovery of American objectivists in the *Revue de littérature générale*.

Cadiot's work, which appears at a time when 'conceptual', later called 'uncreative',[25] writing had imposed itself in the United States, goes beyond the exclusive model of photography.[26] His collage-editing aesthetics, from which photography would of course never be entirely absent, also differs from 'conceptual' or 'non-creative' *mash-up* techniques. It does so, firstly, by its taste for *storytelling* (the absence of a novelistic framework in no way prevents the proliferation of micro-narrative effects), and, secondly, by the omnipresence of a *voice* (even though this instance is no longer comparable to what was once called the 'narrator'). A final distinguishing element, then, is the very *constructed* and calculated nature of its montage effects (Cadiot's texts are always very 'articulated', dismantled and reconstructed at the same time, where the essential movement of the text is grasped exactly at the level of the transition from one sentence to another).

While Cadiot, therefore, borrows the key technique of 'sampling' from the modern heirs of objectivism, it is not the sampling *itself* that interests him. Breaks between samples are not often marked as such, for example by a blank or another sign of obvious rupture; in Cadiot's case, the reader becomes aware of the montage-collage process only as they go along, by following the constantly interrupted and reconstructed thread of the text. It is not always possible, however, to locate exactly where the transition between segments takes place.

Similarly, it is not the accumulation effects themselves that primarily interest Cadiot. He is in that respect a sober, almost parsimonious author, even if excess and loss of control, both equally jubilant, constitute some of the major themes of his work. Cadiot's primary aim is the gesture of sampling insofar as it allows him to compete with the basic mechanism of digital culture: the click. That is to say, he aims to compete with the possibility of instantaneously produced montages by letting himself be led by combinations that are not programmed by the writer but are made possible by machines and their reading/writing software. The main objective is therefore a 'procession' of samples, but always a carefully constructed procession, never a mechanical one. Even if slippage or deviation occur, these always remain fully monitored.

Inspired by the model of digital writing and its clicks from one universe to another, Cadiot's textual writing makes careful use of multimedia hybridizations. However, his writing does not reproduce an endless movement of clicks but proposes instead a model that is more performant, more efficient, more meaningful and, above all, more imbued with rhythm. His 'click', however omnipresent, is never a gesture that simply breaks a continuity in order to stir the reading process into a different direction. Each break also generates significant collusions. In so doing, these breaks create and maintain a particular tension. On the one hand, they propel the text into unexpected territories, and, on the other hand, they oblige the reader to continuously go back and try to identify what 'link' ties each new segment to the one that was just suspended.

The result of this writing is a singular experience of textual velocity, and of immersion in a world that functions like a digital machine. Cadiot's texts recreate the dynamism and vitality of digital technology without succumbing to easy imitation. While they transgress the boundaries of literature in order to compete with the machines of digital culture (in this sense, Cadiot follows in the footsteps of the *demediatization* and *transmedialization* movements), they re-enter it in new, and above all *literary*, ways. In this respect, he is among those who, by approaching it in a different way, rethink the digital fact within textual writing itself. The following comment by Anne-Cécile Guilbard sums it up well:

> The rhythm and distance between the movements announced by the juxtaposition, even in a single phrase, of elements taken from domains that are very far removed from one another, turn this work, manifestly a montage, into an exemplary illustration of the power of language, in the manner of a contemporary Mallarmé who, in the digital age, would lift out absent flowers from any bouquet, now in 3D, by activating the 'Speech' function with a single click.
>
> > 'At one time people wrote like that to save space. [facsimile of an anonymous manuscript reproduced in a format too small to be readable]
> >
> > How to establish a deep space in between these lines? A 3D search?'
>
> The space of the page is no longer called on in the two dimensions of its frontal slimness, it is the thought of the screen that animates it, and while this thought joins the poetic aspiration of making objects appear by virtue of words alone, distributed along the page, it also alters that ambition by integrating modern possibilities: virtuality of the hyperlink, of the click that can automatically bring up, from the bottom of another page, a fragment that was left there.[27]

Two authors facing the digital world (II): Pierre Alferi

Pierre Alferi's (b. 1963) writing, open to a wide range of multimedia genres and practices, often bears the hallmarks of cinema and audiovisual productions.[28] There are many cinematographic references in his work, and the author has played a pioneering role in the genre of the 'cinepoem' (in his case, a variation on the aesthetics of *found footage*). The principles of film editing therefore structure his oeuvre from top to bottom. However, the common traits with Olivier Cadiot's more photographic writing are tangible. Like him, Alferi attaches great importance to the voice, which, in his case, is truly a narrative voice. Even in his poetry, Alferi's writing seems irresistibly attracted to narrative (*récit*), and just like in his colleague's work, a sense of rhythm is omnipresent and touches all themes and techniques of his work.

What specific forms are foregrounded through the primacy of rhythm in Alferi's writing? More than in Cadiot's case, who is above all an author of the 'flux' and energy flows but also of their frequent interruptions, it is worth noting the distinction between the two strata of writing in Alferi's work.

At the level of his oeuvre as a whole, Alferi's fascination with rhythm manifests itself in a profound formal and generic instability. Without confounding them as Cadiot does, the author alternates poetry and prose, essay and fiction, text and multimedia creation, epic and short form, collections of scattered fragments and closely united projects, serials and books. We never precisely know, however, the direction in which the author's work will evolve. This fundamental uncertainty, which certainly adds to the reader's enjoyment, acquires a rhythmic function from the outset. The progression of the work obeys a logic of coming and going between opposing movements, sometimes of continuity, sometimes of discontinuity, which establishes a textual regime of both suspense and revival. Each new episode of his work gives rise to a series of variants and variations, as if each text were governed by an underlying programme or constraint that needs to be fully exploited. At the same time, none of these series seem to come to full completion, as if their author were constantly trying to interrupt one series with yet another one, even if this obliges him, at times, to return to previously abandoned works.

At the micro-textual level, this concern for rhythm is reflected, firstly, in a prolonged hesitation between sentence and narrative (*récit*), which both attract and mutually exclude each other. I apologize in advance for a too lengthy self-citation:

At the beginning of his career as a writer, Pierre Alferi evoked this ambition with the following expression: 'to search for a sentence', and his protean work has never deviated from this programme. In general, a sentence is a singular object, caught between, on the one hand, the stylistic requirements of the old rhetoric, which is very word-centred (a sentence is good when all the words are in their rightful place, when no word is missing or superfluous, and finally, when all the words that are used are the right words) and, on the other hand, more recent approaches to narrative and text (where a sentence is good when it supports the course of the whole text and reinforces its overall emerging architecture). Pierre Alferi's poetry could be defined as an attempt to bring together the 'simple' sentence (i.e., the one governed by the old rhetoric) and the 'multiple' sentence (i.e., the one that makes up the modern text).[29]

Hence the continuous work, in the case of Alferi, on sentence and verse as independent units of writing – not given, but to be constructed – and this, from a perspective that exceeds that of the individual verse or sentence. A verse is created in function of a poem (even a broken one); a sentence is created in function of a story (even an aborted one). This is also why Alferi often plays with the internal organizational principles of his texts. The latter always present themselves as blocks, but they are broken blocks, divided into verses, strophes, sections, chapters, deliveries, even books, or split between various media. This also, then, explains the implementation of a politics of multimedial creation in essentially rhythmic terms. In cinepoems, for example, words and images are not only heterogeneous in themselves, or in order to generate new meanings; they also relate to each other on a temporal axis and can be measured in terms of coincidence or deviation, divergence or simultaneity. These effects are calculated not so much on the level of themes or content but on the level of time. Such montage is mainly a question of rhythm, frequency and duration, and not of the semantic compatibility or incompatibility of the combined elements.

Towards a remediatization of poetic writing?

The primacy of rhythm that deeply binds the writings of Olivier Cadiot and Pierre Alferi can be interpreted as a response to the new mechanisms of production, storage, dissemination and reception of signs, codes and messages in the digital age. It must be repeated, however, that this response in no way implies a rejection or overturning of the printed word or literary culture in the traditional, 'bookish' sense of the term. Of course, neither Cadiot nor Alferi has steered away from digital creation, which they practise in different ways, and both keep a close eye on the technological changes affecting literary expression today. Nevertheless, the two authors are to be situated resolutely in the field of books. Their writing strategy is not one of *demediatization*, nor of *transmedialization*, even if both strive to create a dialogue between different media and adapt their composition techniques in order to support, or even provoke, these types of migration between media. However, in the end – a necessarily provisional end, of course – their politics appear to be much closer to a new form of specificity, which we could describe as one of '*remediatization*':[30] not an attempt to withdraw into what can be considered specific to this or that type of media (indeed, it would be absurd to claim the essentially 'literary' or 'printed' nature of rhythm), but a choice in favour of the necessary reshaping of literary practices, impure and mixed as they often are, in the light of the challenges posed to the latter by the digital revolution that surrounds them.[31]

Notes

1. This chapter was originally published as Jan Baetens, 'Non, la poésie n'est pas en retard: Notes sur l'écriture poétique et la culture digitale'. *Cuadernos de filología francesa* 25 (2015): 39–51.
2. See Lang, *La Conversation transatlantique*; Nachtergael, *Poet Against the Machine*.
3. The volume succeeds an anthology by the same author, Espitallier, *Pièces détachées*. Unlike *Caisse à outils*, this anthology is much more militant, that is to say, more oriented towards defending certain forms of poetry over others (which does not detract from its interest, of course).
4. Reznikoff, *Testimony*, available in French translation by Marc Cholodenko under the title *Témoignage*.
5. See MDRN's collective book, *Modern Times, Literary Change*, as well as, for more details, the group's website: http://www.mdrn.be/. Accessed 25 May 2021.
6. Major theoretical references, but also genealogy, are explored in Perloff, *Unoriginal Genius*.
7. On the medium/media difference, see Baetens, 'Le médium n'est pas soluble dans les médias de masse'.
8. Espitallier, *Caisse à outils*, 227–8. By 'digitists', Espitallier is referring here to a group of writers gathered around the magazines *Alire/Doc(k)s*, led by Philippe Bootz and Jean-Pierre Balpe, and to the 'Manifesto for Digital Poetry', written by Jacques Donguy and published in an issue of *Art Press* in 2002. To these names we should add that of Eric Sadin, an author and theorist of digital culture, as well as a network facilitator of the digital age.
9. We can think here of Quebec, if we want to stay within the domain of Francophonie. For more details, see the archives of the NT2 laboratory at UQAM: http://nt2.uqam.ca/. Accessed 25 May 2021.
10. On the resistance of comic book creators to digital technology, see Groensteen, *Bande dessinée et narration*, and, more generally, the testimonies of many authors gathered in the special issue edited by Chute and Jagoda, *Comics & Media*.
11. Caution suggests it is advisable to keep in mind that media issues are not to be confused with quality issues: a text on-screen is not 'condemnable' because it fails to rely on specifically digital properties, just as a text which does, in turn, is not automatically 'better' than others.
12. A similar question underlies Hayles's *Electronic Literature*: the question is no longer to know whether there is a specialized field within literature, called 'digital literature', but to analyse how the digitization of writing and reading affects all literature.

13. The bibliography on this subject is enormous, but perhaps the best overall study remains Hesmondhalgh, *The Cultural Industries*. In the more specific field of publishing, see Schiffrin, *L'édition sans éditeurs* and Thompson, *Merchants of Culture*. For a more historical perspective, see especially Kalifa, *La Culture de masse en France*, as well as several works by Mollier including, with Letourneux, *La Librairie Tallandier*.
14. See Letourneux, *Fictions à la chaîne*.
15. This foregrounding of space is repeatedly underlined by, for example, post-cinema theorists. Indeed, the latter refuse to consider the disarticulation of narrative and time in post-cinema in purely negative terms, that is, as an erosion of temporality and claim instead that it is just as much a question of promoting the spatial side. See, for example, Cubitt, *The Cinema Effect*.
16. Mallarmé, *Œuvres complètes*, 687.
17. On the often questionable effects of the confusion between poetry and the visual arts, see Baetens, *Pour en finir avec la poésie dite minimaliste*. For an analysis of the writer's 'postures' manifested in videos of authors reading their own work, see Baetens and Truyen, 'Le portrait de l'écrivain'.
18. We will leave aside for the time being any questions about the political dimension of this struggle, which is easier to articulate in theory than in practice (indeed, it goes without saying that we must reject language use as we know it, but does it also go without saying to do so in a language that may discourage the very people we are trying to support?). See the fascinating contributions in the collection Bailly et al., 'Toi aussi, tu as des armes', and the collection edited by Jugnon, *Redrum*.
19. The review had two large issues, in 1995 and 1996.
20. The real discovery of American objectivists in France is due to the anthology of *Vingt poètes américains*, edited by Deguy and Roubaud.
21. Gauthier, *Olivier Cadiot, le facteur vitesse*, 16–17.
22. On the internal evolution of Cadiot's writing, see Alizart, 'Les trois âges du sample'.
23. Denis Roche's collection *Le Mécrit* (1972) contains a sequence of 11 poems, entitled 'La poésie est inadmissible, d'ailleurs elle n'existe pas'. It was under the title *La poésie est inadmissible* that Denis Roche would later bring together his entire poetic production (1995).
24. It should be noted that these texts, while 'appearing' poetic, were not included in Roche, *La poésie est inadmissible*.
25. See the anthology *Against Expression*, edited by Dworkin and Goldsmith, and the volume by Goldsmith, *Uncreative Writing*.
26. The following paragraph owes much to an analysis by Anne-Cécile Guilbard, 'Démontage de l'e-mage', presented at the conference *Montage/Démontage/Remontage*, organized by Aurélie Barre and Olivier Leplâtre in Lyon II (2014), and published in the journal *Textimage* in 2016. I was inspired by this very fine reading of Cadiot, *Un Mage en été*, a text that incorporates many self-reflexive elements.
27. Guilbard, 'Démontage de l'e-mage'. The embedded quotation here is from Cadiot, *Un Mage en été*, 74.
28. A good presentation of Pierre Alferi's protean work can be found in the special issue *Pierre Alferi: Literature's cinematic turn*, edited by Thomas.
29. Baetens, 'Entre récit et rhétorique', 19–20.
30. The term 'remediatization' is borrowed from the work of Bertrand Gervais, who thereby avoids confusion with the Anglicism 'remediation' (based on the concept of Jay David Bolter and Richard Grusin, defended and illustrated in their book *Remediation*). See also Baetens, 'La remédiatisation'.
31. This conclusion is in line with some of the research hypotheses of the 'Back to the Book' programme, led by Prof. Kiene Brillenburg Wurth at the University of Utrecht. The major difference between the trends presented in this chapter and the main thrust of 'Back to the Book' is the overemphasis, in the latter, on the visual dimension of remedial writing – essential to the Anglo-Saxon corpus studied in 'Back to the Book', but not necessarily to the works of Cadiot and Alferi.

Bibliography

Alizart, Mark. 'Les trois âges du sample'. *Critique* 677 (2003): 776–84.
Baetens, Jan. 'Entre récit et rhétorique: la phrase'. *CCP/Cahier Critique de Poésie* 28 (2014): 19–20.

Baetens, Jan. 'La remédiatisation: formes, contextes, enjeux'. In *Introduction à l'étude des cultures numériques*, edited by Raphaël Baroni and Claus Gunti, 239–52. Paris: Colin, 2020.
Baetens, Jan. 'Le médium n'est pas soluble dans les médias de masse'. *Hermès* 70 (2014): 40–5.
Baetens, Jan. 'Non, la poésie n'est pas en retard: Notes sur l'écriture poétique et la culture digitale'. *Cuadernos de filología francesa* 25 (2015): 39–51.
Baetens, Jan. *Pour en finir avec la poésie dite minimaliste*. Brussels: Les Impressions Nouvelles, 2014.
Baetens, Jan, and Fred Truyen. 'Le portrait de l'écrivain: une mythologie pérenne?' In *The Imaginary: Word and image/L'Imaginaire: texte et image*, edited by Claus Clüver, Matthijs Engelberts and Véronique Plesch, 219–29. Amsterdam: Rodopi, 2015.
Bailly, Jean-Christophe et al. *'Toi aussi, tu as des armes': Poésie et politique*. Paris: La Fabrique, 2013.
Bolter, Jay David, and Richard Grusin. *Remediation: Understanding new media*. Cambridge, MA: MIT Press, 1999.
Cadiot, Olivier. *Un Mage en été*. Paris: P.O.L, 2010.
Cadiot, Olivier. *Retour définitif et durable de l'être aimé*. Paris: P.O.L., 2002.
Chute, Hillary, and Patrick Jagoda, eds. *Comics & Media: A Special Issue*. *Critical Inquiry* 40, no. 3 (2014).
Cubitt, Sean, *The Cinema Effect*. Cambridge, MA: MIT Press, 2005.
Deguy, Michel, and Jacques Roubaud, eds. *Vingt poètes américains*. Paris: Gallimard, 1980.
Dworkin, Craig, and Kenneth Goldsmith, eds. *Against Expression: An anthology of conceptual writing*. Evanston, IL: Northwestern University Press, 2011.
Espitallier, Jean-Michel. *Caisse à outils: Un panorama de la poésie française d'aujourd'hui*. Paris: Pocket, 2014 [first edn 2006].
Espitallier, Jean-Michel. *Pièces détachées: Une anthologie de la poésie française*. Paris: Pocket, 2011 [first edn 2000].
Gauthier, Michel. *Olivier Cadiot, le facteur vitesse*. Paris: Les Presses du réel, 2004.
Goldsmith, Kenneth. *Uncreative Writing: Managing language in the digital age*. New York: Columbia University Press, 2011.
Groensteen, Thierry. *Bande dessinée et narration*. Paris: PUF, 2011.
Guilbard, Anne-Cécile. 'Démontage de l'e-mage (Olivier Cadiot)'. *Textimage: Le Conférencier* (2016). Accessed 25 May 2021. http://revue-textimage.com/conferencier/06_montage_demontage_remontage/guilbard1.htm.
Hayles, N. Katherine. *Electronic Literature: New horizons for the literary*. Notre Dame, IN: University of Notre Dame Press, 2008.
Hesmondhalgh, David. *The Cultural Industries*. London: SAGE, 2013.
Jugnon, Alain, ed. *Redrum: À la lettre contre le fascisme*. Brussels: Les Impressions Nouvelles, 2015.
Kalifa, Dominique. *La Culture de masse en France: 1860–1930*. Paris: La Découverte, 2001.
Lang, Abigail. *La Conversation transatlantique: Les échanges franco-américains en poésie depuis 1968*. Dijon: Les Presses du réel, 2020.
Letourneux, Matthieu. *Fictions à la chaîne*. Paris: Seuil, 2017.
Letourneux, Matthieu, and Jean-Yves Mollier. *La Librairie Tallandier: Histoire d'une grande maison d'édition populaire (1870–2000)*. Paris: New World, 2011.
Mallarmé, Stéphane. *Œuvres complètes*, edited by Henri Mondor and Georges Jean-Aubry. Paris: Gallimard, 1945.
MDRN. *Modern Times, Literary Change*. Leuven: Peeters, 2013.
Nachtergael, Magali. *Poet Against the Machine: Une histoire technopolitique de la littérature*. Marseille: Le mot et le reste, 2020.
Perloff, Marjorie. *Unoriginal Genius: Poetry by other means in the new century*. Chicago: University of Chicago Press, 2011.
Reznikoff, Charles. *Témoignage: Les États Unis (1885–1915): Récitatif*, translated by Marc Cholodenko. Paris: P.O.L., 2012.
Reznikoff, Charles. *Testimony: The United States (1885–1915): Recitative*. New York: New Directions, 1965.
Roche, Denis. *La Poésie est inadmissible*. Paris: Seuil, 1995.
Roche, Denis. *Le Mécrit*. Paris: Seuil, 1972.
Roche, Denis. *Les Dépôts de savoir & de technique*. Paris: Seuil, 1980.
Schiffrin, André. *L'édition sans éditeurs*. Paris: La Fabrique, 1999.
Thomas, Jean-Jacques, ed. *Pierre Alferi: Literature's cinematic turn*, *SubStance* 39, no. 3 (2010).
Thompson, John B. *Merchants of Culture: The publishing business in the twenty-first century*. London: Polity, 2010.

Afterword:
Covid-19 or the vulnerability of the future

Florian Mussgnug

> There are days when I feel I've become a Russian Doll, and my centre is a tiny replica of myself with nothing inside.
>
> Andrew Motion[1]

In March 2020, during the early months of the Covid-19 pandemic, novelist Rivka Galchen wrote to the editors of *The New York Times Magazine* to propose a short article on the disturbing relevance of Giovanni Boccaccio's *Decameron*, a story of 10 young people who are forced to shelter in a country house outside Florence while the plague ravages the city. 'We loved the idea', recalls executive producer Caitlin Roper, 'but wondered, instead, what if we made our own Decameron, filled with new fiction written during the quarantine?'[2] What if a sufficient number of authors could be persuaded, like the seven women and three men of Boccaccio's celebrated gathering, to set aside their nervous fascination with illness and mass death and to offer spontaneous tales of grief and laughter, fear and hope, that would accompany them and their readers through the unfolding pandemic? The results of Roper's efforts were published four months later, on 12 July 2020: a magazine issue with 29 texts from authors including Margaret Atwood, Edwidge Danticat, Rachel Kushner, Kamila Shamsie and Colm Tóibín, titled *The Decameron Project: 29 Stories from the Pandemic*. Widely different in tone and style, most of the texts focus on the outbreak of the pandemic, which they variously describe as an experience of shock, vertigo or disorientation. More specifically, several contributors chose to evoke the mood of a brief, extraordinary period in spring 2020, when nearly four billion people – more than half the world's population – lived under strict lockdown.

During that early stage of the pandemic, communal life itself appeared to have come to a standstill. Across regions and nations, people shared the confused intimation of an unfolding catastrophe that, for a while, appeared to exceed their ability to imagine. Unprecedented security and safety measures put an abrupt end to social routines and collective obligations that had governed the interactions between individuals and institutions for years, or even decades. Time no longer seemed to flow naturally into the future. Across the globe, quotidian plotlines of obligation, opportunity and desire were brutally interrupted. As former Poet Laureate Andrew Motion remarked in April 2020, in a brief reflection for the British Comparative Literature Association's *Culture and Quarantine* blog, literature was put to an extreme test by the singular experience of the pandemic. Readers and writers longed for stories that could contain their sense of entropy, stasis, material hardship or social corrosion. Yet it was difficult to find words that captured the sense of a vanishing present and a disappearing future: 'We live in one world, and even before the virus arrived that world was burning', writes Motion. 'If the generations after mine are going to have any chance of saving it, they'd better know each other's languages, and learn the ways that poetry can teach us to hear other's hearts beating.'[3]

Like Motion, many contributors to *The Decameron Project* felt overwhelmed by the novelty of the coronavirus pandemic: a story so new that it could only be told at the level of intimate, lived experience. Of the 29 stories in Roper's edited collection, 11 are autobiographical first-person narratives, written like snapshots of a new, unfamiliar world. Three further stories – by Mona Awad, Tommy Orange and Etgar Keret – address the reader in the second-person singular, thus conjuring a sense of spontaneity and shared destiny. Firmly rooted in the present, these 14 stories – and many others in the volume – foreground the intimate, interlocking temporalities of the emotions: nostalgia, regret, anxiety and fear. By contrast, *The Decameron Project* has surprisingly little to say about life before Covid-19. The past is rarely evoked, and even where it features – as in Téa Obreht's 'The Morningside' – it appears clouded by uncertainty, like a fairy tale: 'Long ago, back when everyone had gone'.[4] Just as surprisingly, none of the authors in the volume engage directly with the future or attempt to imagine how societies and individuals will adapt to the global pandemic or emerge from it. Instead, *The New York Times Magazine*'s edited volume is dominated by a hesitant, almost reluctant acceptance of temporal paralysis. In lieu of complicated plots, the reader is offered slow-paced meditations that seem oblivious to what Walter Benjamin called 'homogenous empty time': the featureless, calendrical time across which progressive history supposedly marches forward.[5] Rich in quotidian settings and intimately personal detail, *The Decameron Project* appears as a collective testimony to the disappearance of the future.

As Marc Augé has explained, Western modernity figures the future as a powerful cultural horizon, shaped by communal traditions and shared knowledge practices, over time. It is assumed that the future gives structure to the present, which would otherwise be experienced as an ungraspable, flickering spectacle of transient shapes that resists explanation. In this manner, the future establishes what the French anthropologist describes as an 'essential solidarity between the individual and society'.[6] In *The Decameron Project*, this solidarity appears to be at the point of unravelling. Mass quarantine is depicted as a condition of dwindling possibilities, which leaves narrators and characters profoundly shaken. Time features as an uncanny, unpredictable and intimately threatening force that subverts and disrupts assumptions about personal identity and social reality. In Tommy Orange's story 'The Team', for instance, the psychological impact of lockdown is described as a traumatic, debilitating experience of time *not* passing. A man ponders the sudden absence of social and sensory stimulation and concludes that time must have come to a standstill or, as he puts it, that 'it was not on your side or anyone's, it was dreaming its waste with you'. According to Orange's narrator:

> Time slipped that way lately, as if behind a curtain, then back out again as something else, here as an internet hole, there as a walk on your street you insisted on calling a hike with your wife and son, here as a book your eyes look at, that you don't comprehend, there as crippling depression, here as observing circling turkey vultures, there as your ever-imminent anxiety, here as a failed Zoom call, there as a homeschooling shift with your son, here as April, May already gone, there as the obsession of the body count, the nameless numbers rising on endless graphics of animated maps.[7]

Anxiety about time, also known as chronophobia or 'prison neurosis', is a common psychiatric condition among individuals held in solitary confinement. Some of its most debilitating symptoms include depression, delusions and feelings of panic. As psychosocial theorist Lisa Baraitser has argued, chronophobia, at its core, is 'a fear that the present time will never come to an end. It is an affective experience of the too-much-ness of time, time that will not pass, will not unfold onto a future of freedom, release or death.'[8] In *The Decameron Project*, this fear is not only expressed in Tommy Orange's short story. It also features, for example, in a text written by Brazilian journalist and literary author Julián Fuks, 'A Time of Death, the Death of Time'. Here, the autobiographical first-person narrator ponders what seems to him to be an apocalyptic watershed moment in the history of his country's tragic experience with the new coronavirus: the day when Brazil tallied 1,001 deaths. As Fuks remarks, 'the symbolism of the number contributed to the failure of time, stealing even the fatal hands of its clocks, exhausting the final unit of measurement'.[9]

Fuks's observation calls for two different interpretative contexts. On the one hand, it conjures the *Arabian Nights*, with its rich and dazzling tapestry of stories: a never-ending tale of enchantment that resists the pressures of time passing. On the other hand, it evokes the biblical book of the Apocalypse and the cultural and religious tradition of millenarian or chiliastic eschatology. In this context (Revelation 20: 4–6), the number one thousand is similarly associated with the end of time and with the monumental idea of a space beyond history: a 'sublime rupture that occurs when time becomes space, when history meets its final antithesis in both a heavenly city and a book', as Steven Goldsmith explains.[10] Fuks, in other words, seems to suggest that the experience of the pandemic can only be understood as a catastrophic singularity: an unspeakable tragedy that resists historical comparison. A similar sense of tragic stasis is also evoked by Moroccan American novelist Laila Lalami, who invites her readers to reflect on the political and symbolic significance of travel restrictions and forced immobility during the Covid-19 pandemic. Lalami's story, 'That Time at My Brother's Wedding', speaks of a short visit to Tangier, on the occasion of a family celebration, during which the protagonist finds herself unable to return to the United States. As Morocco and other states close their national borders to prevent contagion, restrictions on the freedom of movement are suffered by a growing number of people, and not only by those who are most frequently construed as aliens on the grounds of their class, race, ethnicity or nationality. Even privileged travellers such as Lalami's narrator, a resident of San Francisco, or native citizens of the Global North are suddenly exposed to state power, and to the brutal functioning of border regimes that appear to violate their most basic sense of human dignity.[11]

'We are all in this together': during the early months of the pandemic, public officials in different parts of the world reached for this slogan to call for a solidarity that was perhaps inspired more by fears of contagion than by emergent new forms of compassion. Paternalistic models of governance gained attraction and influence. In this context, the discourse of shared vulnerability also acquired strategic importance. Previously used by those in power to justify institutionalized violence – for instance where forced migration was described as a 'menace' to affluent societies – the language of general vulnerability was now employed to introduce new safety measures, but also to advance national and sectoral interests and to promote coercive policies. Since the early months of 2020, the health crisis has inspired new practices of care and fresh modes of wakefulness, but it has also exposed troubling hierarchies and stark social inequalities, within and between nations. These experiences are not sufficiently captured by *The Decameron Project*'s emphasis on near-universal vulnerability and uncertainty, with one remarkable exception: in the final paragraph of Fuks's 'A Time of Death, the Death of Time', the narrator decides to escape his growing anxiety and drives to his parents' house, where he feels a sudden and powerful sense of relief. Against all odds, the ramshackle family home and its two elderly inhabitants are surprisingly unaffected by the pandemic. Their 'pale faces [are] furrowed by the decades', but their expressions are good-humoured, hopeful and calmly attentive. Fuks writes:

> Though they are these peaceable beings, they had themselves once been the dissidents, they had themselves been the subversives, the clandestine militants rising up against the dictatorship of other decades; they are now those most vulnerable to illness, and yet they resist, they survive calmly, ignoring my fear.[12]

Unlike much of *The Decameron Project*, Fuks's description of his parents' calm dignity transcends and decentres conventional ideas of the coronavirus pandemic as an experience of shared vulnerability that erases every form of social difference: a traumatic event without precedent. Instead, Fuks establishes a relation between the narrator's anxiety over Covid-19 and the earlier forms of hardship and oppression that his parents endured. His story links all these experiences to the possible futures that a rich past can inspire. The parents' vulnerability is not 'shared', but rather honoured as a unique, situated experience. Dissociated from discourses of victimization, but also from problematic rhetorical appeals to 'all-togetherness', it enables strategies of resistance that can carry new forms of political agency. In this manner, Fuks's story subverts the seemingly universal sense of shared vulnerability that other writers in the collection attribute to their fictional characters and, at least implicitly, to their intended audiences. He reminds us that the future is of our own making, and that the unfolding health crisis can make each of us, in Rosi Braidotti's words, 'more intelligent about what we are ceasing to be and who we are capable of becoming'.[13]

Notes

1. Motion, 'What is to be done?'
2. Roper, 'Preface', vii. On Boccaccio and the Covid-19 pandemic, see also Rushworth, 'Community, survival and the arts in the Boccaccian tradition'.
3. Motion, 'What is to be done?'
4. Obreht, 'The Morningside', 115.
5. Benjamin, 'Theses on the philosophy of history', 261. For further discussion, see Freeman, *Time Binds*.
6. Augé, *The Future*, 3.
7. Orange, 'The Team', 53.
8. Baraitser, *Enduring Time*, 124.
9. Fuks, 'A Time of Death', 234.
10. Goldsmith, *Unbuilding Jerusalem*, 56.
11. Lalami, 'That Time at My Brother's Wedding'.
12. Fuks, 'A Time of Death', 237.
13. Braidotti, '"We" are in *this* together'.

Bibliography

Augé, Marc. *The Future*, translated by John Howe. London: Verso, 2014.

Baraitser, Lisa. *Enduring Time*. London: Bloomsbury, 2017.

Benjamin, Walter. 'Theses on the philosophy of history'. In *Illuminations*, edited by Hannah Arendt and translated by Harry Zohn, 253–64. New York: Schocken Books, 1968.

Braidotti, Rosi. '"We" are in *this* together, but we are not one and the same'. *Journal of Bioethical Inquiry* 17 (2020): 465–9.

Freeman, Elizabeth. *Time Binds: Queer temporalities, queer histories*. Durham, NC: Duke University Press, 2010.

Fuks, Julián. 'A Time of Death, the Death of Time'. In *The Decameron Project: 29 new stories from the pandemic*, selected by the editors of *The New York Times Magazine*, illustrations by Sophy Hollington, 231–8. New York: Scribner, 2020.

Goldsmith, Steven. *Unbuilding Jerusalem: Apocalypse and Romantic representation*. Ithaca, NY: Cornell University Press, 1993.

Lalami, Laila. 'That Time at My Brother's Wedding'. In *The Decameron Project: 29 new stories from the pandemic*, selected by the editors of *The New York Times Magazine*, illustrations by Sophy Hollington, 225–30. New York: Scribner, 2020.

Motion, Andrew. 'What is to be done?' *Culture & Quarantine*, British Comparative Literature Association. Accessed 25 May 2021. https://bcla.org/reflections/what-is-to-be-done.

Obreht, Téa. 'The Morningside'. In *The Decameron Project: 29 new stories from the pandemic*, selected by the editors of *The New York Times Magazine*, illustrations by Sophy Hollington, 113–22. New York: Scribner, 2020.

Orange, Tommy. 'The Team'. In *The Decameron Project: 29 new stories from the pandemic*, selected by the editors of *The New York Times Magazine*, illustrations by Sophy Hollington, 51–8. New York: Scribner, 2020.

Roper, Caitlin. 'Preface'. In *The Decameron Project: 29 new stories from the pandemic*, selected by the editors of *The New York Times Magazine*, illustrations by Sophy Hollington, vii–ix. New York: Scribner, 2020.

Rushworth, Jennifer. 'Community, survival, and the arts in the Boccaccian tradition'. *Modern Languages Open* (forthcoming).

Index

Abbey, Edward 64
Aesop's fables 19
aesthetics 161–2, 239, 245, 247
Aion 173
Alferi, Pierre 11, 238, 243, 247–9
Aliens Act (1905) 101
animality 6, 20
animal rights 6, 24, 32, 47
    animal studies 5
    animal turn 5
Anthropocene 6
anthropocentric 24, 54
    anthropocentrism 46
anthropomorphism 19, 62
    anthropomorphic 19, 21, 34, 55, 58–60
    anthropomorphization 19, 54
    anthropomorphized 7, 9, 19, 54, 55, 57, 63–4, 125
anxiety 129–30fn2, 164, 253–4, 256
Apollo 11 moon landing 213
Arabian Nights 255
Aramburu, David Varona 210
Argüelles, Agustín 204
Aristotle 224
Assmann, Jan 207
Atwood, Margaret 5–6, 11, 32, 34, 227–9, 231, 252
Augé, Marc 254
Austrian miner's strike of 1934 210
avant-garde poetry 242
Awad, Mona 253
Axia 213
Azevedo, José Pinheiro de 103

Balpe, Jean-Pierre 249fn8
Bambara, Toni Cade 8, 82–4, 86–8, 90–3, 95–6
Baraitser, Lisa 254
Barthes, Roland 187, 194
Baudrillard, Jean 169
BBC 104, 107
Beazley, J. D. 49fn4
Beckett, Samuel 162
Benjamin, Walter 253
Bentham, Jeremy 6
Berg, Jean de (pseud. Cathérine Robbe-Grillet) 196
Bertolucci, Bernardo 106, 108
biopolitics 232
BioShock 172
Boccaccio, Giovanni 252

Bolter, Jay 4, 208, 250fn30
Bootz, Philippe 249fn8
Bordo, Susan 159
Borges, Jorge Luis 244
Boulle, Pierre 6, 30–1
Bourdin, Martial 100
Boyd, Carolyn P. 216
Braidotti, Rosi 235, 256
Brecht, Bertolt 225
bricolage 4
British Comparative Literature Association 253
Brockmeier, Jens 209
Bruno, Giuliana 106
Butler, Brad 105
Butler, Judith, 1, 3, 7–8, 14fn5, 84, 92–3, 95, 150, 233
Buell, Lawrence 54
Bulgakov, Mikhail 6, 21, 22, 24, 27

Cadiot, Olivier 11, 243–9, 250fn31
Caesar, Julia 168
Callahan, Daniel 6
Call of Cthulhu: Dark corners of the Earth 140
Camporesi, Silvia 36fn46
Caraion, Marta 188
Carr, Kris 166fn37
Casares, Adolfo Bioy 244
Casid, Jill 130fn13
Catan 173
capitalism, capitalist 32, 96
Carroll, Noël 138
Cawthon, Scott 10, 177, 180, 182–3
Cervantes, Miguel de 206, 216
Cervantes Prize 211
Christian, Christianity 209, 217
    Catholic Church 73, 103
    Christian art 40
Civil Rights Movement 82
class 86, 234, 255
    lower class(es) 234–5
    middle class(es) 232, 104
    upper class(es) 25, 160
Clark, Kenneth 135
climate emergency 2
cognition 225
Cold War 30, 99, 103
colonialism 73, 116–17, 119, 121, 128–9, 186
    colonial epistemology 73, 77
    colonial history 72
    colonizers 72, 116, 118

European colonizers 116, 118
  neo-colonial 79
comics studies 150
Communist Party 104
Conrad, Joseph 8–9, 100–2, 104–6, 111–12
Connor, James 169
corporeality 143–4, 233–4
Corso, Lucia 2, 12–13
Covid-19 pandemic 2, 12, 252–3, 255–6
Creative Assembly 174
creolization 4
Crichton, Michael 30
Crisp, Quentin 157
critical theory 224
cryptography, cryptographic 168–83
cultural studies 2–4
  cultural forms 5
  cultural memory 5, 11, 203, 207–13
  cultural plastic 159
  cultural translation 4
  cultural self 86
  print culture 238
  popular culture 157, 207–8
  Western culture 87
Cunhal, Álvaro 103
Curry, Tommy J. 91, 93
cyberspace 145

Dalí, Salvador 216
Daily Mirror 105
Danticat, Edwidge 8, 71, 75–9, 252
Darwin, Charles 21, 23, 59, 60
Daston, Lorraine 34fn1
De Bezige Bij 196
De Ferrari, Guillermina 8, 72
Deleuze, Gilles 10, 153, 161, 163–4
Dell'Agata, Giuseppe 39
demediatization 12, 241–3, 246, 249
democracy 107, 218
demonic 54
Derrida, Jacques 11, 48–9
DeShazer, Mary 152
Dessalines, Jean-Jacques 72
Dewitt, Anne 35fn6
diegetic 143
Dick, Philip K. 6, 20, 28–9
Die Hard 208
Diego Valor 205
digital culture 242–3, 245–6, 249fn8
digital revolution 249
digitization 12, 241–2, 249fn12
Dodds, Susan 6–7, 35fn24
Donguy, Jacques 249fn8
Douglas, Stan 8–9, 99–100, 102–9, 111–12
Duff, David 223–4
Dune, Anthony 229–30
dystopia(s), dystopian 30, 228, 230
  dystopian society(ies) 223, 232, 235

Eames, Charles and Ray 109–10, 113fn45
Echols, W. C. 60
Eco, Umberto 169
ekphrasis 10–11, 186, 189–92, 194–9
El Cantar de Mio Cid 208
El Greco (painter) 213–4

El Ministerio del Tiempo 11, 203–13, 216, 218–19
empathy 24, 38–9, 41–2, 42, 45, 47–8, 86, 231, 234–5
  empathetic perspective-shifting 47–8
Engelberg, Miriam 9–10, 151–2, 154–65
Ensemble Studios 174
Environment 7, 54–62, 65, 137, 144, 232–3, 236
  environmental humanities 3–4
ephemerality 238, 243
Erll, Astrid 207–8
Eskelinen, Markku 140
Espadas, Javier Figuero 214
Espitallier, Jean-Michel 238–40, 243, 249fn3
Euripides 50fn6
ethics, ethical 19, 22, 47–8, 155, 162–3, 233
  bioethics, bioethical 3, 231–2
expanded cinema 105
extradiegetic 173
Extradition Act (1870) 101

Five Nights at Freddy's (*FNaF*) 170, 177–83
Felman, Shoshana 124
feminism(s) 234
  Black feminism 82
  feminist cultural production 150
  psychoanalytic feminists 93
  second-wave feminism 156
Fenians 102
Ferrarese, Estelle 2
First World War 40
Fishelov, David 225
folklore 52
  folk tales 54
Foucault, Michel 186, 230
Fowler, Alastair 224
Franco, Francisco 216
Frankenstein, Victor 21–2, 25–7, 32
Freud, Sigmund 20, 44, 45, 213
Fuks, Julián 255–6

Galbe, Jorge Miranda 214
Galchen, Rivka 252
Gambetti, Zeynep 3, 7–8, 92–3, 95
Ganteau, Jean-Michel 5, 8, 71, 76, 78, 79
Garland-Thomson, Rosemarie 85–6
Gasol, Pau 211
Gauthier, Michel 244
Geeraerts, Jef 10, 185–6, 194, 196–7
gender studies 234
  gender roles 82
genericity 224, 229
genre, 1–2, 4–5, 10–12, 54–5, 82–3, 92, 99, 105, 135, 143, 146–7, 150, 157, 162–3, 170, 176, 181, 185–9, 199, 203–4, 213–5, 223–9, 231, 235, 247
  adventure novel 203
  Bildungsroman genre 83
  costumbrista fiction 203
  detective fiction, detective story 168–71, 181–2, 203
  fantasy 19–20, 23, 30, 30, 89, 137, 159, 203
  fantastic literature 225
  genre ecology 4
  genre theory 11, 223–4

genre (*continued*)
   historical fiction, genre 204–5
   horror genre 135, 146
   horror game genre 176
   literary fiction 229
   literary genre 224
   period drama 203
   poetry as vulnerable genre 11
   science fiction 203, 206, 224–30, 235
   sci-fi, SF 19–21, 24, 27–8, 30, 32, 225–30
   SF writers 27–8
   speculative fiction 227–9
genetic mutation 27, 29
Gervais, Bertrand 250fn30
Global North 255
Gilroy, Paul 75
Girodias, Maurice 185
Gitelman, Lisa 205, 219fn2
Godzilla 21
Goldie, Peter 47–8
Goldsmith, Steven 255
Gospodinov, Georgi 6–7, 38, 44, 48–9, 49–50fn5
government 231
Goya, Francisco de 213
globalization 32, 102
Glissant, Édouard 74
graphic medicine 149
Great Depression 107
Greenberg, Clement 241
Greene, Eric 14fn11, 33fn42
Groot, Jerome De 214
Grusin, Richard 4, 208, 250fn30
Guardians of the Galaxy 21
Guardian, The 106, 227
Guattari, Félix 10, 161, 163–4
Guilbard, Anne-Cécile 246

Hades 43
Halberstam, Jack 157–9
Halo Wars 174
Hamon, Philippe 188, 194
Hand, Richard J. 105
Hall, Alice 86
Hall, Stuart 213, 215
Harris-Perry, Melissa 86
Harry Potter 214
Headfirst Productions 140
Heffernan, James 189–90
Herman, David 142
Haraway, Donna 232, 235
Harris, Trudier 86–7
Hiroshima 27
Hitchcock, Alfred 107, 113fn35
Holmes, Martha Stoddard 152
Homer 189
homosexuality 218
Hoskins, Andrew 207
'Hot Summer' of 1975 99, 103
Huizinga, Johan 139–40
Human-Animal Studies 21
Hutcheon, Linda 106
Huxley, Thomas Henry 22
hybridity 4
   hybridization 29, 79, 239, 241–2, 245

identity 86–7, 234, 254
imperialist 96, 116–17, 209
industrialization 241
infantilization 89–92
intermediality, intermedial 190, 194
intertextuality 195
Irving, Washington 213
Isabel II of Spain 216

Jameson, Frederic 35fn35
Jenkins, Henry 110, 171, 215
Jesus 40
Johnson, Kelli Lyon 78
Joyce, Richard 139
Jung, Carl 213
Jurassic Park 21, 30
Juul, Jesper 140–1

Kafka, Franz 161–2
Karastathi, Sylvia 190
Keats, John 189
Keret, Etgar 253
Kerouac, Jack 162
Konami 9, 136
King, Stephen 137
Kissinger, Henry 104
Kushner, Rachel 252

Lacan, Jacques 43, 44, 110
Laffond, José Carlos Rueda 213
Lalami, Laila 255
Landsberg, Alison 209, 212
landscape writing 238
Laub, Dori 124
Lazarillo de Tormes 205, 208
Le Guin, Ursula K. 227–8
Lehan, Richard 137–8
Lennon, Brian 169
Leonard, David J. 91
Letourneux, Matthieu 241
Linfield, Susie 128–9
literary studies 2–4, 5, 140, 146
literary theory 224
London, Jack 7, 52, 54, 58, 61, 63–4
Lopez, Barry 53, 65fn13
Lorca, Federico García 213
Lorde, Audre 157
Lovecraft, H. P. 9, 136–7, 143–4
Louverture, Toussaint 72
Lull, Ramon 106

Mackenzie, Catriona 6–7, 233
Makkonen, Olli-Erkki
male gaze 197
Mallarmé, Stéphane 242, 246
Manichaean dualities 223
Manning, Erin 153
Manso, Margarita 213
Marchetto, Marisa Acocella 156, 159
Marcos, Natalia 212
Marsden, John 9, 116
Martí, Enriqueta 213
mass extinction 33, 232
Matute, Ana María 211
Marx, Karl 112fn10
   Marxist socialism 60

Matrix, The 174
Mbembe, Achille 74
McCarthy, Cormac 5, 7, 52, 54, 60–5
McCoy, Marina 14fn11, 77
McDowell, Graham 14fn5
medical research 232
Meintjes, Libby 74
memory scholars, studies 207–8
Menard, Pierre 244
Mezzeroff (Professor) 102, 113fn15
Mickey Mouse 20
Millennialism (or chiliasm) 255
Miller, Jacques-Alain 110–11
minor literature 161, 164, 166fn60
Minos 7, 42–5, 49–50fn5
Mitchell, David T. 8, 84, 90
Mitchell, W. J. T. 197
Mitman, Gregg 34fn1
Mittell, Jason 211
Minotaur 6–7, 38–49, 49–50fn5
Mizra, Karen 105
modernity 155
modernist 189
Montesa earthquake (1748) 213
Moore, G. E. 50fn11
Morgan, Jack 144
Morrison, Toni 83, 85, 90
Morton, Timothy 63
Motion, Andrew 252–3
Muther, Elizabeth 83
myth 6, 38, 40–2, 44, 49fn4, 50fn6, 54, 59, 63, 217
    mythical 58, 62
mysticism 60

Nanay, Bence 189
nationhood 71–2
NATO 104
Nature 6, 22, 29, 44, 52–61, 63–5, 118
    animal nature
    human nature 41
    laws of 23
    nature writing 54
    photos of 4
neo-avant-garde 239
neoliberal 158
neo-lyricism 238
new world 116, 121, 126–7, 198
New York Times Magazine, The 252–3
Nietzsche, Friedrich 60
non-human 6, 19, 21, 27, 38, 41, 47, 54, 231
non-playable characters (NPCs) 172, 174
nuclear fallout 27
nuclear holocaust 27
nuclear catastrophe 29
Nussbaum, Martha 1

Obreht, Téa 253
O'Donovan, Rossa 102
Oedipal 46
Olivares, Javier 212
Olympia Press 185
Olympic Games (1992) 211
Onega, Susana 8, 71, 76, 78–9
Orange, Tommy 253–4
Orlando, Francesco 38, 47fn6

Other (the Other) 43–4, 48–9
Oudart, Jean-Pierre 100, 111
Ovid 40, 49fn5, 50fn6
Oxford English Dictionary 135

Paladio, César 244
Palmer, William 218
Pankhurst, Emmeline 102
Parsley Massacre 8, 11, 71, 73, 76
Pasiphaë 7, 40, 44
patriarchy 91, 96
Pease, Allison 199
Phillip II of Spain 218
Phillip V of Spain 216
Phillips, Dana 53
philosophy 3, 117
    analytical philosophy 45
    epistemology 72
    moral philosophy 46
    moral feminist philosophy 7
photography, photographic 10, 31, 128, 185–99
Pick, Anat 6, 64
Pita, María 204, 213
Planet of the Apes 6, 21, 30–1
Plunkett, John 188
Poe, Edgar Allan 168–9
P.O.L. Editions 243
political theory 2–3
pornography, pornographic 185–93, 195–9
post-human 6, 34
postmodernism
    postmodern body 159
    postmodern novel 38
    postmodernist 170
PREC – Processo Revolucionário em Curso 103
pseudo-science 226
psychiatry 44
psychology 19, 43–4, 47, 155
Puritan era 53

Raby, Fiona 230
race 71, 86, 255
    black nationalism 91
    institutionalized racism 73
    racialized people 86
    racial identities 87
    racism 91
    racist police officers 88
    racist society 90
    racist stereotypes 93, 95
    white supremacy 92
Racine, Jean 50fn6
Radcliffe, Ann 135
Radford, Colin 139
Rádio Renascença 103
realism, realist 189, 195
    realist literature, novels 188, 195
Reddit 182
Reeve, Clara 135
Rehberg, Peter 187
relativism 223
remediatization 249
Reznikoff, Charles 239
Ricardou, Jean 241
Rigney, Ann 207–8

Ritvo, Harriet 35fn6
Roberts, Adam 224–7
Robisch, S. K. 55
Roche, Denis 244
romanticism 135
Roper, Caitlin
Rogers, Wendy 6–7, 35fn24
role playing games (RPGs) 173
Rosenheim, Shawn James 169
Ruiz, Carlota Coronado 213
Rwandan genocide 9, 116–17, 119
Ryan, Marie-Laure 135, 142

Sabsay, Leticia, 3, 7–8, 92–3, 95
Sade, Donatien Alphonse François de 187
Sadin, Eric 249fn8
Said, Edward 117, 128, 129fn1
Sanders, Wim 197
satire 227
Scarry, Elaine 62
Schaffner, Franklin 36fn39
Schreckenberg, Stefan 209
scientia sexualis 187, 192
Scholes, Robert 226
Schubert, Damion 171
Scolari, Carlos Alberto 214
Seneca 50fn6
serialization 241–2
Seton, Ernest Thompson 7, 52, 54–9, 61–4
sex 47–8, 108, 186–9, 193, 195–8
  sexuality 86, 185, 192
  sexual abuse 84
  sexual morals 186
Shadowbane 171
Shakespeare, William 31, 213
Shelley, Mary 21, 25
Sidney, Sylvia 107
Siege of Baler 204
Siege of Breda 209
Silent Hill 2 9, 136, 140–4
Spanish-American War 210–11
Spanish Armada 218
Spanish Civil War 214–15
Spanish Empire 209, 218
Spanish Golden Age 206
sphynx 58
Spínola, Ambrosio 208–9, 216
Singh, Julietta 2
slavery 91
Smith, Paul Julian 216
Soares, Mário 103
social media 210, 212, 215
Sontag, Susan 223
Spanish Armada 204
Squier, Susan 149
Star Wars 211
Stassen, J. P. 9, 116
Steiner, Gary 27
Stockwell, Peter 144
Super Mario Bros. 136
Suvin, Darko 20, 225–6, 230
Svec, Michael 228

Svirsky, Marcelo 153, 155
syncretism 4
Szép, Eszter 150

Tan, Shaun 9, 116, 118, 129, 129fn2
Tani, Stefano 170
Tapp und Tastkino (Touch Cinema) 105, 113fn27
telos 24
terrorism
  2004 terrorist attacks (Madrid) 213
  9/11 2, 213
Tóibín, Colm 252
Toledo, Pablo Lara 210
trapper story 54, 58, 60
transmedia 9, 174, 179, 182, 203–4, 210–12, 214–15, 240
transmedialization 12, 241–3, 246, 249
trauma 5, 60, 71, 79, 119, 124
Trouillot, Michel-Rolph 72, 77
Trujillo, Rafael Leonidas 8, 71, 73, 74, 76
Trum, Claus 10, 186

unheimlich (uncanny) 20, 124, 138, 164, 143
unconscious, the 39, 44, 170
utopia(s), utopian 28, 30, 107, 225, 230–2

vegetarianism 47
Velázquez, Diego 205–6, 208–9
  The Surrender of Breda 208–9
Venaille, Franck 238
Verne, Jules 229
Vertovec, Steven 4
Victorian Britain 22, 102
victimization 3, 38, 256
Vint, Sherryl 30
visual arts 242
Vivar, Rodrigo Díaz de 208

Walpole, Horace 135
Walter Soethoudt 185
Waples, Emily 152, 156, 159
Weinbren, Grahame 142
Wells, H. G. 6, 21–3, 27, 229
Williams, Ian 149–50
Williams, Linda 143, 186–7, 197
Willis, Bruce 208
Winiski, Mike 228
westward expansion 52, 54
Winter, Douglas E. 146
Wolf, J. P. 145
Women's Social and Political Union 102
World of Warcraft 40
Wright, Richard 91

Youngblood, Gene 105
YouTube, YouTuber 185, 205, 211

Zelazny, Roger 29
Zeus 42
Zoom 254
Zootopia, Zootropolis 19

Lightning Source UK Ltd.
Milton Keynes UK
UKHW021551150222
398729UK00014B/261